LEADERSHIP

Leadership: The Key Concepts is an indispensable and authoritative guide to the most crucial ideas, concepts and debates surrounding the study and exercise of leadership.

Topics covered in this guide include:

- Authority
- Creativity
- Cross-cultural Leadership
- Motivation
- Emotional Intelligence
- Group Dynamics.

Bringing together entries written by a wide range of international experts, this is an essential desktop resource for managers and leaders in all kinds of institutions and organizations, as well as students of business, sociology and politics.

Antonio Marturano is Research Fellow in the Centre for Leadership Studies at the University of Exeter. The focus of his research and his writing is on Leadership ethics.

Jonathan Gosling is the Director of the Centre for Leadership Studies at the University of Exeter and has written widely on the subject of Leadership in the public and private spheres.

ALSO AVAILABLE
FROM ROUTLEDGE

Management: The Basics
Morgen Witzel
978–0–415–32018–4

Fifty Key Figures in Management
Morgen Witzel
978–0–415–36978–7

Business: The Key Concepts
Mark Vernon
978–0–415–25324–6

The Routledge Dictionary of Business Management
David Statt
978–0–415–32819–7

Marketing: The Basics
Karl Moore and Niketh Pareek
978–0–415–38079–9

Finance: The Basics
Erik Banks
978–0–415–38463–6

Economics: The Basics
Tony Cleaver
978–0–415–31412–1

Economics: The Key Concepts
Donald Rutherford
978–0–415–40057–2

Fifty Major Economists, 2nd edition
Steven Pressman
978–0–415–36649–6

Globalisation: The Key Concepts
Edited by Annabelle Mooney and Betsy Evans
978–0–415–36860–5

LEADERSHIP

The Key Concepts

Edited by
Antonio Marturano
and Jonathan Gosling

6/08
Routledge
Taylor & Francis Group

LONDON AND NEW YORK

First published 2008
by Routledge
2 Park Square, Milton Park, Abingdon, Oxon OX14 4RN

Simultaneously published in the USA and Canada
by Routledge
270 Madison Ave, New York, NY 10016

Routledge is an imprint of the Taylor & Francis Group, an informa business

Typeset in Bembo by
Book Now Ltd, London
Printed and bound in Great Britain by
Antony Rowe Ltd, Chippenham, Wiltshire

British Library Cataloguing in Publication Data
A catalogue record for this book is available from the British Library

Library of Congress Cataloging in Publication Data
Leadership: the key concepts/edited by Antonio Marturano and Jonathan Gosling.
p. cm.
"Simultaneously published in the USA and Canada by Routledge."
Includes bibliographical references and index.
1. Leadership. I. Marturano, Antonio. II. Gosling, Jonathan.
HD57.7.L413 2008
658.4′092–dc22   2007018146

ISBN10: 0–415–38365–X (hbk)
ISBN10: 0–415–38364–1 (pbk)
ISBN10: 0–203–09964–8 (ebk)

ISBN13: 978–0–415–38365–3 (hbk)
ISBN13: 978–0–415–38364–6 (pbk)
ISBN13: 978–0–203–09964–3 (ebk)

Wars, conflict, it's all business. One murder makes a villain. Millions a hero. Numbers sanctify.

(Sir Charlie Chaplin, *Monsieur Verdoux*, 1947)

Mankind will find no cessation from evil until either the real philosophers gain political control or else the politicians become by some miracle real philosophers.

(Plato, *Republic*, 326d)

CONTENTS

CONTRIBUTORS

Scott J. Allen, PhD, is the founder of the Center for Leader Development (www.centerforleaderdevelopment.com) – an organization dedicated to advancing the theory and practice of leadership development. Scott co-authored *The Little Book of Leadership: 50 Tips to Unlock Leadership Potential* (Moonlight Publishing, 2007) and *A Charge Nurse's Guide: Navigating the Path of Leadership* (Center for Leader Development, 2005). In addition, Scott serves as a Visiting Assistant Professor of Business Communications at John Carroll University and a Presidential Fellow at Case Western Reserve University.

Mats Alvesson holds a chair in the Department of Business Administration, Lund University, Sweden. He is one of the world's foremost researchers into managerial and leadership processes, currently concentrating on how specialists secure and enhance their managerial identity – what he calls 'identity work'. He is leading a large-scale Europe-wide study, co-ordinating the efforts of top-rate researchers in several countries. He has published a large number of books on a variety of topics, including *Understanding Organizational Culture* (Sage, 2002), *Postmodernism and Social Research* (Open University Press, 2002) and *Knowledge Work and Knowledge-intensive Firms* (Oxford University Press, 2004). He has published a large number of journal articles and contributed to many handbooks. He is on the editorial board of *Academy of Management Review*, *Journal of Management Studies*, *Strategic Organization*, *Management Communication Quarterly* and *Organizational Research Methods* and is a co-editor of *Organization*.

Jon Aarum Andersen is Professor of Business Administration at Lillehammer University, Norway. He holds two Master's degrees from Norway as well as a PhD from Lund University, Sweden. The title of his dissertation is 'Leadership and Effectiveness'. He was regional manager of a Norwegian consultancy and vice chancellor of a Norwegian university college. Professor Andersen has written twelve university level textbooks and has a number of international research publications. He has completed several foreign aid assignments in Africa and Asia and has work experience from nine countries. For five years he was Director of the doctoral programme at the School of Management and Economics. He is now engaged in lecturing and tutoring at the master and doctoral levels as well as in research on leadership and organizational issues.

Paul Arsenault holds a PhD from Temple University, an MBA in general management from the Babcock School of Management at Wake Forest University and a Master's degree in Psychology from Vanderbilt University. Dr Arsenault is presently an Assistant Professor in Marketing at West Chester University and an active consultant. Previous to his present position, Paul taught at the University of Delaware and St Joseph's University. He has constantly received excellent teaching evaluations at these institutions. Dr Arsenault has extensive experience in the corporate world. He has held various product management and consulting positions with concentration in new product development and strategic planning. He has either worked for or consulted with several companies. His research interests include team and individual leadership, personality as a moderator in the leadership and consumer buyer process and charismatic leadership.

Ruth H. Axelrod, PhD, is Assistant Professor of Management at Gettysburg College. She earned Master's and PhD degrees at The George Washington University School of Business. Her primary field of expertise is organizational behaviour and development, specializing in leadership and interpersonal dynamics. Prior to becoming an academic, she acquired more than fifteen years of experience in management positions, directing day-to-day operations, developing new programmes and serving as an internal consultant in large, complex organizations. More recently, as an independent consultant, she has facilitated leadership and organizational development for clients in the not-for-profit sector. Her current research focuses on trust-based decision-making and women's leadership development. Ruth is a member of numerous professional associations and virtual discussion groups, and a founding member and associate of the GWU Women's Leadership Institute.

JoAnn Danelo Barbour is Professor in Educational Administration and Leadership at Texas Woman's University. She has taught, advised or worked with educational leaders for over thirty years. She earned doctorate and Master's degrees at Stanford University in educational administration and policy analysis, and anthropology, respectively. Areas of inquiry for Dr Barbour include leadership theory, teaching others to lead, team leadership, organizational and work culture leadership, ethnography and the case study method. Dr Barbour published on team building in the *Journal of Cases in Educational Leadership*, and has ten entries published in the new *Sage Encyclopedia of Educational Leadership* and was on the editorial review board for this reference text. She is on the review board of the *Journal for Research on Leadership Education*, and is the 'Leadership' issue editor for *Academic Exchange Quarterly*. Currently Dr Barbour is the International Leadership Association's Convener for the Leadership Education Global Learning Community.

Cynthia J. Bean received her PhD in Organizational Communication from the University of South Florida, Tampa. She holds an MBA from the University of St Thomas in St Paul. Since January 2003, she has been Assistant Professor of Management in the College of Business at the University of South Florida, St Petersburg campus. Her scholarly interests are focused on organizational change, organizational communication and leadership. Her research in these areas has been published in a variety of scholarly journals including *The Journal of Business Ethics*, the *Journal of Organizational Change Management*, *Human Relations* and *Business Ethics: A European Review*. She teaches undergraduate and graduate courses in organizational development, organizational behaviour and leadership. She also provides consulting services to clients. Dr Bean speaks to community organizations and business audiences about leadership, leadership development and organizational change topics.

Jeremy Black is Professor of History at the University of Exeter. He studied at Queens' College Cambridge, St John's College Oxford and Merton College Oxford before joining the University of Durham as a lecturer in 1980. There he gained his PhD and ultimately his professorship in 1994. He joined Exeter University as Established Chair in History in 1996. He is interested in early modern British and continental European history, with particular interest in international relations, military history, the press and historical atlases. His publications include *Parliament and Foreign Policy in the Eighteenth Century* (CUP, 2004), *The English Seaborne*

Empire (Yale University Press, 2004), *World War Two: A Military History* (Routledge, 2003), *Italy and the Grand Tour* (Yale University Press, 2003), *France and the Grand Tour* (Palgrave, 2003), *Visions of the World: A History of Maps* (Mitchell Beazley, 2003), *The British Abroad: The Grand Tour in the Eighteenth Century* (Sutton, 2003).

Richard Bolden is a Research Fellow at the Centre for Leadership Studies, University of Exeter, UK. His current research explores the interface and interplay between individual and collective approaches to leadership and leadership development and how they contribute towards social change.

Diane Boston MBA Chartered FCIPD and **Jackie Hunt** BA Chartered MCIPD are experienced and qualified practitioners who have been working together for seven years. During that time they have designed and run training and development interventions for a wide variety of clients, particularly in the not-for-profit sector. Diane has a background in general management and human resources. She also specializes in issues related to governance and is a Board Member of a Housing Association. Jackie's experience includes teaching, management training and development and human resources consultancy. She is also a Certified NLP (Neuro Linguistic Programming) Practitioner.

John S. Burns is Associate Professor at the School of Education, Whitworth University, Spokane (WA). He holds a PhD in Higher Education Administration, Washington State University. He is Coordinator and Instructor for the Interdisciplinary Minor in Leadership Studies and Instructor in the Graduate School of Education.

Peter Case, Professor of Organisation Studies at Bristol Business School, holds higher degrees from the University of Massachusetts and the University of Bath. His academic studies encompass the ethics of leadership, organization theory, methodology and multicultural aspects of management learning and development. Peter is also interested in the social and organizational impact of information and communication technologies and has published in such journals as *Organization, Human Relations, Journal of Management Studies, Management Learning* and *Culture and Organization*. In addition to receiving international invitations to lecture and run doctoral workshops on a regular basis, he has held visiting scholarships at Helsinki School of Economics and the Royal Institute of Technology of Stockholm. Peter is chairperson of the *Standing*

Conference on Organizational Symbolism and is a member of the editorial boards of *Leadership, Culture and Organization* and the *Leadership and Organizational Development Journal.*

Joanne B. Ciulla is one of the founding faculty members of the Jepson School, and teaches courses on ethics, critical thinking, conflict resolution and leadership in international contexts. She was honoured in 2003 with the Outstanding Faculty Award from The State Council of Higher Education for Virginia. Professor Ciulla has held the UNESCO Chair in Leadership Studies at the United Nations International Leadership Academy in Jordan and academic appointments at La Salle University, the Harvard Business School, The Wharton School and Oxford University. Her research interests are leadership ethics, business ethics, international leadership and the philosophy of work. Her books include *Ethics, The Heart of Leadership* (Praeger, 1998), *The Working Life: The Promise and Betrayal of Modern Work* (Three Rivers Press, 2001) and *The Ethics of Leadership* (Wadsworth, 2002). The book critics at Amazon.com ranked *The Working Life* as No. 2 in their list of the ten best business books of 2000.

Richard A. Couto is a Professor and founding faculty member of the Antioch University PhD programme in Leadership and Change. Previously he was a founding faculty member of Jepson School of Leadership Studies at the University of Richmond, where he held the George M. and Virginia B. Modlin Chair. He has published books and articles on leadership in community health, community change efforts, the Appalachian region and civil rights. He co-edited *Teaching Democracy by Being Democratic* (Praeger, 1996) with Ted Becker. His most recent book on community health leadership, *To Give Their Gifts*, was published by Vanderbilt University Press in 2002. He acquired an MA in political science at Boston College, and received his PhD in political science from the University of Kentucky in 1974.

Christian De Cock is Professor of Organization Studies at the University of Wales, Swansea. He started out his academic career in 1990 researching the impact of creativity training and he has found himself increasingly drawn to the concept of creativity in his current research.

Elaine Dunn is Assistant Director of the Centre for Leadership Studies. Elaine joined the Centre in 1999 initially as Programme Manager for the Master's and Diploma programmes. She was subsequently appointed as the Centre's Assistant Director, taking on responsibility for its management and business development. Since 2003 she has been a part-time student on Lancaster's MPhil/ PhD in Critical Management, researching contemporary conceptions of management, the influences of gender and power in organizational settings, adult education, and the philosophy and sociology of management education. Elaine is currently researching critical management education and approaches for identifying and evaluating team/organizational performance arising from relational (as opposed to rational and competency based) forms of management practice.

Donelson R. Forsyth holds the Leo K. and Gaylee Thorsness Chair in Ethical Leadership in the Jepson School of Leadership Studies at the University of Richmond. A social psychologist, his interests include reactions to success and failure, individual difference in moral thought, applications of social psychology in clinical settings and group dynamics. His research has been published in such journals as *Journal of Personality and Social Psychology*, *American Psychologist*, *Journal of Educational Psychology* and *Contemporary Educational Psychology*. He has also written and edited several books, including *Our Social World* (Brooks/Cole, 1995) and *Group Dynamics* (Brooks/Cole, 2006). He was the founding editor of the journal *Group Dynamics*.

Jonathan Gosling is Professor and Director of the Centre for Leadership Studies. Prior to this appointment he was Director of the Strategic Leaders Unit at Lancaster University and the International Masters in Practicing Management, a collaboration of seven business schools around the world that share in the delivery of taught modules for experienced managers in multinational companies. Jonathan's research focuses on leadership and ethics in current strategic changes, and on contemporary innovations in leadership development. Jonathan's academic career includes MBA Director for British Airways, Director of the Strategic Leaders Programme for BAE Systems, Director of Lancaster University's PhD programme in Critical Management and Visiting Professor at McGill University in Montreal. He is a Trustee of the Fintry Trust and The J H Levy Trust.

Frank Hamilton, PhD, is an Assistant Professor of Management at Eckerd College in St Petersburg, Florida. A retired Army Lieutenant Colonel, he spent 22 years in a variety of leadership positions, including an assignment to the Pentagon in the Secretary of the Army's Office. His current research interest focuses on leadership development and the creation of shared values in organizations.

Tim Harle is a management ecologist, working with leaders to build sustainable change in organizations. He applies insights from natural ecosystems and complexity thinking to improve business performance. Reflecting on his broad experience of corporate life, he also writes and speaks at business schools and seminaries. He has published on business ethics and contributed to *John Adair: Fundamentals of Leadership* (Palgrave Macmillan, 2007).

Nathan Harter is Associate Professor in Organizational Leadership at the College of Technology, Purdue University. He was hired away from the practice of law in 1989 to join the Department of Organizational Leadership at Purdue University, where he was subsequently tenured. He lives and works in Greensburg, Indiana, teaching adult undergraduates.

Crystal L. Hoyt is Assistant Professor at the Jepson School of Leadership, University of Richmond. She brings a psychological perspective to the study and teaching of leadership. Her curricular interests include social behaviour, leadership and group dynamics, and research methodology in the social sciences. Her research interests include examining the effects of stereotypes and discrimination on women and minority leaders, the role of confidence in shaping group leadership, transformational and transactional leadership, and new methodological tools for social scientists. Her research has appeared in journals including *Psychological Inquiry*, *Presence* and *Leadership Review*. She has presented her research at invited talks and professional conferences, including the Western Psychological Association, the American Psychological Society and the Society for Personality and Social Psychology.

Brad Jackson is the Fletcher Building Education Trust Professor of Leadership at the University of Auckland Business School. Prior to this he was the Director of the Centre for the Study of Leadership and Head of School of the Management School at Victoria University of Wellington in New Zealand. Brad has been a Visiting Associate Professor with the Copenhagen Business School in Denmark and an Associate Professor of Continuing Education at the University of Calgary in Canada.

Stephanie Jones is an Associate Professor at Maastricht School of Management in the Netherlands. Previously she taught at the Kuwait Maastricht Business School, and before then was teaching at the University of Wollongong in Dubai and the American University in Dubai. Specializing in teaching HRM and organizational behaviour, she also lectures in quality management, change management, international business, entrepreneurship and business ethics. Before returning to academic life around the year 2000, Dr Jones was a senior consultant with a global HR consultancy. She specialized in consulting projects for the banking and oil/gas industries across the GCC. Prior to this she worked in India, Hong Kong, PRC and Sydney, Australia. She lectured at the London School of Economics, having graduated with a PhD in Economics from University College London. She has published more than 20 internationally known books on business and management. Dr Jones is a member of the Editorial Committee of *Human Assets Middle East*, and served twice as an assessor for the Dubai Human Development Awards.

John Jupp set up the Royal Air Force Leadership Centre, which has the remit to design the policy and strategy for through-life leadership training for all personnel in the RAF. He has written the doctrine for leadership in the RAF and researched and explained the leadership attributes that are considered important within the organization. He delivers talks on leadership to a wide variety of internal and external audiences and has edited two books on the subject. Before being asked to set up the RAF Leadership Centre, John held a wide variety of leadership positions in the Royal Air Force in his capacity as a Tornado pilot, weapons expert and instrument flying examiner. Other appointments have included responsibility for the avionics in the Typhoon procurement project and Tornado F3 operational fleet management.

Donna Ladkin joined the Centre for Leadership Studies in January 2005 as Programme Director for the Master's and Diploma programmes. She has a background as a lecturer in organisational behaviour at Cranfield School of Management, where she focused primarily on developing effective learning interventions for senior managers, particularly aimed at developing personal effectiveness. For the last seven years she has run her own consulting business, Learning Matters, which specializes in coaching senior managers and their teams. As well as working with a range of clients in this capacity, she has been part of the teaching team at the University of

Bath's Centre for Action Research in Professional Practice, where she supervises professionals as they undertake MPhil and PhD studies.

Robin Ladkin is a Fellow of the Centre for Leadership Studies at the University of Exeter, an Associate Consultant with Ashridge Consulting Limited and a Partner in Learning Matters. For many years Robin has been developing his own practice in the development of leaders in an organizational context of strategic change. He is particularly interested in the development of professionals in leadership and his clients include global multi stakeholder agencies as well as commercial and public sector organizations.

Kenneth J. Levine holds a PhD in Organizational and Small Group Communication from Michigan State University and a JD from Case Western Reserve University School of Law. He is an Assistant Professor in the School of Communication Studies at the University of Tennessee. Levine's research agenda concentrates on leadership, organizational communication and small group communication within organizations. His research into leadership looks at the perceptions of what makes a person a leader and what makes a leader effective. Further, he is currently examining the methods used to properly define and measure leadership and leadership communication. Additionally, his research in organizational communication centres on anticipatory socialization, specifically looking at the messages sent by and received from the various sources of socialization and the impact of these messages on work, worklife and career aspirations.

Pat Lyons is a Fellow of the Centre for Leadership Studies at the University of Exeter and Chief Executive of Europa Academy. With a background in human resource, marketing and commercial management, his career has encompassed senior positions within several multinational organizations. An experienced leadership development professional, he has a proven track record in creating and delivering high value and effective business solutions for clients, especially within leadership, team and personal effectiveness projects. He holds postgraduate degrees from University College Cork and the University of Warwick and his professional and research interests lie in the areas of leadership, emotion in organizations and team development.

Antonio Marturano holds a PhD in Philosophy of Law from Milan University. He has held several academic posts at universities in the

UK, Italy and the USA. His main areas of interest are in applied ethics (including the ethical and legal problems crossing genetics and ITCs, for which he was awarded a Marie Curie Fellowship) and leadership ethics. Antonio has published a large number of papers for international journals and conferences, and is on the editorial board of the *Journal of Information, Communication and Ethics in Society*. Antonio holds several academic responsibilities in the field of professional ethics: he is Ethics Officer for the School of Business and Economics at the University of Exeter and is a member of the ethics committee of the Ministry of Defence in Italy.

Mindy S. McNutt is an Associate Professor of Organizational Leadership and the dean at the Wright State University, Lake Campus. She was promoted to dean after her sixth year as a faculty member, and had previously held a variety of administrative positions in both four- and two-year institutions. In addition to expertise in capstone courses, capstone projects and transfer students, her areas of interest include the study of leadership in higher education, women in leadership, transformational leadership and team leadership. She earned her Bachelor's, Master's and Educational Specialist degrees at Wright State University, and her PhD at Bowling Green State University.

Thomas Mengel is Associate Professor at Renaissance College, University of New Brunswick.

Chris Miller is Director of the Centre for Local Democracy at the University of the West of England, Bristol.

Dale Pfeifer is a Research Fellow at the Centre for the Study of Leadership, Victoria University of Wellington, New Zealand. Dale's research interests include cross-cultural leadership, public leadership, strategic leadership and co-leadership. She has taught a postgraduate course in Leadership Studies.

Terry L. Price is Associate Professor at the Jepson School of Leadership Studies at the University of Richmond, Virginia and Visiting Associate Professor of Philosophy at the University of North Carolina at Chapel Hill for the 2006–7 academic year. He has degrees in philosophy, politics and psychology from the University of North Carolina at Chapel Hill and the University of Oxford, and he completed his doctorate in philosophy at the University of Arizona. His work has been published in outlets such as *American Philosophical Quarterly, Encyclopaedia of Leadership, Journal of Political Philosophy, Journal of Value Inquiry, Leadership and Organization Development Journal* and *Leadership Quarterly*. He is co-editor of the three-volume reference set *The International Library of Leadership* (Edward Elgar, 2004) and author of *Understanding Ethical Failures in Leadership* (Cambridge University Press, 2006).

Kuldip S. Reyatt is Founder/Director of Strategic Visioning Partners. His prior career involves senior management in blue chip corporations and international management consultancies. He has also served on the board of a charity that provides pro bono consultancy to help improve the performance of NGOs that operate in the field of alleviating human suffering and deprivation. He holds an MBA from a leading UK business school; he works across many business sectors with strategic leaders to improve their individual, group and organizational performance. Practice and scholarship focuses on excellence in board leadership, strategic leadership, visioning and transformation for developing successful organizational futures. His research has undergone external scholarly review with several papers published, or accepted for publication, and presented at UK, European and international leadership conferences.

Joseph C. Rost is Professor Emeritus of Leadership Studies in the School of Education at the University of San Diego, California. He is one of the most prominent scholars in leadership studies. He wrote seminal articles and provocative books such as *Leadership for the Twenty-First Century* (Praeger, 1993).

Jonathan E. Schroeder is Professor at the School of Business and Economics, University of Exeter. He is also a Visiting Professor in Marketing Semiotics at Bocconi University in Milan, Visiting Professor in Design Management at the Indian School of Business, Hyderabad and Research Associate, Centre for Advanced Study of Leadership, Stockholm School of Economics. His research focuses on the production and consumption of images, and has been widely cited in marketing, organization, psychology, design and law journals. He is the author of *Visual Consumption* (Routledge, 2002) and co-editor of *Brand Culture* (Routledge, 2006). He is an editor of *Consumption Markets and Culture*, and serves on the editorial boards of *Journal of Business Research, European Journal of Marketing, Marketing Theory* and *Advertising and Society Review*.

Sen Sendjaya is Lecturer in the Department of Management, Monash University. He teaches leadership subjects at the undergraduate and graduate level and conducts research on leadership, ethics, management and spirituality, and e-leadership. He has published in a number of journals including *Journal of Academic Ethics* and *Journal of Leadership and Organizational Studies*.

Marco Tavanti teaches for the international Master of Science (MS) degree at DePaul University's Public Services Graduate Program (MPS) and co-directs the William and Mary Pat Gannon Hay, Vincent de Paul Leadership Project (DLP). Dr Tavanti received his PhD in Sociology from Loyola University, Chicago, in 2001. Since 1997, Dr Tavanti has been conducting collaborative research, leading delegations and teaching courses abroad in Chiapas, Mexico. In the past 15 years he has consulted for and collaborated with various international nongovernmental organizations. He developed unique perspectives in globalization, religious identities, international movements and organizations while living, working, teaching and researching in many European and developing countries. Dr Tavanti's publications include *Las Abejas: Pacifist Resistance and Syncretic Identities in a Globalizing Chiapas* (Routledge, 2003).

Michael Walton is Fellow of the Centre for Leadership Studies at the University of Exeter and a Chartered Occupational and a Chartered Counselling Psychologist, and for several years has worked as an independent consultant supporting top and senior executives – and their teams – through personal and organizational change. He is particularly interested in helping executives become less prone to derailment and collapse. He has a background in HR, management training and OD and worked for many years in the NHS, at operational and at policy levels, before returning to the commercial field when he joined a respected management consultancy. During his time at the International Monetary Fund in Washington, DC he worked as their management development consultant on a range of change and development initiatives with senior professionals.

Martin Wood is senior lecturer at the University of York. Previously a member of faculty in the Centre for Leadership Studies, University of Exeter and prior to this a Research Fellow at Warwick Business School. He was awarded a PhD for work on the production and consumption of knowledge in the public sector area of health care. He has published in academic journals of the highest international standing, including *Academy of Management Journal, Human Relations, Journal of Management Studies, Organization* and *Organization Studies*.

LIST OF KEY CONCEPTS

advice and dissent
aesthetic leadership
authority

behavioural theories of
  leadership

change and continuity
charisma
complexity theory
contingency theories
creativity
cross-cultural leadership

delegation
derailment
distributed leadership

effectiveness
elite theory
emotional intelligence
empowerment
ethics

followers

gender and leadership
great man theory
group dynamics

heroic leadership
hierarchy

identity
impression management
influence

leader–follower relations
leadership definition
leadership development

measurement
military leadership
motivation

need for leadership

organizational culture

participatory leadership
philosophical approaches to leadership
power
process theory

quiet leadership

religious meaning
responsibility

self-awareness
servant leadership
situational leadership
strategic visioning
style theories

toxic leadership
trait theory
transactional leadership
transformational leadership
trust

wisdom

INTRODUCTION

Leadership is the topic of a vast literature, and is a central concern of all the social sciences and most of the humanities. Yet this book is an attempt to summarize some of the key concepts employed by theorists across this very broad range of disciplines, each a metaphorical battle-field of competing vocabularies and interpretations. We might well be mad to try, but we draw strength from the tradition of leadership studies itself, which seems to proceed with a blithe disregard for – or at least a healthy scepticism of – the sensitivities of theoretical purists. Leadership studies are a domain for those who revel in their hybrid status. We may be academic mongrels, but we have a lot of fun with some of the most exciting problems in social science. In editing this volume we seek to communicate the inventiveness of the field, as well as its thoughtfulness. Contributors include many of the most promi-nent writers in the field today, as well as some of the most controver-sial. As editors we have tried to maintain the original authorial voice of the contributors while ensuring a reasonably comprehensive treat-ment of each 'key concept'.

This book includes 18 main entries, each about 1,500 words or more, and 36 shorter articles, of about 1,000 words. Main entries are about the core concepts of leadership, while the shorter articles are about more peripheral, but still important, or new and emerging concepts and paradigms. This division, as well as the overall selection of terms, is certainly open to criticism, but is not entirely whimsical. We consulted widely with both academic and practitioner networks to create, extend and finally to prioritize the list of key concepts. Even as we go to press we are fielding well-argued suggestions for more inclusions: this collection is inevitably defined by its time as well as its authors. However, each entry is provided with cross references to other cognate entries available in the book, and further readings which would help the reader to have a holistic idea of the discipline. The book also contains short biographies for all the contributors and, at the end, a further bibliography.

Because leadership is a contested field, enriched by constantly revolving fads, hotly disputed definitions and wildly optimistic (and pessimistic) claims, there is no objective point at which to stand to survey the field. Any book that claimed to do so would be controversial on those grounds alone, regardless of what else it contained. But a book that is organized simply by the alphabetic ordering of its key terms must surely surrender to a certain arbitrariness and happenstance. By what intellectual argument would we otherwise justify following an essay on R with one on S? This is most definitely not a book to be read front-to-back.

Leadership studies: what is it all about?

A lot of things. What makes a good leader, what it means to be a good leader, why people follow bad leaders, how to develop the ability to lead, what enables groups to give authority to one of their number, how inequalities of power and privilege affect and are affected by those in charge, and many, many other questions. In spite of the plethora of issues, it is possible to discern a number of trajectories in the way the field has developed.

First, there has always been a strong concern with the moral and intellectual qualities of leaders – classically a political philosophy question, more recently informed by psychology. In this volume the entry on traits deals directly with this concern, although many other entries balance a concern *for* leaders with a more curious and sometimes critical concern *about* leaders. This is reflected in the entry on toxic leadership, for example. Some theorists go further, suggesting that our focus on the personal qualities of leaders is a mistaken cultural bias; they propose a more diffuse perspective on processes that give rise to the impression that some individuals are leading.

Second, there is a concern with the different conditions under which work is conducted and the impact this has on the exercise and effectiveness of leadership. At its simplest, this is an attempt to take into account the tremendous differences of *context*. This is generally taken to include factors as diverse as: pace of change, national or corporate culture, professional mores, standardization or uniqueness of work processes, educational standing of staff, and just about anything else that marks one situation apart from another. A perennial question in leadership studies is precisely to determine what is common to all situations: are there any generally applicable rules, norms or types? The idea of 'leadership studies' would suggest there must be; but the experience of studying leadership is of extreme variety. While many attempts have been made to define factors to measure across all situations (the most common being the leader's attention to task or to relationships), these frameworks inevitably become reified and perhaps self-serving if taken to extremes.

Third, leadership studies contribute to our understanding of the political arrangements likely to produce effective leadership while curbing its excesses, in various cultural and economic circumstances. Governance (corporate and political) has become a significant aspect of leadership studies, certainly amongst practitioners and policy-makers. These concerns are also expressed in studies of the way in which leadership is distributed throughout an organization or community. This has given rise to a particularly lively literature, fuelled perhaps by academic suspicion of hierarchical dispensations of authority, and a desire to legitimize professional autonomy. We might expect future studies to borrow more from political science to address some of the classical structural questions about centralization, devolution, representation and subsidiarity. The relevance of this is obvious in relation to some of the most prominent leadership examples, not least in the realm of international relations, in which the mitigating authority of the United Nations and international law seems to be under threat from unilateralism. This would, in our view, be a healthy extension to the current tendency to focus on the style and policy of individual leaders when it comes to sharing their power.

Fourth, the causal link between leadership capability and organizational performance is hard to pin down. Organizational effects are produced by many forces and influenced by innumerable factors – just one of which may be leadership by the few or by the many. Corporations reward their managers on the assumptions of a strong causal link, so leadership scholars contribute definitions of competencies, measures of performance, and occasionally critical reappraisals of these assumptions.

Fifth, scholars love defining and re-defining their field and spend an inordinate amount of time and energy trying to state what leadership *is*. Conferences and internet mail-lists are replete with arcane debate on the matter – which is fortunate for us, as this is precisely the domain into which this book plunges headlong, with over 50 definitions of key concepts.

Sixth, it is worth noting one of the abiding characteristics of the field of leadership studies: the tendency to confuse *description* with *prescription*. Almost every major contribution to leadership studies moves quickly from analysing *what* leadership is to asserting a model of *how* it gets done, and thence to prescriptions for what leaders *should* do. And all too often the studies start at the end, with value-laden notions of what *ought* to be the case. In compiling this collection and editing the entries we have urged authors to be as even handed and descriptive as possible. But strong moral convictions about leadership are the life-blood of this community of scholars, and it would be quite wrong, we feel, to drive this purposefulness out of these essays. Readers will be well advised, therefore, to approach this volume with a willingness to engage and debate with the authors. You may not agree with their opinions, but, having read each entry, you should know why they hold to them.

Finally, many crucial theoretical questions are just touched on in this book. One abiding issue is the possibility of a general theory of leadership; that is, a holistic theory which would offer a comprehensive idea of all leadership phenomena, homogenizing all the different – often contrasting – perspectives around the same paradigm. Many writers on the subject lay claim to having devised just such a theory, while others argue that the socially constructed nature of the concept makes it neither possible nor desirable. Nonetheless the belief that we are all talking about more or less the same thing would seem to imply a common idea. This volume is a kind of testament to the motivating force of the search for a unifying theory of leadership, at the same time as being a celebration of its complexity.

Acknowledgements

We are grateful for the editorial assistance of Tricia Doherty and Ian Sutherland. Moreover, we would thank the School of Leadership Studies, University of Richmond and the International Leadership Association (ILA) for the assistance given to providing and recruiting many of the contributors.

Jonathan Gosling and Antonio Marturano
Centre for Leadership Studies
Exeter University, UK
April 2007

LEADERSHIP

The Key Concepts

ADVICE AND DISSENT

Ruth H. Axelrod

In this complex world, no single leader has the knowledge and ability to effectively envision, plan and achieve social, political or organizational goals entirely on his or her own. Modern leadership demands collaboration with many people, each of whom has special knowledge, skills and expertise that generate unique insights and perspectives. One of the crucial aspects of a leader's job, therefore, is to foster open communication among her collaborators and involve them in decision-making at all levels. To function effectively, collaborators must feel free to participate fully in the process, providing information, giving advice and expressing dissent.

All too often, however, people do not feel free to speak their minds, particularly in situations where there is an asymmetry of social **power**. The problem is widespread not only in organizations but also in public dialogues. In his observations on early nineteenth-century democracy in America, de Tocqueville (1835/1956) warned of the tyranny of the majority, a phenomenon which continues to threaten freedom of speech in favour of political correctness. In the 1950s, a booklet issued by the American Society of Friends challenged prevailing societal attitudes in a report entitled *Speak Truth to Power* (Cary 1955). This directive has since become a rallying cry for the disenfranchised who seek to voice their aspirations for social change.

How often do we avoid speaking truth to power, especially when it is truth that we believe those in power do not want to hear? We invoke endless reasons for not speaking out, asserting that the issue is not important enough to bring to the notice of the leader or arguing that if the leader does not want to hear it, she won't, so why bother. We rarely admit to ourselves that it is anxiety that keeps us silent, but most of our rationalizations are grounded in fear of reprisal if we speak out – at best, of being disregarded or ostracized and, at worst, of being fired. History, as couched in legend, tells us that the recipient of unwelcome news often strikes out brutally at the messenger. Our fears teach us to believe it.

Surveys of what leaders and **followers** want from each other in hierarchical organizations inevitably place loyalty high on the list (see, for example, Kouzes and Posner 2003). The wise subordinate carefully considers what his manager might mean by loyalty and may err on the side of risk-aversion. Some seek safety in acquiescence, but that self-protection may be purchased at high cost to the organization. For it is only when organizations, like societies, welcome dissent and promote

3

openness that they are likely to prosper. Yet dissenters are often derided for being selfish and disloyal even though they adhere to their beliefs and values at their own expense (Sunstein 2003).

Much has been written about radical, public forms of dissent, such as whistle-blowing, but many studies of dissent in every-day decision-making have focused on decisions that were poorly conceived because of the failure of those involved to fully evaluate all relevant information, including contrarian views. The powerful social forces that produce the Abilene Paradox (Harvey 1988a, b) and groupthink (Janis 1982) – the desire to be accepted as part of an in-group and the fear of ostracism for expressing dissenting views – are salient in all interpersonal relationships.

Some leaders signal their subordinates, whether intentionally or not, that they are uncomfortable with dissent and may even consider it to be an expression of insubordination. But it is essential that they discriminate clearly between constructive dissent and insubordination. To dissent is to express a difference of opinion, to disagree. To be insubordinate is to be disobedient. The former is part of an effective decision-making process; the latter is a rejection of its outcome. The former supports legitimate **authority**; the latter contests it.

There are, of course, limits to constructive dissent. At some point, if a consensus is not reached, the prudent dissenter must either accept the decision of those in authority or continue to voice his dissent in another arena. Certainly, some circumstances warrant bypassing the normal chain of command in a **hierarchy** or even going outside of the organization to major stakeholders, the courts or the press. Each dissenter must make that decision for himself. However, it is far less likely that matters will progress to such a pyrrhic struggle if the dissenter believes that he has been heard and engaged in an open dialogue.

What can be done by leaders of organizations and societies to encourage constructive dissent? First, leaders must demonstrate that they welcome viewpoints that challenge their own. This requires that they treat others as collaborators, rather than reflexive or reactive followers, and be willing to share thought leadership, admitting that their associates may have better ideas then they do. Second, they must encourage open dialogue, ensuring that there are no undiscussables that compel a collusion of silence (Ryan and Oestreich 1998). This requires that they be willing to bear a close examination of all aspects of their organization and their own leadership. Third, they must suppress ideacide by rewarding innovative thinking and discouraging habitual conformity (Hornstein 1986). This requires that they be willing to consider radically new ways of thinking and accept failure as a cost of experimentation. This is not an easy approach to take. It requires personal courage, psychological hardiness and a strong sense of purpose.

A key part of a leader's job is to establish an effective **organizational culture** that supports the values that she espouses (Schein 1985). People learn to **trust** that the leader means what she says only when there is evidence of it in practice, when the values are operationalized in policies, procedures and reward systems that are verified by collective experience. For it is through the stories that exemplify 'the way we do things around here', the rituals and legends, that culture is transmitted in any social group. Through these mechanisms, the organization and its leaders cultivate, or deplete, the interpersonal trust that is at the heart of all effective social relationships (Jaques 2002). Trust, in turn, enriches the organizational decision-making processes by allowing employees to communicate even bad news, with confidence, upward through the hierarchy (Roberts and O'Reilly 1976) and work groups to abandon self-censorship (Friedlander 1970; Gibb 1978). When people trust each other, they feel free to speak their minds.

Thus, the challenge for leaders who wish to make the most of the knowledge and talent that is available in their organizations is to build trust throughout their constituencies by clearly and consistently conceptualizing their associates as collaborators rather than followers and welcoming both advice and dissent.

See also: **authority**, **leader–follower relations**, **cross-cultural leadership**, **ethics**, **hierarchy**

Further reading: Chaleff 1995; Hornstein 1986; Rosenbach and Taylor 1998; Ryan and Oestreich 1998; Sunstein 2003

AESTHETIC LEADERSHIP

Jonathan E. Schroeder

Aesthetic leadership concerns the manner in which artists, and other aesthetic workers, perform leadership functions within groups, communities and culture, often outside established positions of **authority**. Aesthetics has generally been concerned with questions of beauty and the notion of universal tastes. Kant argued that human response to art is disinterested, which led to an ongoing debate about the relationship with visual culture. Others have argued that there is a distinct aesthetic realm, which allows people to respond to beauty in terms of colour and form. Recently, artists have been called upon for aesthetic leadership in management – as leaders, practitioners, visionaries and inspirers (e.g. Austin and Devin 2003; Hatch *et al.* 2004; Schroeder 2005). Thus, aesthetic leadership need not refer merely to **creativity** or vision, rather aesthetic leadership may emerge from insight into cultural, political or interpersonal issues; aesthetic statements on social injustice or crucial cultural concerns; or, at a more general level, provide alternative ways of seeing problems, history or received **wisdom**. In this way, aesthetic leadership may either complement or contradict more traditional leadership forms, such as politics, religion or management. It may be that aesthetic leadership draws some of its **power** from the position of the aesthetic producer outside conventional leadership positions.

Well-known examples include Jacques-Louis David, whose famous painting *The Death of Marat* (1793) catalysed support for the French revolution by shrewdly mixing fine art with propaganda. During the bloody eighteenth-century uprising, David reorganized the Académie, an important national institution – critical for authenticating and disseminating cultural and political opinions and trends – and he produced many spectacular propagandistic events, eventually being imprisoned for his political views. Another iconic aesthetic leader, Nobel Prize-winning poet Czeslaw Milosz, drew attention to repression in Poland, and helped spark the Solidarity movement's success. A final example concerns the Asian-American sculptor and architect Maya Lin, whose haunting Vietnam Veteran's memorial in Washington DC helped a nation – especially Vietnam veterans and their families – begin to come to terms with a tremendously debilitating and divisive epoch in American history. Lin, who, an undergraduate university student at the time, steadfastly refused to compromise her aesthetic principles during a bitter battle over her minimalist design, held to her strong, clear vision, as described in the Academy Award winning documentary of the rancorous debates about how the war should be memorialized (Mock 1995).

Research and thinking about aesthetic leadership spans several disciplines, and often encompasses management studies, art history and sociology – aesthetic leadership represents one strand within the growing field of aesthetics and management. In the field of organization studies, Rafaël Ramirez's *Beauty of Social Organization* (1991) inspired many scholars in an aesthetic turn. *Organization and Aesthetics* by Antonio Strati (1999) has become well respected, its contribution resting on applying aesthetics to understanding organizations from a psychologically informed organizational theory point of view. Heather Höpfl and Stephen Linstead's edited volume, *The Aesthetics of Organization* (2000), offers a useful, well-conceived introduction to the issue of aesthetic leadership. Pierre Guillet de Monthoux's *The Art Firm: Aesthetic Management and Metaphysical Marketing from Wagner to Wilson* (2004) provides several case studies of aesthetic leadership, providing a useful genealogy of aesthetics within the economy. Stephen Taylor and Hans Hansen (2005) provide a useful review of this emergent field, focused on aesthetic inquiry.

Aesthetic leadership may rest in leadership qualities of **charisma**, interpersonal skill or vision, yet remains elusive, and difficult to categorize or contain. Often, aesthetic leaders have trained in areas somewhat distant from typical leadership or management disciplines – literature, art or theatre, for example – and this training may offer a capacity for innovative insight. However, insight or vision alone remains insufficient; aesthetic leadership requires a rare combination of desire, determination and drive, along with a prodigious aesthetic gift.

See also: **charisma**, **creativity**, **cross-cultural leadership**, **ethics**, **wisdom**

Further reading: Austin and Devin 2003; Guillet de Monthoux 2004; Hatch *et al.* 2004; Lin 2000

AUTHORITY

Chris Miller

Few attempts have been made to analyse the concept of authority since Max Weber's (1947) classical study (see Sennett 1980; Raz 1979, 1990). Weber identified legitimate authority as resting on one of three systems of social control: tradition, **charisma** and legal-rational authority underpinned by expertise and formal rules. Those with **power** are accorded authority by virtue of the legitimacy of the principles by which they hold power. Subsequent political science literature has explored authority in relation to the state and problems of social coordination. Lukes (1987) notes that the focus has either been analytical, concerned with identifying the elements of authority, or normative and directed on the legitimacy of authority. For some these are distinctly separate with legitimacy understood as context-related and therefore subject to change. Others argue that any study of authority must be that of legitimate authority and thus the key question is the basis on which authoritative pronouncements should be recognized as such.

Carter suggests that authority is the antithesis of force (1979: 17) and implies the capacity to command respect and elicit a variety of forms of voluntary compliance or 'followership'. For Raz (1979) authority is normative power, consisting of the ability to change behaviour by providing other overriding reasons for action legitimized by a sufficient number of people.

A key assumption is that authority belongs primarily to a sanctioned and mutually recognized role (Friedman 1990). Such positional authority depends on the recognition of those subject to it and the capacity and desire of the occupant to take up the role (Lukes 1987: 209). Yet mutual recognition is not always necessary to sustain authority, its exercise may not always be apparent, the criteria by which the credentials of authority are chosen may be unclear and the nature of the recognition accorded can result in the surrender of judgement (Lukes 1987). The relational nature of authority by which legitimacy is established, maintained or lost and new voices of authority emerge continues to be a fruitful area of enquiry, as is the capacity for multiple sources of authority to co-exist (Lovell 2003).

Raz (1979, 1985) argues that authority and reason are bound together. Compliance is ceded on the grounds that what is proposed offers 'a more reliable and successful guide to right reason' (Raz 1985: 25). Lukes insists that the objectives an authority wishes to pursue cannot be determined a priori and are often contested. Consequently, the identification of relations of authority is complex, involves a process of interpretation, and is perspective related. Authority is here inherently unstable, subject to conflict, negotiation and change.

Within the 'group relations' tradition, authority is given a specific meaning within an organizational context where it is understood as a function of self-management in relation to role and task performance (Miller 1993: 310). It does not imply a 'commitment to the prevailing power structure or to the established way of doing things' (p. 311) and its exercise can involve personal risk to the individual concerned. Authority is derived from personal competence and commitment to the task that is constantly prone to corruption from collusive patterns of behaviour involving both those in authority and their subordinates (Chapman 2003). However, the task cannot always be straightforwardly deduced (Silverman 1968), although when contested the stress on 'personal authority' resonates precisely because there are no fixed and durable definitions.

Within civil society, where informal roles predominate within horizontal relationships, the part played by the individual, both in establishing and maintaining authority, or 'reputation', is critical. Here it remains useful to distinguish between someone who has an inner authority that appears to be embodied in the individual personality, someone who is an authority, and commands a respectful hearing, and someone who is in authority. These three forms of authority refer to the self, to reputation and to position respectively and while each is distinct there is likely to be some relationship between them. Although such relations take place within a social context marked by structural inequalities, relations of authority cannot simply be reduced to these, nor is the impact of underlying power structures so evident in specific contexts.

Analyses that focus on the dynamically unfolding relations of authority can better account for those in which authority is transitional, when those with authority no longer command it nor have the need to do so. Here the exercise of authority is itself an authorizing process, enabling the other to become autonomous, sensing and acting upon his/her own authority. To invest in a sustainable relationship of authority, albeit one that contains the seeds of its own dissolution, the relationship must be available for challenge and the transactions and the rationale for these transparent. To the extent that the boundaries of authority are ambiguous, these need to be negotiated and re-negotiated. Such relationships can neither assume a compliant subject nor succeed through the use of sanctions, but are inherently fragile and require repeated demonstrations of authority reliability.

Responses to authority or the use of one's own authority will be applied inconsistently dependent on time and context. Such relationships are a shifting terrain fluctuating from resistance to compliance and are difficult to transfer from one context to another. Further, while in a role of relative dependency we may be simultaneously in 'authority' in relation to someone else. What we seek in the other we may hope for in ourselves. We remain cautious about authorizing a role, institution or person anticipating disappointment or worse. Good authority is hard to find and disappointments are all too frequent. The need for authority, and the sense of dependency that results, conflicts with individual freedom, another powerful need, and can generate a strong antipathy toward or fear of authority, often reinforced by the behaviour of those 'in authority'.

Freud highlighted the fundamental importance of an internalized authority and its origins in the family, arguing that the child exists initially in a state of total dependence on its parents. Such early experiences leave traces that continue to surface in adult life and interact with subsequent experiences of authority, often unconsciously. There is always some reworking to be done in distinguishing between our perception of the authority of parental figures, our 'authority in the mind', and our selves, while those who experienced difficult relationships may continue to struggle to find either an authoritative voice or engage effectively with other authority figures.

Too much authority becomes authoritarianism, encouraging submission and the projection of frustrated aggression onto others who are perceived to be weaker (Adorno *et al.* 1964). Too little authority is said to provide no strength or solidity against which to react (Lasch 1977, 1979). For those whose internal authority is either too weak or too powerful, the task of creating an authoritative voice can become a life's project. To find and act upon our own sense of authority it is important to have experienced sufficient and 'good enough' relationships of authority. Their absence, however, does not preclude other compensatory relationships significant enough to address 'hidden injuries' and provide a sense of internal authority. Others face the more demanding challenge of abusive forms of authority when authority breaches, invades or violates our personal physical or emotional selves, our bodily integrity (Williams 1999).

Sennett (1980) explores the impasse between bad authority and resistance to it. Resistance is the recourse of the weak expressed 'by being the negative of whatever the powerful wanted them to be' (p. 72) that binds the antagonists together. A good authority symbolizes strength, solidity and stability over time, using that strength to care for others (p. 82). It offers shelter from the storms of growing independence and a place of recuperation, reflection and re-learning. It contains the hopes, fears and fantasies, contradictory perceptions and experiences toward authority. What remains for the active subject is a respect and appreciation for the work undertaken by the mentor or guide in fulfilling the obligations of that role.

At the heart of Sennett's analysis is the concept of 'recognition', a concept central to Hegelian thought, to contemporary political theory (Honneth 1995) and psychoanalysis (Benjamin 1990, 2004). Good authority promotes mutual recognition of the independent existence of the other and her/his needs and experiences, where recognition has elements of both acceptance and valuation. Following Hegel, Sennett (1980: 128–9) outlines a four-stage journey of liberty that offers a way in which 'the experience of authority might become less humiliating, more free in everyday life' (p. 127). For Benjamin the struggle for recognition corresponds to a pre-depressive mode of relating in which each party assumes that virtue is almost entirely on its side. Mutual recognition does not eradicate asymmetries of authority and dependency but does offer a relationship where each now feels respected. With each shift in the consciousness of self and other there comes a change in behaviour toward others and in turn this produces a change in the other's behaviour. We can act cooperatively if we play neither the victim nor the master (Benjamin 2004).

Marx criticized Hegel's idealism in which self-consciousness was the essence of humankind (Marx 1970: 176). Rather, human history was the struggle of real people in organized relations to each other. Sennett attempts to connect the journey of liberty to the structure of large-scale institutions. He argues that with consciousness of the link between strength and time comes the realization that no authority lasts forever. Awareness of the other's fallibility generates two demands: public authorities must be 'visible' and 'legible'. Citizens must themselves, through periodic disruptions to the chain of command, 'read', understand, collectively discuss, judge and revise the actions of authority, and authority becomes a process. Critical to this is a sense of inner authority, and the continuing struggle to secure and maintain this, if subjects are to challenge the misuse of authority whilst enabling others to find their own voice and construct relations of authority founded upon recognition and social justice.

See also: **advice and dissent, charisma, followers, group dynamics, power**

Further reading: Honneth 1995; Lovell 2003; Raz 1985

BEHAVIOURAL THEORIES OF LEADERSHIP

Thomas Mengel

In the middle of the twentieth century, the focus of leadership theory shifted from trying to identify personal characteristics of leaders to studying the behaviour as demonstrated by leaders. This can partially be explained by the failure of the **trait theory** of leadership to identify a clear and unique set of personal characteristics that would identify great leaders. Furthermore, it also reflects the general shift towards the study of observable behaviour in psychological research.

While groundbreaking studies on leadership behaviour were conducted at Ohio State University and the University of Michigan, probably the best known model of leadership behaviour was introduced to leadership practice and **leadership development** by

Blake and Mouton (1964). The major result and contribution to leadership theory of all three approaches is the discussion and presentation of two distinct dimensions of leadership behaviour: the focus on tasks and performance on one side and the concern for people and the relationship among them on the other.

Starting with a list of 1,800 descriptors of leadership behaviour, the researchers finally composed a questionnaire consisting of 150 items and respective questions: the Leader Behaviour Description Questionnaire (Hemphill and Coons 1957; Stogdill 1963). The questionnaire was widely used in various settings (e.g. industrial, educational and military contexts) and identified two clusters of typical leadership behaviour: 'consideration' and 'initiation structure'. Consideration behaviour (CB) emphasizes the relationship aspect of leadership behaviour. Considerate leaders support their **followers**, include them in the decison-making processes, treat them as equal, and foster open communication and teamwork. Initiation structure behaviour (IB) focuses on the tasks to be accomplished. Leaders who score high in this dimension structure tasks and schedules, clarify roles and responsibilities, and set and control standards for work completion.

As the two identified clusters of behaviour have proven to be independent of each other, four different combinations were studied in regard to their **effectiveness**: High CB–High IB (HH), High CB–Low IB (HL), Low CB–High IB (LH) and Low CB–Low IB (LL). While some research has shown the HH to be the most effective combination of leadership behaviour – very considerate toward the people involved and highly structured toward task completion – other research has indicated that in some situations HL or LH respectively will be the better choice.

In parallel with the research conducted at Ohio State, scholars at the University of Michigan were studying the potential impact of leadership behaviour on small group performance (Katz and Kahn 1952; Likert 1961, 1967). Again, leadership behaviour was conceptualized as either 'employee oriented' or 'production oriented' and the research was conducted in field studies within different settings (e.g. insurance company, manufacturing company, railroad section gangs). As the most interesting result, three different types of effective leadership behaviour could be identified: Effective managers demonstrated task-oriented behaviour similar to the behaviour characterized as IB in the Ohio State research. In particular, effective managers focused on planning and coordinating activities and supported their subordinates in setting challenging yet achievable goals. Effective leaders also scored high in demonstrating relations-oriented behaviours that were similar to the CB of the Ohio State studies. Their extensive support towards subordinates was built on **trust**, confidence, appreciation and recognition. Finally, effective managers would demonstrate a participative approach to leadership, preferring the supervision of groups over closer control of individuals, and fostering cooperation and joint decision-making. However, subsequent studies presented contradictory results and remained inconclusive (Northouse 2004).

When extending their research toward the survey of 'peer leadership', Bowers and Seashore (1966) also presented the first results on the effectiveness of sharing particular leadership behaviours with subordinates and of including them in the facilitation of group and work processes.

The Leadership Grid® (called Managerial Grid in its earlier version; Blake and Mouton 1964, 1978, 1985) was another, more practical approach mirroring the findings of the research done at the Universities of Michigan and Ohio State. This grid appears to be 'the most well-known model of managerial behavior' (Northouse 2004: 68) and is still being used in leadership development and consulting practices around the world.

This model and the respective questionnaire identify manager behaviour within two dimensions – 'concern for people' and 'concern for production' – on a scale from 1 (minimum concern) to 9 (maximum concern). The resulting scores are then combined and located on a two-dimensional grid. Most leaders' behaviour combinations fall within five major management styles:

- 'Impoverished management' (1, 1 score): Minimum effort is being exerted in regard to both dimensions by rather indifferent or even apathetic managers.
- 'Middle-of-the-road management' (5, 5 score): Managers exercising this style seek to balance their concern for people and their concern for the tasks involved on a level of adequacy and moderation.
- 'Country-club management' (1, 9 score): Highly friendly relations and a very good atmosphere have the clear prevalence over low concern for productivity and task completion within this leadership style.
- 'Authority-compliance management' (9, 1 score): Job performance and task completion are the major focus of this result-driven leadership style. Relationship and communication with people is reduced to the minimum necessary for clear instructions and performance control.

- 'Team management' (9, 9 score): This leadership style has a very high consideration for both tasks and people. Fostering commitment through supportive relationships and teamwork is equally important to promoting the efficiency and effectiveness of the organization.

While according to the authors of the Leadership Grid® most leaders have a clear propensity toward one dominant leadership style, they often have a secondary style which they particularly apply in situations of high pressure or when their preferred style doesn't appear to be effective. Furthermore, two additional patterns of behaviour have been identified by Blake and McCanse (1991):

- Paternalism/Maternalism: Some leaders appear to use both the 'Country-club management' as well as the 'Authority-compliance management' style without integrating them. Benevolent behaviour is demonstrated only to secure goal achievement and job performance.
- Opportunism: Any combination of leadership styles can be demonstrated at various times by managers who strive for personal advancement rather than for job performance or relationship building.

While the model and the finding of some researchers suggest the Team-management style (9, 9 score) to be most effective and the preferred objective of leadership development, this is not supported by the majority of studies based on the Leadership Grid® (Shriberg *et al.* 2005).

The behavioural theories have introduced two powerful concepts into the development of a comprehensive theory of leadership as well as into the practice of leadership training and development: the focus on tasks and the emphasis on relationships. Thus, 'evidence has been provided that adding managerial activities to leader behaviors increased the ability to understand employee satisfaction, commitment, and performance' (Wren 2005). By enhancing the earlier focus on personal characteristics of leaders in trait theory through the study of leadership styles, the behavioural approach has clearly added an important dimension to the discussion and understanding of the impact of leaders on the leadership process; there also is some first evidence on the effectiveness of participative leadership. However, by and large the many studies have failed to identify a sufficiently consistent pattern in regard to the link between people and task-oriented leadership styles or the relationship between leadership behaviour and its impact on followers or organizational effectiveness. Furthermore, the respective research could not identify a universally effective set of leadership behaviours (Yukl 2002). Finally, this approach focuses on the leader and his or her behaviour and fails to comprehensively consider and incorporate the situational context of as well as the values and motives underlying the various leadership behaviours.

See also: **authority**, **group dynamics**, **leadership development**, **leader–follower relations**, **participatory leadership**, **style theories**

Further reading: Blake and McCanse 1991; Northouse 2004; Shriberg *et al.* 2005

CHANGE AND CONTINUITY

Jonathan Gosling

Left on their own, organizations tend towards stability and stagnation; leaders incite and direct change. This view of organizational life has become so dominant that leadership is sometimes defined precisely as 'creating change' in contrast to the work involved in maintaining the status quo, which is merely 'management'. There is clearly some sense in this, although taken to extremes it becomes ridiculous; does change and evolution really depend on leaders? Most forms of organizational activity have as much to do with continuity as change – for example, people communicate with each other to build **trust**, decide what to do and check on progress. Does leadership have nothing to do with these continuing activities? On the other hand, some aspects of 'moving onwards' often arise from someone seeing new opportunities and articulating a sense of the future in ways that arouse the enthusiasm and confidence of others. So 'vision' is often said to be a quality of leadership, and many observers also emphasize the role of leaders in implementing new priorities, changing the work people do or how they relate to their colleagues and the sense of purpose they bring to it all. Some go so far as to claim that leaders are solely responsible for making change happen, for the way in which it is conducted and the eventual outcomes. Efforts to change things fail, they say, because leaders fail in certain functions – a seminal article by John Kotter (1995), for example, claims that corporate transformation fails because leaders don't do eight key things: instil a sense of urgency, build a guiding coalition, develop a clear vision of the future, communicate this vision remorselessly, remove obstructive people, ensure some short-term wins, sustain the effort for long enough and build the changes into the collective culture.

The link between leadership and change is not always drawn so strongly. Many small innovations arise from people solving problems simply to get a job done, but then give rise to new ways of working and the discovery of new opportunities. The people in leadership roles may recognize these adaptations as emerging new patterns of activity, and honour them with the title of 'strategies' (Mintzberg 1978). Even quite significant new directions such as acquisitions, disposals or entry into new markets often come about as the result of apparently insignificant events and chance conversations, so if leadership is really closely associated with 'making change', it must be widely distributed.

Regardless of who creates or initiates change, individuals and groups differ in how they respond. New fashions, customer demands, competitor behaviours, environmental crises and many other factors force us to do things differently, and much of the literature on 'leading change' is really addressing the role of leaders in helping others to make these transitions. In fact it might make more sense to focus on the leadership of continuity, sustaining a sense of **identity** and purpose in spite of continuous and sometimes life-threatening changes (Barry 1997). This perspective emphasizes the narrative processes by which people negotiate their place in unfolding events. Changes that seem to follow some kind of logic are easier to comprehend, so leaders provide some of this narrative continuity when they articulate a 'strategy'. Senior people in an organization or community also tend to be important characters in the storyline itself, and the way they behave influences the ways in which the other 'actors' develop their characters and contributions to the emerging plot-line. What kind of narrative is this, though? Are leaders acting out archetypal heroic myths? Sometimes the way in which leadership is written about might lead one to imagine organizational life to be scripted like a Hollywood thriller, with neat definitions of good and bad, and everything leading towards a clear-cut *dénouement*. A more realistic metaphor, if one is needed, would be a soap-opera in which a number of interweaving plot-lines develop through intermittent cliff-hangers and teases, involving a limited number of characters deeply rooted in the particularity of their place and time. Leaders may figure as characters in this process, although significant changes (plot developments) may be initiated in a number of ways. The main problem with this metaphor is that if overall leadership of the effort is shared by all the characters, do we really need the concept of leadership?

Change and continuity feature strongly in contemporary organization theory. For example:

> Wishing to highlight the pervasiveness of change in organizations, we talk about organizational becoming. Change, we argue, is the reweaving of actors' webs of beliefs and habits of action to accommodate new experiences obtained through interactions. Insofar as this is an ongoing process, that is to the extent actors try to make sense of and act coherently in the world, change is inherent in human action, and organizations are sites of continuously evolving human action.
>
> (Tsoukas and Chia 2002: 567)

According to this perspective, change is a continuous process of sense-making (Weick 1995). Individuals manage themselves in relation to changes within and around them, and in so doing they are constantly re-creating themselves. There is, as it were, no dry land on which to stand, clear of the constant flow; or to return to our earlier metaphor, no script-writer, producer or director exempt from the action of the story-line. Leaders of groups, organizations and countries may be distinguished by their more-than-usual **influence** on the sense-making process and the shared identities that emerge from it.

A related but quite distinct approach emphasizes the centrality of personal development in any kind of organizational development (Owen 1987). Many courses on 'change leadership' include a significant focus on **self-awareness**, reflection and priority-setting in one's own life, on the assumption that 'self-mastery' is a necessary corollary to leading change in a group. Participants find that this encourages greater thoughtfulness about what they hope to achieve, an awareness of their own energy and resilience for the work involved, and the likely responses of other people who may be affected by change. However, it is not really clear that personal development is an accurate analogue for organizational or social change, except in the very abstract terms implied by **process theory**. Particularly, whereas self-mastery may be a desirable goal for many people, social systems that seek control by a single super-ordinate leader are rightly termed totalitarian, and tend to be highly resistant to change in the emergent sense mentioned above. Although democracy requires a degree of self-discipline on the part of citizens, as a system of governance it is inherently 'messy' and ambivalent about centrally planned management of change.

Nonetheless real events are affected by people who manage to exert their influence. The problem of agency seems to be perennial: where does change start, and how do we define the limits to the factors that we believe influence it? Put like this, the problem is clearly complex, and the recent interest in 'complexity sciences' has enabled theorists to accommodate both the influence and the dependency of individual agents. But of course there is no simple answer to the complexity of change. Some writers stress the centrality of conversation, mediating internal and external worlds (Shaw 2002); others turn to the auto-poetic powers of social as well as natural systems, in which individual agency is effective if inspired by a universal informing spirit (Wheatley 1999).

In conclusion: leadership is a term applied to a very diverse set of human actions – perhaps evenly spread between those that seem to be initiating and managing change, and those that provide continuity and direction in spite of change.

See also: **complexity theory**, **identity**, **process theory**, **self-awareness**, **strategic visioning**

Further reading: Kotter 1995; Mintzberg 1978; Tsoukas and Chia 2002; Weick 1995; Wheatley 1999

CHARISMA

Antonio Marturano and Paul Arsenault

For years, social scientists have analysed and debated the concept of charisma and why people gravitate toward charismatic leaders. Traditionally, the notion of charisma comes from 'gift', which was semantically linked to another Greek word 'Karis' to mean 'gift of grace': a donation by the Holy Spirit to all believers. However there is more than one idea of charisma. In the apostolic writings we find several 'charismas', such as the ability to make prophecies, the power to perform miracles, discernment of spirits, and some particular capac-ities to lead a society. According to St Paul (Corinthians, 12.7 foll.), charisma is given to the individual in order *to serve the whole community* (in its original formulation, therefore, such a notion has a strong moral flavour) and it reaches its apogee when a charismatic person serves with inner willingness and gentleness.

Max Weber, a famous sociologist, revised this religious concept of charisma in the following way to not only fit the religious notion of charisma but with a kind of legitimate **authority** that was also applicable to multiple contexts, including political, administrative and economic institutions: Weber stated

> The term 'charisma' will be applied to a certain quality of an individual personality of which he is considered extraordinary and treated as endowed with supernatural, superhuman, or at least specifically exceptional powers or qualities. These are such as not to be accessible to the ordinary person, but are regarded as of divine origin or as exemplary, and on the basis of them the individual concerned is treated as a 'leader'.
>
> (Weber 1968: 241).

Talcott Parsons (see Tuccari 1991) attempted to clarify the differences by stating that there are two notions of charisma. One is focused anthropologically as a world in which religion and magic play a fundamental role in the social sphere. The second notion applies to a disenchanted world where what is extraordinary loses its metaphysical *raison d'être*. (A fundamental Weberian notion is that modernity is characterized by World disenchantment – *Entzauberung der Welt*.)

More recent critical German editions of Weber (Winckelmann 1956) suggest a translation more along the lines of

> 'Charisma' is a quality of a person that is so extraordinary that it leads others to believe that he has powers or abilities that are supernatural, superhuman or at least exceedingly rare; OR that he is sent by God; OR that he is worthy of emulation; OR, that as a result of these beliefs, he is accepted as their 'leader'.
>
> (Bullen 1987: np)

In other words, Weber aimed at describing an inter-subjective and sociological notion of charismatic leadership. (In support of this interpretation, see Dow 1978; Tucker 1968; Tuccari 1991.)

The concept of charisma has continued to be modified by sociological, political and organizational scholars (Shils 1965); even into the postmodern era we lack a solid understanding of charisma in relation to organizations (Bryman 1992). This lack of understanding of charisma has indeed kept it mysterious. As Nozick stated, 'by its own nature (charisma) does not invite analysis; in fact, it discourages it' (1990: 76). The aura surrounding charisma has also created a serious worry of what happens when this personal quality gets out of control and turns to evil (Keeley 1995). Solomon (2004) concluded, after looking at the moral and ethical issues of charisma, that maybe charisma should not be let out of the bottle as it can be so dangerous.

To gain a better understanding of charisma, modern researchers began to reexamine the classic work of Max Weber. This new focus on Weber's work began to question the role of the follower and organization in creating charisma. The three major questions are: Is there everyday charisma? Can charisma be rational? Can charisma function effectively within a formal organization? Conger (1988) helped to answer these questions by distinguishing Weber's types further by the following comparisons:

- *Rational vs Heroic* – Both the charismatic and rational types are revolting against the tyranny of tradition. The charismatic revolution depends on beliefs and revelation. Charismatic authority seeks to overturn the existing social order that is stagnant or in crisis. Its goal is to appeal to **followers**' emotions and mind.
- *Stable vs Transitory* – Charismatic authority is transitory; its purpose is to be a transition from one stable type of authority to another.
- *Formal vs Informal Organization* – While the traditional and rational work around permanent organizations, the charismatic authority operates through informal organizations. It is unencumbered by formalities and organized arrangements.

Conger further stated that Weber was ultimately concerned with understanding the creation and transformation of institutional arrangements. Under this guise, the German sociologist wanted to explain the forces of individual **creativity** that completely contradicted the other two systems. In order to do this, it was natural that Weber got very interested in the role of the follower in charismatic authority.

House (1977) made a major contribution to the study of charisma in formal organizations. By establishing testable hypotheses about the behaviour of charismatic leaders, follower effects and situation factors, he was the first to empirically examine these relationships (Bryman 1992). This seminal work offered a very intricate model based on the interaction of leader characteristics (i.e. self-confidence and need for **influence**) and the ability to establish favourable perceptions of followers.

The impact of House's study was tremendous. The study represented the basis for the way the new leadership theorists initially viewed how charisma could function within the organization. This study generated several studies to identify charismatic leaders in organizations and to characterize their behaviour and effects (Shamir

1991). In addition, the study was instrumental in showing the profound impact followers have in the relationship.

Peters and Waterman's (1982) work on the role of charisma in excellent organizations was also influential in illustrating how charismatic leaders can function within an organization. Called antibureaucrats, the authors saw them as championing innovation and bringing about change. The idea of charismatic leaders being change agents has brought about an increased interest in the charismatic process primarily due to the inflexible bureaucratic organizational climate in the United States (Conger 1993).

The work of House (1977), Peters and Waterman (1982), and the emergence of **transformational leadership**, have reduced the confusion and ambiguity surrounding charisma. The realization that charisma cannot function in a vacuum but as a social relationship has become more accepted. As Bryman explained,

> charisma is a social relationship in three ways; the importance of followers in the affirmation of charisma, the leader and follower find a greater purpose in charisma than is typically the case and charismatic relationship is antithetical to the notion that charisma is purely attribution.
>
> (Bryman 1992: 69)

The dynamics of charismatic **leader–follower relations** continues to gain attention. Burns (1978) and Bass (1988) quickly advocated the need for charisma in every leader to transform and revitalize organizations. They introduced the concepts of transactional and transformational leadership. Coined by Bryman (1992) as the new leadership approach, transformational leaders achieve results through followers in one or more ways. For example, transformational leaders inspire followers through charisma, meet their emotional needs through individual consideration and stimulate them intellectually by stirring their awareness of problems (Pierce and Newstrom 1994).

The most important impact of Bass and later Avolio has been their systematic research of leadership using a reliable and valid instrument. The Multifactor Leadership Questionnaire (MLQ) was based on Bass' original work with the purpose of 'capturing the broadest range of leadership behaviors while differentiating ineffective and effective leaders' (Bass 1985: 135). The instrument comprised 10 factors under four categories; transformational leadership which includes charisma as a significant component. Most importantly, the instrument has been found to be a reliable measure of charisma (Avolio *et al.* 1991).

The work of the modern authors led to a more in-depth investigation of charisma. Graham (1988) believed that research which measures both charismatic leaders and their followers is the best way to remove the perception of charisma as mysterious and magical, believing along with Howell (1988) and Klein and House (1995) that followers of charismatic leaders have been largely ignored. Believing that charisma resided in the relationship between the leader and follower and not in the leader only, Klein and House found differences in the relationships between the levels of charisma and the homogeneity of followers. Furthermore, many leadership researchers have theorized that a social construction perspective is necessary to better understand the relationship of charismatic leaders, followers and the environment. As Bryman (1993) stated, the social constructive perspective creates an opportunity to illuminate the understanding of how charismatic leadership works in organizations. Meindl (1995) stated that charisma cannot be viewed as predetermined based on a specific definition, but viewed as a social relationship that is a function of the leader, follower and environment. Therefore, Drath and Palus (1994) defined charisma as part of a highly emotional and socially charged process by which this leader embodies what members within the community have in their minds and hearts, and in return these people legitimize this leader with special characteristics.

See also: **organizational culture, power, religious meaning, situational leadership, transformational leadership**

Further reading: Bryman 1992; Bullen 1987; House 1977; Klein and House 1995; Weber 1947

COMPLEXITY THEORY

John S. Burns

Though often unrecognized, paradigms from classical science inform social sciences like leadership studies. Based on equations developed by Galileo Galilei and Descartes, Newton invented the calculus of differential equations in the 1600s. Newton's calculus allowed him to describe the motion of solid bodies (Capra 1996), which led to the development of the mechanical-universe paradigm. The universe Newton described was a 'machine' made up of myriad components, each playing out a role rooted in cause and effect determinism. The job of science was to employ reductionist methodologies to explore increasingly intricate parts of the machine in order to discover fundamental causes. Theoretically, it might be possible to determine the underlying causes for everything and indeed, through the lens of this paradigm, science and technology made unprecedented advances for more than three centuries.

At the close of the nineteenth century, the universe of the Newtonians began to crumble as physicists began their explorations in the quantum world. In other fields, such as biology, modelling nature through linear equations also had severe limitations. Capra explains: 'Exact solutions were restricted to a few simple and regular phenomena, while the complexity of vast areas of nature seemed to elude all mechanistic modelling' (1996: 121). Thus, cause and effect determinism borders on mythology as a credible description for complex natural phenomena. Through quantum and later chaos theory discoveries in physics, and through complexity theory in biology, the twentieth century witnessed physical and natural scientists rethinking their fundamental paradigms. Instead of presenting the idea of a deterministic machine, the emerging paradigms describe a living universe that is continually changing through adaptation.

In leadership studies, the suppositions from Newton's mechanical paradigm are as invisible, pervasive and unexamined as the air we breathe. Even the verbs used in reference to leadership describe the assumption of a mechanical 'nature' of organizations. For example, organizations are *run*, systems are *operated*, **followers** are *developed*, and lines of communication are *built*. Management theorists jumped headlong into the Cartesian mechanistic paradigm during the Industrial Revolution. They examined organizations, and through scientific management, experimented with ways to manipulate workers and organizational structures to increase efficiency. For more than a century, management and leadership theorists have employed Newtonian reductionist methodologies as they have investigated ideas about charismatic, democratic, autocratic, humanistic, collaborative, team, community, feminist, male, modern, post-modern, transforming, transactional, top-down, bottom-up and middle-of-the-road leadership. They have conducted countless studies about the traits of good and bad leaders and followers, about **power** and its characteristics, environmental factors, social ills and a host of other atomized topics. Over the last 15 years, some social scientists have begun to re-evaluate their fundamental paradigms in light of the demise of the mechanical-universe paradigm (Burns 2002; Lewin and Regine 2001; Lissack 2002; Stacey 1996; Wheatley 1999). Most social scientists, however, are still steeped in scientific reductionism, believing underlying causes can be discovered; and if they are known, effects can be predicted and possibly controlled.

The emerging paradigm based in complexity theory from biology and quantum and chaos theories from physics allows social scientists to understand human organizations as complex adaptive systems. The new complexity/chaos paradigm teaches that organizations function not as machines, but as organic entities in a web of living complex adaptive systems, all capable of learning and transforming in response to environmental challenges. As this new paradigm gains traction, there will be profound changes in the ways in which people think about leadership in human organizations.

A living organization needs to be nurtured. Healthy organizations remain healthy as they continually adapt to the ever-turbulent environment. In the new paradigm, reductionist analysis and manipulation of the various components of the organization is not crucial. Instead, conducting leadership depends on the richness of the web of relationships, the free flow of critical information, and individual-agent and organizational learning, which leads to an adaptive response to the environment. Constrained by the mission and values of the organization, these are the things that nurture an organization, and they conspire to facilitate its long-term survival.

An organization's ultimate purpose and its core values are the essence of the 'strange attractor' (from chaos theory) that functions to keep the organization from either ossifying or flying into completely random behaviour. This middle ground between ossification and randomness is where the organization can continually self-organize. In this creative zone, it holds in dynamic tension the inclination to implode – by 'managing' the organization so closely that it is no longer responsive to environmental influences – or to explode into total chaos, by being so responsive to the environment that the organization loses its focus and purpose (Burns 2000; Stacey 1996; Wheatley 1999).

In the new paradigm, leadership is not reduced to the 'leadership' behaviour or traits of a leader or team of 'top' people. Leadership is conducted as the complex adaptive system learns from and successfully adapts to environmental challenges. Thus, leadership is conducted throughout and by the entire organization (Rost 1991), because in turbulent environments, any agent might have access to vital information about the organization's relationship with the environment.

Leaders (key position holders) have important functions that facilitate the adaptive process of a complex adaptive system. The first function is to continually revisit and uphold the ultimate shared purpose and core values of the organization. Second, key position holders must assure that the organization is engaged in continuous assessment of environmental demands as they relate to the primary mission and values of the organization, testing adaptive strategies that could potentially satisfy those demands. The third function is to ensure that information, the 'food' that keeps the organization alive and growing (Wheatley 1999), flows throughout the organization.

As an organization continually grows and adapts to environmental demands, its ultimate purpose and core values become clearer because they are viewed in multiple environmental contexts over time. Thus, the organization is able to lift its collective vision to discover creative ways to continually adapt in order to fulfil its enduring essential purpose.

See also: **creativity, distributed leadership, leadership definition, organizational culture, transformational leadership**

Further reading: Burns 2002; Kauffman 1995; Lewin and Regine 2001; Stacey 1996; Wheatley 1999

CONTINGENCY THEORIES

JoAnn Danelo Barbour

Following criticism in leadership studies that the 'great man' theories and behavioural theories do not take into account the context of leadership, contingency theory has been an attempt to assess and discuss leadership from two perspectives. From an organizational perspective in systems theory, contingency theorists view organizational and administrative processes and choices as contingent upon the particular character or nature of the organization itself, the environment of the organization at that particular moment, and the specific task or tasks the organization seeks to accomplish at a particular time. Scott (1987) suggests that when Lawrence and Lorsch (1967) coined the term 'contingency theory' their argument was that different environments place differing requirements on organizations, and, accordingly, on the leaders of those organizations. From the leader's perspective grounded in behavioural theory, contingency theorists contend that there is no one best way of leading, that a leadership style that is effective in some situations may not be successful in others. The leader's ability to lead, consequently, is contingent upon various situational factors, including the leader's preferred style, the capabilities and behaviours of **followers** and also various other situational factors. Contingency theories will be discussed from the leader's perspective noting the contributions of key theorists, the chief criticisms of contingency theories, and emerging theories.

Contingency theorists stress several key concepts. There is no universal or one best way to lead. There is, however, some common ground among the universal principles of leadership that fits all situations. Organizationally, the design and its subsystems must be a 'fit' for the leader; the organization, its subsystems and leader must have a proper 'fit' with the environment; and each situation within the organizational environment is unique and therefore must be studied and treated as unique. The success of the leader is a function of various organizational contingencies in the form of subordinate, task and/or group variables. The **effectiveness** of a given pattern of leader behaviour is contingent upon the demands imposed by the situation. For an individual leader, contingency theory assumes that leadership is changeable and should be variable for different situations; thus, these theories stress using different styles of leadership appropriate to the needs created by different organizational situations. The contingency theories noted below include grid, continuum and decision tree models, and focus on three variables: leader's style, follower's **motivation** and skill, and nature of the task.

Fred Fiedler (1967, 1973, 1974), generally considered the father of leadership contingency theory, departed from trait and behavioural models by asserting that three organizational contingencies determine appropriate leadership behaviour: leader–member relations (the degree to which a leader is accepted and supported by group members), task structure (the extent to which tasks are structured and defined with clear goals and procedures), and leader positional **power** (the ability of a leader to control subordinates through reward and punishment). Fiedler argued that combinations of the three contingencies create favourable or unfavourable conditions for leadership, that is, situations in which the leader can exert **influence** over the group. High levels of leader–member relations, task structure and positional power provide the most favourable situation to exert influence over others; low levels of the three contingencies provide the least favourable leadership situation to exert influence. Fiedler determined that a task-oriented style is more effective in situations wherein the leader has very much or very little influence; a relationship–oriented leader is more effective in situations only moderately favourable to influence.

Fiedler concluded that the organization should match up a particular manager or leader and style to the demands of the situation, or alter the variables within the situation, that is the power that goes with the leadership position, so that the situation becomes more conducive to one's style of influence. In other words, it may be easier for leaders to change a situation to achieve effectiveness, rather than change leadership style.

Introducing a variation to Fiedler's model, two examples of continuum models include House and Mitchell (1974, 1997) and Tannenbaum and Schmidt (1973). Influenced by expectancy theories of motivation, House and Mitchell developed the Path-Goal contingency model, asserting that the leader's behaviour is acceptable to subordinates insofar as they view the behaviour as a source of immediate or future satisfaction. They suggest the leader affects the performance, satisfaction and motivation of a group in a number of ways. The **responsibility** of the leader is to observe and understand the situation and choose appropriate leadership styles and actions (paths) depending upon goals of subordinates and leader. The responsibilities of the leader, to offer rewards for achievement of performance goals, to clarify paths towards these goals, and to remove obstacles, are accomplished by adopting certain leadership styles according to the situation. Leader styles will be directive, supportive, participative and achievement-oriented, depending on subordinate needs and abilities. Leadership behaviours are matched along a continuum of subordinate and environmental characteristics, from structured to unstructured situations; thus, if group members have a high need for motivation, directive leadership is provided, specific advice is given and ground rules are established to provide structure. If members have a low need for motivation, achievement-oriented leadership is provided and challenging goals are set with high performance encouraged while showing confidence in members' ability, a more unstructured situation. Effective leaders adjust their leadership to fit these contingencies of group and environment and to motivate subordinates. House and Mitchell add that leaders who have influence upon their superiors can increase group satisfaction and performance. Additionally, Tannenbaum and Schmidt describe a range of behavioural patterns available to a manager or leader, from democratic (relationship-oriented) leadership to authoritarian (task-oriented) leadership. The choice of leader actions relates to the degree of **authority** used by the leader and the amount of freedom available to the subordinates. The leader's actions described on the left of the continuum characterize one who maintains a high degree of control, while those on the right describe a leader who delegates authority. They believe a leader should be flexible and adapt the leadership style to the situation.

Hersey and Blanchard (1974, 1993) developed the Situational Leadership Grid which contains two dimensions of leadership: task behaviour, wherein the leader delineates the duties and responsibilities of an individual or group, and relationship behaviour, the extent a leader participates in two-way or multi-level communication, that is, listening, facilitating behaviours and providing socioemotional support with behavioural choices to include giving support, communicating, facilitating interactions, active listening and providing feedback. Hersey and Blanchard suggest that leadership style should be matched to the maturity of the subordinates (psychological maturity, subordinate self-confidence and ability and readiness to accept responsibility) and job maturity (relevant skills and technical knowledge). As the subordinate maturity increases, leaders should be more relationship-motivated than task-motivated. Leadership will vary with the situation and the leader may delegate to, participate with, sell ideas to, or tell subordinates what to do.

Vroom and Yetton (1973) and Vroom and Jago (1988) developed a decision tree contingency model for leader decision–making, a normative model that emphasizes leader behaviour from authoritative to participative. According to this model, the effectiveness of a decision procedure depends upon a number of aspects of the situation: the importance of the decision quality and acceptance; the amount of relevant information possessed by the leader and subordinates; the likelihood that subordinates will accept an autocratic decision or cooperate in trying to make a good decision if allowed to participate; and the amount of disagreement among subordinates with respect to their preferred alternatives. The Vroom-Yetton Leadership Model includes the selection of one of five leadership styles for making a decision: Autocratic 1 when the problem is solved using information already available; Autocratic 2 when additional information is obtained from the group before the leader makes a decision; Consultative 1 when the leader discusses the problem with subordinates individually before making a decision; Consultative 2 when the problem is discussed with the group before deciding; and Group 2 when the group makes the decision with the leader simply acting as facilitator. The leadership style is chosen by considering seven questions that form the decision tree. Vroom and Yetton suggest that the overall effectiveness of a decision depends on two intervening variables: decision quality, the objective aspects of the decision that affect group performance regardless of any effects mediated by decision acceptance, and decision acceptance by followers, the degree of follower commitment in implementing a decision effectively. They maintain that both decision quality and acceptance are affected by follower participation during decision-making.

While contingency theories have been a valuable approach to understanding leadership behaviours, there have been criticisms of the approach. Critics suggest contingency theorists are limited in their conceptualization of leadership and the empirical strength to support the various arguments. Circumstances do not stay fixed for long, for example, which would necessitate a constant renegotiating of leadership behaviours and styles. The interactions of all factors are very complex and unpredictable. Fiedler and others suggest that further research is needed to encompass more variables that may be within various situations. Bolman and Deal (1991) suggest that contingency theorists fail to distinguish between manager and leader behaviour, and support for a person or support for specific actions. Often there is an oversimplification of options available to leaders and the range of situations that leaders encounter, with some theorists providing illusory promises to make leaders' lives less confusing and perplexing.

Studies in the area of contingency theories seem to have diminished, due, in part, to the increase in contextual approaches to studying leadership, whereby contextual factors are seen as a basis for certain leadership behaviours or their dispositional antecedents. These contextual factors can include leader hierarchical level, national culture, leader–follower gender or organizational characteristics, among others (Antonakis *et al.* 2003). Research is ongoing within the realm of chaos, chaordic and complexity theories, including spiral dynamics. Behavioural complexity from the notion of paradox (Denison *et al.* 1995), symbolic behaviours (Schein 1985; Hofstede 1980), contingencies within systems (Senge 1990) are also promising approaches.

See also: **behavioural theories of leadership, complexity theory, great man theory, leader–follower relations, trait theory**

Further reading: Fiedler 1973, 1974; Hersey and Blanchard 1993; Vroom and Jago 1988; Vroom and Yetton 1973

CREATIVITY

Christian De Cock

The concept of creativity has very much re-established itself on both corporate and political radars since its heyday of the 1950s and 1960s. In recent years we have witnessed a surge of books exploring creativity in a business context (Bills and Genasi 2003; de Brabandere 2005; Gogatz and Mondejar 2005; Kelley 2001; Proctor 2005), and in response to the *Cox Review of Creativity in Business* (Cox 2005) the 2006 UK Budget Report included the launch of a feasibility study for a London creativity and innovation hub at the centre of a wider network of creativity and innovation centres. The same year saw a joint initiative from the Department of Trade and Industry and various UK Research Councils called *Exploring the Nature of Creativity*. This programme provided substantial funding 'to support researchers in setting up workshops and networks which will stimulate discussion and research to enhance our understanding about the nature of creativity and . . . the conditions which underpin creativity' (Arts and Humanities Research Council, 3 February 2006, www.ahrc.ac. uk/news/news_pr/2006/exploring_the_nature_of_creativity.asp Accessed 2 August 2007).

Various commentators (Bills and Genasi 2003; De Cock 1996; Mumford and Gustafson 1988) have pointed out that creativity is a rather slippery concept. One of the founding fathers of creativity research summed it up rather nicely at the end of his career: 'The very essence of creativity will, I believe, always elude us. That, however, is no reason for giving up on our research; rather, it is all the more reason for continuing our research' (MacKinnon 1978: xvi). Apart from definitional vagueness, creativity as a subject for scientific study also struggles with what Rickards and De Cock have called the ontological paradox: 'How might the generative process of creativity be expressed within a model or theory seeking some generalizability if an essential property of the process is its uniqueness from that which existed before?' (1999: 239). More recently a special issue of the journal *Creativity and Innovation Management* (vol. 15, no. 2) was devoted to this thorny issue of 'novelty' (De Cock and Rehn 2006). Such reservations have not held back practitioners generating a multitude of 'working definitions' and the one provided in the Cox report is a recent typical example: '*Creativity* is the generation of new ideas – either new ways of looking at existing problems, or of seeing new opportunities, perhaps by exploiting emerging technologies or changes in markets' (Cox 2005: 2). Thus creativity involves looking differently at what we normally take for granted: 'It's the ability consistently to generate novel responses to all sorts of issues, problems, situations and challenges . . . ' (Gogatz and Mondejar 2005: 9).

Tudor Rickards (1999: 26–36) provided an instructive overview of historical landmarks in creativity research. One such landmark was JP Guilford's speech to the American Psychological Association which was widely reported outside the confines of academia. The background was the successful launch of the Soviet satellite Sputnik and the perceived loss of national technological advantage.[1] Federal funds were attracted to researching the creativity phenomenon and to educational initiatives for stimulating creativity. Other key landmarks include Arthur Koestler's investigation of the creative process in *The Act of Creation* (1964); Edward de Bono's writings on lateral thinking, Torrance's Test of Creative Thinking (TTCT – these were designed to assess and codify originality as well as fluency and flexibility in idea generation), and the introduction of brainstorming.

Brainstorming is without doubt the best known way of stimulating creativity in the workplace. In 1953 advertising executive Alex Osborn collected the techniques used to stimulate 'everyday creativity' in his practice, which he labelled 'brainstorming', in a book called *Applied Imagination*. The three major principles for generating ideas in the work environment were: *postpone judgement*, *quantity breeds quality* and *hitchhike* (building on others' ideas). The status of brainstorming has been controversial since it was lampooned by the business magazine *Fortune* as 'cerebral popcorn' in the 1950s. Many academic studies have shown since that nominal (non-interacting) groups seem to produce more ideas than brainstorming groups and no conclusive evidence has been offered to date as to the quality of the ideas produced. Yet, virtually all of these critical studies were 'laboratory' or 'classroom' based. A seminal article by Sutton and Hargadon (1996) based on research in an organizational setting (the American design company IDEO) outlined a range of '**effectiveness** outcomes' ranging far beyond simple idea generation. These included: supporting the organizational memory of design solutions; providing skill variety; supporting an attitude of **wisdom** (acting with knowledge while doubting what one knows); and impressing clients. Alex Osborn went on to establish the Creative Education Foundation at Buffalo, New York. Here Sid Parnes was influential in further developing the CPS model. Consisting of six stages – objective finding, fact finding, problem finding, idea finding, solution finding and acceptance finding – the CPS model is designed to give an understanding of the scope of a project, and find new perspectives to generate novel, actionable ideas. One of the best practical guides on running a CPS session is still Parnes' (1985) 50-page booklet *A Creative Style of Leadership*. The CPS model has proved very influential (Puccio *et al.* (2006) provide a comprehensive longitudinal review of the effectiveness of CPS training in a workplace environment) and has been adapted to suit various contexts (e.g. Rickards and De Cock (1994) sketch out the mutation of CPS into the MPIA model and explore its effectiveness in a European context). The Center for Creative Leadership based in Greensboro, North Carolina (www.ccl.org/leadership) has been at the forefront of integrating research into stimulating creativity (and the CPS model in particular) with leadership research. Rickards and Moger (2006) recently wrote an overview article on the understanding of leadership as a process contributing to creativity and innovation, and their research serves as a useful point of departure for those wishing to explore the links between leadership and creativity.

See also: **effectiveness**, **leadership definition**, **organizational culture**, **process theory**, **wisdom**

Further reading: Bilton 2007; de Brabandere 2005; De Cock and Rehn 2006; Rickards and Moger 2006; Rickards *et al.* forthcoming

CROSS-CULTURAL LEADERSHIP

Dale Pfeifer and Brad Jackson

This term refers to leadership in which a leader endeavours to **influence** the activities and goals of a culturally diverse group by appealing to their systems of shared knowledge and meaning. Cross-cultural leadership recognizes the moderating effect that culture can have on leadership processes. It also seeks to discover the similarities and differences between cultures as to what is generally considered to constitute appropriate and inappropriate **leader–follower relations**.

Interest in cross-cultural leadership was initially prompted by the rapid expansion of a large expatriate work force driven to the far corners of an increasingly globalized world. These managers often experienced 'culture shock', as they set about trying to adjust their management and leadership styles to a different set of dominant norms and expectations of the host society (Frederick and Rodrigues 1994; Harris and Moran 1987). The expatriate's need to understand the fundamentals of intercultural interactions combined with their sponsoring organization's need to successfully manage international assignments drove the demand for cross-cultural leadership theory and skill development. In response, cross-cultural leadership theorists tended to focus their efforts on providing broad-based descriptions of the characteristics of a particular national culture, combined with an account of the specific idiosyncrasies of conducting business within that national culture (Hickson and Pugh 2001). These were replete with case studies and guidelines as to what to do and not do in order to survive and excel in a culturally different context. This type of work continues to be an important staple of the popular management book market, but has been superseded by more sophisticated attempts to develop universal theoretical models of cross-cultural leadership.

One major line of inquiry has been to seek to identify the persistent behavioural patterns exhibited by leaders from different national cultures. Specifically, the focus of this work has been to identify the ways in which predominant cultural values moderate leadership behavioural patterns (Dorfman and Howell 1988). Differences are systematically described by systems that categorize and compare cultural values. Several influential universal frameworks comprised of cultural value dimensions emerged from this work including Kluckhohn and Strodtbeck (1961), Trompenaars and Hampden-Turner (1997) and Hofstede (1980). Hofstede's five dimensions of power distance, individualism/collectivism, uncertainty avoidance, masculinity/femininity and long- vs short-term orientation have been highly influential and continue to shape a great deal of contemporary cross-cultural leadership research.

Another major line of inquiry has sought to identify and delimit the shared prototypes or profiles of outstanding leadership that might be distinctive to specific national cultures. This has been done primarily by examining **followers**' perceptions of leaders' behaviour, values, attitudes and personality traits (Shaw 1990), referred to generally as implicit leadership theories. Prototypes contain a set of attributes that define the essential characteristics of a category, for example, an effective business leader. Leadership categorization theory (Lord and Maher 1991) suggests that the better the match between a perceived individual and the leadership concept held by the perceiver, the more likely it is that the perceiver actually 'sees' the individual as a leader. Followers who categorize a manager as a prototypical leader are likely to allow him or her to exert leadership influence on them. If leadership concepts differ as a function of cultural differences, they can constrain the influence of expatriate managers: in other words, the more leadership conceptions diverge between managers and subordinates or colleagues, the less referent influence will likely be exerted by the manager.

Unquestionably the most ambitious piece of cross-cultural leadership research conducted to date has been undertaken by the Global Leadership and Organisational Behaviour Effective (GLOBE) Project led by Robert House. This long-term programmatic research project involved approximately 170 scholars from more than 62 nations over an 11-year time period. Field data were collected from more than 17,000 managers, in 900 organizations, across three industries, using quantitative and qualitative methods. It assessed the relationship between nine culture dimensions (uncertainty avoidance, power distance, institutional collectivism, in-group collectivism, gender egalitarianism, assertiveness, future orientation, performance orientation and humane orientation) and six global leadership dimensions (charismatic/value-based, team-oriented, participatory, humane-oriented, autonomous and self-protective). Systematically testing more than 20 hypotheses, the GLOBE has added significant depth to our understanding of cross-cultural leadership.

Although significant progress has been made towards developing universal models of cross-cultural leadership, Dorfman (2004) has offered a timely warning about the limitations of this research in the form of four caveats he believes should be borne in mind when applying a cross-cultural lens to leadership research. With the first caveat, he warns leadership researchers against the perils of ignoring significant differences within a country as well as significant differences between countries that are considered part of a country cluster. With the second caveat he points out that a cultural dimension that has been identified as being associated with a particular national culture may, in fact, vary and seem contradictory at times. The third caveat is that individual differences will still exist in the adherence to cultural values and, as such, not all individuals will display the cultural values of their indigenous culture. Osland and Bird (2000) have similarly warned against the dangers of blindly applying 'sophisticated stereotypes' when trying to understand and lead in culturally diverse contexts. Related to this, the final caveat for leadership researchers offered by Dorfman is to consider that cultures are not static but are dynamic and continually evolving.

Perceptions of what it means to be a successful 'global leader' are changing. No longer are the 'geocentric globetrotters' who were transferred from country to country to manage foreign operations seen as being the exemplars of good global leadership. Instead, global leaders need to endeavour to become transcultural creative leaders (Graen and Hui 1999). These leaders have the ability to learn how to transcend their childhood acculturation; respect very different cultures; build cross-cultural partnerships based on mutual **trust**, respect and obligation; actively engage in cross-cultural problem-solving conflicts; and help to construct new cultures based around projects, networks and transitory organizations.

See also: **behavioural theories of leadership, leader–follower relations, leadership definition, transformational theory**

Further reading: Den Hartog *et al.* 1999; Dorfman 2004; Hofstede 2004; House *et al.* 2004; Thomas and Inkson 2004

DELEGATION

Mindy S. McNutt

Today's manager is being called upon to work in a rapid-paced environment, where more and more productivity is expected. In fact, over 20 years ago, McCormack commented: 'If executives were asked to list their greatest frustrations, I suspect that not having enough time would be very near the top of the list' (1984: 209). The demands on the manager's time have only increased in the years since. In today's work environment, managers find it both necessary and beneficial to delegate work to others. Not only is it beneficial to the manager, but it benefits the employee and the organization as well.

The process of delegation involves the transfer of carefully selected tasks or activities from the manager to an appropriately selected individual. According to Yukl, delegating is 'allowing subordinates to have substantial responsibility and discretion in carrying out work activities, handling problems, and making important decisions' (1998: 60). Hunsaker indicated that 'delegation occurs when a manager transfers **authority** to a subordinate for achieving goals and making decisions about how to do a job' (2001: 430). Moreover, Lussier and Achua wrote that 'delegation is the process of assigning responsibility and authority for accomplishing objectives' (2001: 229).

Clearly, the transfer of authority to carry out the assigned tasks is essential. Individuals who have been given specific assignments must have the **power** to make decisions, and have full access to all the resources necessary to accomplish the objectives (Yukl 1998). According to Portny, authority is 'the ability to make decisions', where **responsibility** is 'the obligation to ensure certain results are achieved' (2002: 62). He felt that authority can be transferred to the employee, but ultimate responsibility for completion of the task lies with the manager.

There are three primary reasons why managers utilize delegation; to manage their workload, for the professional development of the employee and to benefit the organization. From the manager's perspective, the act of delegation frees him or her to focus on more critical or higher-priority goals and tasks for the organization (Hughes *et al*. 2002; Lussier and Achua 2001). This not only provides a means of time management, but it also allows the manager to increase his or her productivity (Lussier and Achua 2001; Yukl 1998). Additionally, it is important for managers to recognize that, at times, the employee may have more expertise in the area of the specific task, and it would benefit the organization more by delegating that specific task (Yukl 1998).

For the employee, delegation provides an important developmental opportunity. It can make the job more interesting, challenging and meaningful (Hughes *et al*. 2002). The employee can develop or enhance existing skills and abilities, and work toward gaining new skills that will benefit not only him or her, but the organization as well (Yukl 1998). Additionally, it provides the opportunity to learn more about the work unit and can assist in developing new capabilities, talents and interests on the part of the employee (Ponder 2005; Quinn *et al*. 2003). Employees who work on delegated tasks are more committed to the task at hand. Moreover, successful completion of delegated tasks provides a means for building **trust** with the manager and self-esteem for the employee (Quallich 2005; Yukl 1998).

Organizationally, delegation can lead to higher productivity, higher quality decisions and increase the tasks accomplished and thereby strengthen the organization (Bass 1990b; Hughes *et al*. 2002; Lussier and Achua 2001; Yukl 1998). By providing these new opportunities for the employee, there can be a better allocation of organizational resources, and this management development opportunity can increase the pool of potential managers for the future (Lussier and Achua 2001).

It is important to recognize that there are some caveats related to delegation. For all the benefits that seemed to be gained, some managers avoid delegation for a variety of reasons. Related to the self, some managers have power needs, and may feel that giving up tasks diminishes that power, or feel that it could be too much of a career risk (Hughes *et al*. 2002; Portny 2002; Yukl 1998). Moreover, certain tasks that might be delegated may have some prestige associated with them and therefore the manager wants to keep them for him or herself (Hughes *et al*. 2002; Yukl 1998). Additionally, some managers may be used to doing certain tasks themselves, or simply do not know how or what to delegate (Lussier and Achua 2001). Yet others may feel that delegating is too time-consuming to oversee, and assume that they can do the job better and faster (Hughes *et al.* 2002).

Related to the employee, some managers may doubt the subordinate's ability to complete the task, feel the job will not be done as well, and fear being blamed if something goes wrong (Hughes *et al.* 2002). Subordinates may have different values and goals than the manager, and sometimes others are just simply too busy to take on a new task (Yukl 1998).

The first principle in learning how to delegate is for the manager to understand the strengths and weaknesses of each employee. This process allows the manager to select the best person for each of the tasks that will be delegated (Hughes *et al.* 2002; Lussier and Achua 2001; Ponder 2005; Portny 2002).

Second, the manager must decide what to delegate with an awareness of what can and cannot be assigned to someone else (Quallich 2005; Quinn *et al.* 2003). Tasks that can be delegated include: those that are better done by the employee, given his or her skills and abilities; those relevant to the employee's career; and those not central to the manager (Yukl 1998). Not all tasks are appropriate to be assigned to an employee. For example, matters related to personnel should not be delegated, nor should confidential issues, crises or situations in which it is difficult to coordinate interdependent individuals (Lussier and Achua 2001; Portny 2002; Yukl 1998).

Third, the manager must be an effective communicator. Not only will he or she need to effectively communicate the task to be accomplished, but also the parameters for successful completion of the task, noting any constraints and the resources available (Ponder 2005; Portny 2002). There must be openness for the employee to be able to come to the manager to discuss any issues or problems that fall outside of the employee's area of expertise (Portny 2002). Delegating must allow for the employee to work autonomously, but with monitors on progress (Hughes *et al.* 2002; Ponder 2005).

Fourth, the manager must assign the objective of the task, but not the means to accomplish it. There is no 'one best way' to accomplish a task, and this allows the employee the opportunity to stretch his or her skills and learning opportunities (Portny 2002). Finally, the manager must be willing to let go, and understand that delegation involves a learning process for the employee and a chance for professional growth (Quallich 2005).

Managers should ensure that employees, to whom tasks have been delegated, understand the context and importance of the job (Portny 2002; Quinn *et al.* 2003). Moreover, throughout the whole process employees should be supported and encouraged. In fact, Peters emphasized the 'role of faith, belief, vision, caring, intensity' (1987: 456) related to delegation. Additionally he noted that 'paradoxes abound, such as really letting go, but establishing an inspiring moral context for the importance of the task – including the leader's obvious confidence and caring' (Peters 1987: 456).

Quinn *et al.* (2003: 49–50) offered managers these important keys to effective delegation:

1 Clarify, in your own mind, what it is that you want done.
2 Match the desired task with the most appropriate employee.
3 In assigning the task, be sure you communicate clearly.
4 Make sure that the employee has the time to do the assignment.
5 Keep the communication channels open.
6 Allow employees to do the task the way they feel comfortable doing it.
7 Check on the progress of the assignment, but do not rush to the rescue at the first sign of failure.
8 Hold the person responsible for the work and any difficulties that may emerge.
9 Make sure that the person has appropriate authority to carry out the task and obtain the resources and cooperation required for its successful completion.
10 Recognize the employee's accomplishments.

Finally, in the end, it is important for the manager and the employee to evaluate both the success of the results, and the learning opportunities that were gained by the employee. This provides a feedback loop that will allow the employee to grow from the experience and be better able to contribute to the organization in the future.

See also: **authority**, **leader–follower relations**, **leadership development**, **organizational culture**, **responsibility**

Further reading: Blanchard *et al.* 2001; Heller 1998; Huppe 1994; Nelson 1994; Taylor 1991

DERAILMENT

Michael Walton

Instances of successful and prominent leaders who self-destruct are increasingly and regularly reported in the media. Investigation of the bases for 'derailment' – the involuntary failure of able and successful senior executives – remains an intriguing area of leadership research. The term 'derailment' – associated with the groundbreaking research into this phenomenon conducted by the Center for Creative Leadership (CCL) in the 1980s – refers to leaders with a strong track record of success who, involuntarily, fail to fulfil their career potential and their corporation's expectations. Such instances are: (i) unintentional, (ii) come as a surprise (although there may well have been clues of impending disaster in their past work) and (iii) will cause considerable collateral damage both to the organization and the individual(s) affected (McCall 1998).

> Few people reach the top of a major corporation without considerable talent and an impressive list of accomplishments. Still, many talented executives rise *near* the top yet are denied the ultimate positions. The quick answers to why this can happen include the ever-popular Peter Principle – rising past one's level of competence – or more darkly, that some managers possess a fatal flaw.
>
> (McCall and Lombardo 1983a: 1)

Early research studies, which examined derailment cases from Fortune 100 companies and compared derailed leaders with those who were continuing to function successfully at the top, contributed insights into the developmental needs of managers aspiring to senior leadership positions (Lombardo and McCall 1984; McCall and Lombardo 1983a, b; CCL 2002). In their initial studies, CCL defined a successful executive as a manager who had made it to at least general manager level and who was considered by senior executives to have potential for further promotion. In contrast, a derailed executive was defined as a manager who had made it to the same general management level but who – despite all expectations – had failed to progress further and had then involuntarily left the company or plateaued-out into a position that was less senior than expected. The derailment was seen as indicating a perceived lack of 'fit' between the derailed leader's personal characteristics and the skills and demands of the job at the more senior level. The research highlights how even very senior and successful people with a strong track record remain prone to failure in spite of significant career and professional success.

The CCL research found that both successful and derailed managers shared many of the same skills and limitations. Those who remained successful, however, evidenced five underlying characteristics in that they (i) had more diversity in their career paths, (ii) maintained composure under stress, (iii) handled mistakes with poise, (iv) were focused problem-solvers and (v) got along with all kinds of people (Lombardo and McCauley 1988; McCall and Lombardo 1983a, b).

Corporate seniority increases the potential for the exposure and amplification of leadership behaviours that could become dysfunctional if exaggerated or overused. The studies noted how strengths become weaknesses, how previously unimportant blind-spots come to matter when occupying more senior and exposed positions, how success led to arrogance and in some instances how bad luck conspired to derail the leader (McCall 1998). Susceptibility to the so-called 'Success Trap' in which over-reliance on strengths and past successes, combined with a reluctance to admit and overcome weaknesses and limitations, was seen to lead to derailment (Sloan 1994).

Research by Personnel Decisions Inc. (PDI) suggests that: (i) the competences that help managers do their job well may not get them to the Executive Suite, (ii) factors which get managers ahead may not keep them out of trouble, (iii) managers risk being blind-sighted by their blind spots, (iv) managers who want to do well and stay out of trouble should get feedback and take steps to develop in all of the key areas (of executive competence), (v) an executive's inability to hear and take action on feedback is a primary source of career jeopardy and (vi) organizations can create a climate of continuous management improvement by providing ongoing feedback and development opportunities. The implication is that addressing each of these points would reduce the likelihood of derailment at the top (PDI 1992).

Four enduring derailment themes, seen to recur across industries, organizations and hierarchical levels, were identified by CCL:

(i)   problems with interpersonal relationships,
(ii) failure to meet business objectives and make strategic transitions,
(iii) failure to build, mould and lead a team, and
(iv) an inability to change or adapt to changing operational and personal conditions.

(See also Charan and Colvin 1999; Finkelstein 2003; Kets de Vries 1989a, b; Kofodimos 1989, 1990; Lowman 1993; McCalley 2002; Sperry 2002, amongst others, in support of these findings.)

CCL derailment studies in Europe showed no significant differences from the North American work with the top two derailment factors being 'poor working relations' (top in the European study) and 'an inability to develop or adapt' (top in the North American studies).

The European study identified an additional derailment factor called 'organizational isolation', whereby such leaders were described as individually isolated and always placing boundaries around their unit or department (Leslie and Van Velsor 1996; Van Velsor and Leslie 1995).

Whilst the derailment themes may have remained largely consistent, the wider business context facing leaders has not; this is evidenced through the leadership challenges generated by globalization. Such challenges reinforce the importance of the quality of a leader's relationship with those around him and the need for style flexibility and personal sensitivity to enable him to adjust and adapt swiftly to contextual changes both within the organization and externally. The ability to deal with complex and ambiguous business situations whilst maintaining composure under pressure is critically important because the role is larger, the cost of mistakes is greater and the consequences of failure are more severe (Lombardo *et al.* 1988; Lombardo and McCauley 1988; Ludeman and Erlandson 2004; McCall 1998). Derailment is not seen as career-limiting, nor as precluding subsequent successful senior appointments, albeit probably in different contexts.

Contrary, and complementary, explanations for the derailment of senior executives would emphasize contextual changes and cultural dissonances (Schein 1985; Trompenaars 1997), life-stage approaches to individual development (Dotlich *et al.* 2004; Drucker 1999; Levinson *et al.* 1978; Levinson 1978), and consideration of the psychological differences between those who derail from those who do not (Babiak 1995; Babiak and Hare 2006; Conger 1990; Dotlich and Cairo 2003; Hogan and Hogan 2001; Kets de Vries 1989a, 1995; Maccoby 2000, 2004).

In addition, 'derailment' prompts consideration of psychological features which may find expression in the overt behaviours highlighted by CCL and other researchers in this area, but which may point to more toxic psychological dimensions underpinning the behaviour of the executives described. More research is now emerging explicitly about leadership toxicity and its underpinnings (Cavaiola and Lavender 2000; Drucker 2004; Frost 2003; Kellerman 2004a; Lipman-Blumen 2005a).

Executive derailment remains an important and continuing facet of business life. A key challenge for all successful leaders is to maintain self-insight, adaptability and personal development in the face of transitions during times of turbulence, ambiguity and relative chaos. Reducing an executive's susceptibility to derailment remains a matter of prime corporate importance as the negative consequences of such collapses remain significant and are dramatically increased at the highest levels within organizations.

See also: **change and continuity**, **hierarchy**, **leadership development**, **organizational culture**

Further reading: Dotlich and Cairo 2003; Finkelstein 2003; Kofodimos 1990; Lipman-Blumen 2005b; Lowman 1993

DISTRIBUTED LEADERSHIP

Richard Bolden

The concept of 'distributed leadership' has become popular in recent years as an alternative to models of leadership that concern themselves primarily with the attributes and behaviours of individual 'leaders' (e.g. trait, situational, style and transformational theories). This approach argues for a more systemic perspective, whereby leadership **responsibility** is dissociated from formal organizational roles, and the action and **influence** of people at all levels is recognized as integral to the overall direction and functioning of the organization. Spillane suggests that a distributed perspective 'puts leadership practice centre stage' (2006: 25), thereby encouraging a shift in focus from the traits and characteristics of 'leaders' to the shared activities and functions of 'leadership'.

The call for a more collectively embedded notion of leadership has arisen from research, theory and practice that highlights the limitations of the traditional 'leader–follower' dualism that places the responsibility for leadership firmly in the hands of the 'leader' and represents the 'follower' as somewhat passive and subservient. Instead, it is argued that: 'leadership is probably best conceived as a group quality, as a set of functions which must be carried out by the group' (Gibb 1954, cited in Gronn 2000: 324). As such, this approach demands a dramatic reconsideration of the distribution of **power** and influence within organizations. It isn't simply about creating more 'leaders' (a numerical/additive function) but facilitating 'concertive action' and pluralistic engagement (Gronn 2000, 2002a). In effect, distributed leadership is far more than the sum of its parts.

That said, distributed leadership does not deny the key role played by people in formal leadership positions, but proposes that this is only the tip of the iceberg. Spillane *et al.* (2004: 5) argue that leadership is 'stretched over the social and situational contexts' of the organization and extend the notion to include material and cultural artefacts (language, organizational systems, physical environment, etc.). The situated nature of leadership is viewed as 'constitutive of leadership practice' (*ibid*.: 20–1) and hence demands recognition of leadership acts within their wider context.

Such a perspective draws heavily on systems and **process theory** and locates leadership clearly beyond the individual leader and within the relationships and interactions of multiple actors and the situations in which they find themselves. A useful analogy is given by Wilfred Drath in his book *The Deep Blue Sea* (2001), where he urges us to look beyond the wave crests (formal 'leaders') to the deep blue sea from whence they come (the latent leadership potential within the organization).

In a review of the literature, Bennett *et al.* (2003) suggest that, despite some variations in definition, distributed leadership is based on three main premises: first, that leadership is an emergent property of a group or network of interacting individuals; second, that there is openness to the boundaries of leadership (i.e. who has a part to play both within and beyond the organization); and third, that varieties of expertise are distributed across the many, not the few. Thus, distributed leadership is represented as dynamic, relational, inclusive, collaborative and contextually situated. It requires a system-wide perspective that not only transcends organizational levels and roles but also organizational boundaries. Thus, for example, in the field of education, where distributed leadership is being actively promoted, one might consider the contribution of parents, students and the local community as well as teachers and governors in school leadership.

> Taking this view, leadership is about learning together and constructing meaning and knowledge collectively and collaboratively. It involves opportunities to surface and mediate perceptions, values, beliefs, information and assumptions through continuing conversations. It means generating ideas together; seeking to reflect upon and make sense of work in the light of shared beliefs and new information; and creating actions that grow out of these new understandings. It implies that leadership is socially constructed and culturally sensitive. It does not imply a leader/follower divide, neither does it point towards the leadership potential of just one person.
>
> (Harris 2003: 314)

In addition to extending the boundaries of leadership, the above quote indicates the centrality of dialogue and the construction of shared meaning within social groups. As such, the concept has much in common with notions of democratic and inclusive leadership (Woods 2004).

Of the authors who have attempted to develop a conceptual model of distributed leadership, Gronn (2000, 2002a) and Spillane *et al.* (2004) are perhaps the most comprehensive. In each case, they have used Activity Theory (Engestrom 1999) as a theoretical tool to frame the idea of distributed leadership practice, using it as a bridge between agency and structure (in Gronn's case) and distributed cognition and action (in Spillane *et al.*'s case). Leadership, therefore, is seen as an integral part of the daily activities and interactions of everyone across the enterprise, irrespective of position. It is revealed equally within small, incremental, informal and emergent acts as within large-scale transformational change from the top. The more members across the organization exercise their influence, the greater the leadership distribution. This is not a zero sum equation where developing the agency of **followers** diminishes the power of formal leaders, but one where each can mutually reinforce the other.

In practice, there are many forms that distributed leadership can take and the literature does not generally prescribe one over the other. Within schools, for example, MacBeath (2005) identifies six forms of distributed leadership (formal, pragmatic, strategic, incremental, opportunistic and cultural), but argues that the most appropriate and effective form will depend upon the situation. There are, however, some serious challenges to the practical implementation of distributed leadership. MacBeath (2005) argues that distributed leadership is premised on **trust**, implies a mutual acceptance of one another's leadership potential, requires formal leaders to 'let go' of some of their control and **authority**, and favours consultation and consensus over command and control. Each of these poses a serious challenge to traditional hierarchical models of authority and control in organizations and can place severe physical and psychological demands on designated managers.

There are also serious implications for **leadership development**. Whilst the majority of investment continues to be for individuals in formal leadership roles, a distributed perspective would argue for the development of leadership capacity throughout the organization. This distinction is captured by Day (2001) in his comparison between 'leader' and 'leadership development'. Whereas 'leader development' is an investment in *human capital* to enhance intrapersonal competence for selected individuals, 'leadership development' is an investment in *social capital* to develop interpersonal networks and cooperation within organizations and other social systems. In his account both of these are necessary, but the latter is all too often neglected.

By considering leadership practice as both thinking and activity that 'emerges in the execution of leadership tasks in and through the inter-action of leaders, followers and situation' (Spillane *et al.* 2004: 27), distributed leadership offers a powerful post-heroic representation of leadership well suited to complex, changing and inter-dependent environments. The challenge will be whether or not organizations and the holders of power will be sufficiently flexible to enable this to occur in practice.

See also: **change and continuity, group dynamics, leadership definition, leadership development, power**

Further reading: Bennett *et al.* 2003; Drath 2001; Engestrom 1999; Gronn 2002a; Spillane 2006

EFFECTIVENESS

Richard A. Couto

Style, process and outcomes provide three lenses with which to examine the effectiveness of leadership. The first centres on the action of a leader and resembles **trait theory** but with a focus on the interac-tion of leaders with their environments, including **followers**. The second has an element of leader-centricity but also gives followers a larger role in leadership effectiveness. Process looks at effectiveness through a lens of mutual and reflexive relationship of leaders and followers. The last lens looks for results. Again followers are key. The outcome may be the improved and increased production of widgets, in which case effective leadership makes followers better instruments to meet the goals of others. The outcome may be the development of or some benefit for followers, in which case effective leadership is explicitly or implicitly moral action for positive change.

Edwin Hollander (2004), one of the first scholars in recent times to treat leadership as a mutual and reflexive process, combines the three lenses of style, reflexive processes and outcomes. He suggests that the needs we have for **authority** and our socialization to its legitimacy lead us to place expectations upon people in positions of authority. Hollander calls these expectations 'credits' and from it he fashioned a model of Idiosyncrasy Credit (IC), which 'deals with the latitude followers provide a leader for action by giving or withdrawing support' (Hollander 2004: 695). IC permits people in authority to innovate and deviate from the norm. Success brings more credits and failure depletes them. Effectiveness, in this instance, measures the ability of leaders to maintain their credit with followers and thus keep their positions or introduce innovation.

Hollander's model begs the questions: How do we judge success and failure for the award of credit? Who makes those judgements? In answer, every leadership model implies criteria of leadership effectiveness and the source of judgement; people in authority over the leader or people without authority who work with the leader and for whose benefit leaders work. Needless to say, the criteria for and determination of effectiveness varies widely from model to model.

Some models posit elements of personal style. Robert Blake, Anne McCanse and Jane Mouton provide a grid with Concern for People and Concern for Results and identify some totally ineffective styles, low regard for both, and most effective, high regard for both (Blake and Mouton 1964; Northouse 2001: 40). The grid suggests a vector such as Pareto's optimization by which one attempts to increase an increment of concern on one measure without sacrificing the other. Effectiveness on this grid is to move towards the quadrant of high regard for task and touch. Both followers and hierarchical authority have a say on effectiveness.

Some models of style include environmental factors, including followers, thus complicating a simple grid. **Situational leadership** proposes a grid with horizontal and vertical axes of supportive and directive behaviour that gives rise to four styles of leadership: delegating, supporting, coaching and directing. Effective leaders match the right style to the capability of followers to conduct a task; a third factor. Low capability requires more direction and high development more **delegation** (Hersey and Blanchard 1969, 1974; Northouse 2001: 56). Contingency theory complicates the environment further by adding the nature of relationships between leaders and followers – positive or negative; the high or low structure of the task involved; the amount of **power** and the preferred leadership style of the person in authority. Leadership effectiveness now depends upon the leader to align these factors correctly from one task to another (Northouse 2001: 77). Robert House's path-goal theory combines leadership behaviours, the characteristics of followers and a task, and the **motivation** of followers to do a task that they feel they are able to, for an expected outcome, and a reward for that outcome (House 1971: 32–9; Northouse 2001: 91–2).

We may distinguish models of style from models of process by the capacity they give followers to act and the instrumentality of **leader–follower relations**. Certainly, leaders take followers into account in leader-centric models. However, leaders make judgements about and for followers as part of the environment of the leadership challenge in a manner that followers' behaviours and performance become an output of leadership (Bass 1990b: 906–7). The path-goal model gives leaders the task of keeping followers' motivation high, for example. Leadership effectiveness in models of leader-centric style depends upon getting others to conduct a task from producing widgets to riding into the valley of death. Models of process posit some degree of mutual relationship between leaders and followers and give the latter more importance in determining leadership effectiveness. Hollander explains, for example, that charismatic leadership requires followers to invest a great deal of hope and credit (Hollander 2004: 697). The very notion of **charisma** requires the capacity to attract followers; without the action of followers, however, charisma is ineffective. In the same manner, Howard Gardner's work (Gardner with Laskin 1995) on the role of narratives in leadership suggests that leaders and followers share specific stories in which common values are embedded.

Followers' behaviours and performance are much more clearly inputs, more independent variables, in leadership models of process that emphasize mutual and reflexive relationships between leaders and followers. These mutual process models require interacting with followers and take into account followers' needs and wants as well as the task. Gardner's (Gardner with Laskin 1995) innovative leadership, for example, requires a shared narrative of increased and improved human bonds. According to Ronald Heifetz (1994, 2007) some of that innovative narrative also explains that leaders do not have all the answers and that some leadership tasks must be shared between leaders and followers. Thus, mutual process models suggest that effective leadership requires that people with authority recognize the difference between technical work of authority and the adaptive work of leadership. Thus effective leadership of mutual process gives the work of dealing with a task back to the people by mobilizing a group's resources to identify and address the gap between values and practice, needs and conditions.

So far the models that we have examined offer effective styles and processes of leadership with secondary attention to outcomes. Other models of leadership judge effectiveness by direct benefits for followers. For James MacGregor Burns the litmus test of effective transforming leadership is 'significant change' (Burns 1978: 425). Leaders may take any style or process, but their effective use is not enough unless it lifts some caste-like restriction from a group of people. Instrumentality has no place in transforming leadership. Likewise, mutual and reflexive processes of leaders and followers are necessary for effective transforming leadership, but not sufficient unless both are raised to a high moral plane. Adam Yarmolinsky takes issue with Burns and insists on the need to uncouple change from leadership. Leadership is effective not for initiating change but for mediating the changes that are always occurring and for reconciling system change and stability (Yarmolinsky 2006: 45). Robert Greenleaf (1977b), writing at about the same time as Burns and in a somewhat compatible manner to Yarmolinsky, offers stewardship as a process and style of effective leadership but also a distinct outcome; effective servant-leadership shows other people their capabilities for stewardship and leadership.

Each of our three lenses may overlap and offer deeper insight into the effectiveness of leadership. They are also handy to keep separate, as well, so that we may keep in mind whether the criteria for effectiveness is instrumental or developmental and leader-centric or mutual and reflexive and who makes the judgement about effectiveness.

See also: **hierarchy**, **leader–follower relations**, **process theory**, **style theories**, **transformational leadership**

Further reading: Burns 2003; Erkut and Winds of Change Foundation 2001; Heifetz 2007; Hollander 2007; Northouse 2004

ELITE THEORY

Nathan Harter

Political history describes the tendency of one group to dominate another by means of virtue, conquest or divine intervention, depending on one's point of view. The pattern keeps recurring. At the dawn of sociology, a strand of Italians (Pareto, Mosca and others) took it upon themselves to study these group distinctions. Why do certain groups prevail – amassing **power** and privilege out of proportion to their numbers? Their studies have since coalesced into what has come to be known as Elite Theory. Elite Theory, in turn, makes indirect contributions to leadership studies.

Early in his analysis of politics, Aristotle had observed that by nature there must be 'a union of the naturally ruling element with the element which is naturally ruled, for the preservation of both. The element which is able, by virtue of its intelligence, to exercise forethought, is naturally a ruling and master element' (*Politics* I, 2, §1,

Aristotle 1946). By the time of the Renaissance, Machiavelli stressed the importance of acknowledging, as a matter of empirical observation, that only certain people govern based on their demonstrable competence. Who are they? What sets them apart?

A variety of influences converged in the nineteenth century on two Italian scholars working independently on the same basic theoretical problem (Voegelin 2001: 117–19). Both Vilfredo Pareto (1991) and Gaetano Mosca (1939) arrived at the earliest formulations of elite theory.

They noted that all societies split into two basic groups or classes, one of which dominates the other. Monarchies premised on a single leader and democracies premised on the absence of leaders are both illusions, forms of organization that obscure the persisting **influence** of an oligarchy. Later, Robert Michels would test this hypothesis and conclude with his famous 'Iron Law of Oligarchy' (1915/1949). Even in organizations dedicated to equality, he found, the static structure of any society shows this gross division.

The structure of societies is obviously more complex than a simple division between elites and masses. Sociologists differentiated, for example, within the two classes. Mosca subdivided the elites into clerks, celebrities and partisans. Antonio Gramsci (1957/1992) described a layered pyramid, descending from intellectuals through lieutenants and true believers, down to the masses. In each case, nevertheless, elite theorists offer a hierarchical division, reflecting the same basic tendency.

Elite theory also seeks to understand the dynamics by which this happens. The dominant group secures and preserves its position, creating what Gramsci refers to as their 'hegemony' over the community, a condition of widespread consent. They do this by means of two things: ordinary competence and non-scientific beliefs intended to induce loyalty (Levine 1995: 236). This elite organizes, trying to amass power and increase its permanence in a pattern of consolidation subsequently described by Bertrand de Jouvenel (1945/1993). With time, however, we could trace the circulation of new elites into dominance, separately as individuals or together as a group, partly as a result of their striving but also as a result of the dissipation of the existing elite. The new group enters into prominence and displaces the old.

An *understanding* of these dynamics does not require a student of leadership to *endorse* them (see Nye 1977). Elite theorists have frequently objected to patterns of domination they were especially qualified to detect, protesting the unfairness of institutions such as slavery, apartheid and later the Soviet *nomenklatura*. Elite theorists are not necessarily elitists. The philosopher Eric Voegelin describes a continuum from (a) theorists of an elite merely trying to understand the structures and processes of society to (b) activists, including communists and fascists, who took it upon themselves to thrust a new elite into power because they perceived inadequacy in the dominant minority. The activists might have understood the basic dynamics of society, as one elite displaces another, but to varying degrees they overlooked the 'deep foundations' of the legitimacy of the existing social order. It is not enough simply to replace the actors (Voegelin 1999: 132f.). As more than one author has noted, leadership is grounded on more than position in a structure. Theorists sought the origins and legitimations of these structures.

Because leadership takes place within social structures, it also shapes these social structures. These structures are, according to elite theory, hierarchical. For this reason alone, leadership studies is advised to consult elite theory. More directly, elite theory provides a framework for the historical patterns of leadership. Leaders emerge into the elite, whether invited by the powers-that-be as heirs to the system or provoked by the status quo to contest the system. Once in power, so to speak, leaders then find themselves interested in managing the system because they have a stake in it.

Embedded in these inquiries would be the role of an elite in shaping prospective leaders, whether directly or indirectly. By virtue of its status, the elite enjoys a disproportionate influence over the laws, customs, mores and fashions of a community. It often intervenes in education. Even if an elite did nothing overt to recruit and prepare leaders, nevertheless it exerts an attraction on the ambitious simply by possessing more of the tangible and intangible goods of a community. Of course, the elite also act to frustrate leadership on occasion, as the Parliament of 1642 revoked the privilege of Charles I.

Elites shape leaders directly and indirectly, and leaders shape elites as well, sometimes simply by rising to preeminence and sometimes more directly by shaping the elite – its composition, number, wealth, reputation and so forth. Four years after the death of Charles I, Oliver Cromwell cleared Parliament at the point of a sword.

One leadership theory in particular bears a close resemblance to elite theory, and that is Leader-Member Exchange theory or LMX, in which groups are understood to split into in-groups and out-groups, depending on the members' particular relationship with the group's overall leader. The so-called in-group becomes for all intents and purposes an elite (Harter and Evanecky 2002). As LMX demonstrates, elite theory has the potential to assist in understanding the phenom-enon of leadership in context over time.

See also: **behavioural theories of leadership**, **hierarchy**, **philosophical approaches to leadership**, **power**, **situational leadership**

Further reading: Levine 1995; Michels 1915/1949; Nye 1977; Pareto 1991

EMOTIONAL INTELLIGENCE

Pat Lyons

The term 'emotional intelligence' (EI) has achieved widespread usage in both fashionable and academic literature over the past 15 or so years. Popularization of the term owes much to the mid and late twentieth-century humanistic psychology and feminist response to the Western tradition of anti-emotionalism (Maslow 1969; Rogers 1961). In particular, since the publication of Daniel Goleman's *Emotional Intelligence* in 1995, the subject has achieved something of the status of a zeitgeist that fits neatly within the contemporary enthusiasm for **self-awareness** and understanding.

Set against the cognitive tradition which regards intelligence as 'the aggregate or global capacity of the individual to act purposefully, to think rationally and to deal effectively with his environment' (Wechsler 1958: 7), the importance of non-cognitive aspects of intelligence had been posited as early as the mid 1930s by Thorndike through reference to 'social intelligence' (Thorndike and Stein 1937), as 'affective and conative abilities' by Wechsler (1943), and by Leuner, who had highlighted the importance of the concept in the context of social role adaptation (Leuner 1966). By 1983, the work of these early pioneers received a fillip when Howard Gardner proposed the concept of multiple intelligences and in particular through his description of 'intrapersonal' and 'interpersonal' intelligences (Gardner 1983). By 1990, the construct entered the mainstream academic literature when Salovey and Mayer coined the term emotional intelligence to refer to 'the ability to monitor one's own and others' feelings and emotions, to discriminate among them, and to use this information to guide one's thinking and action' (Salovey and Mayer 1990: 189, quoted in Bar-On and Parker 2000: 45).

But it was the publication of Daniel Goleman's book *Emotional Intelligence* in 1995 and a subsequent article in the *Harvard Business Review* of November–December 1998, in which Goleman claimed that, in terms of business performance across a large number of companies, emotional intelligence 'proved to be twice as important' as technical skills and IQ 'as ingredients of excellent performance', that substantially sparked the popular imagination and encouraged significant lay and scientific interest in the subject (Goleman 1995, 1998a: 94). At around the same time, Reuven Bar-On, who had coined the term 'EQ' (Emotional Quotient) in 1985, had been attempting to operationalize the construct, and in 1997 published the first instrument designed to measure aspects of noncognitive intelligence, the Emotional Quotient Inventory – *The BarOn EQ-i* (Bar-On 1997). Bar-On's research in clinical contexts had sought to explain the noncognitive capabilities, competencies and skills factors that contributed to success in life.

In subsequent years a burgeoning literature has emerged with research results ranging from claims that emotional intelligence can correlate with less subjective workplace stress, better health and well-being (Slaski and Cartwright 2002), to a large body of findings by members of The Consortium for Emotional Intelligence in Organizations which claim that emotional intelligence can significantly contribute to bottom line business results (www.eiconsortium. org/research/business_case_for_ei.htm). At the same time, claims surrounding the pliable nature of emotional intelligence by Goleman and others has led to the emergence of a veritable industry of human resource development professionals promoting the role of EI assessment and enhancement in (a) personal development, (b) occupational and career assessment, (c) occupational stress management, (d) job performance and satisfaction and (e) work–life balance. In particular, assertions that EI contains strong links to leadership and executive competency by Goleman, Boyatzis and McKee and others have witnessed an associated upsurge in executive training prescriptions across Western organization environments (Cherniss and Goleman 2001; Dearborn 2002; Goleman *et al.* 2002; Higgs and Rowland 2002; Orme and Bar-On 2002).

Since the publication of Bar-On's EQ-i, a number of additional definitions of the construct and associated psychometric measures have been developed (see, for example, Cooper 1996/1997, Higgs and Dulewicz 1999; Goleman 1998b; Mayer and Salovey 1997; Mayer *et al.* 2000), with a differentiation drawn between two distinct approaches. The first group of personality-like approaches are referred to as *mixed models* (e.g. the Bar-On and Goleman models), which combine a range of mental capabilities (such as reality testing and problem solving) and personality traits (such as assertiveness and optimism). The second group of performance-based models are generally described as *ability models* (Mayer *et al.* 2000), and focus on emotional intelligence as a set of abilities relating to emotional identification-perception, assimilation of emotions, understanding emotions and managing emotions.

Much of the debate among the academic community has focused on the actuality of the emotional intelligence construct as a distinct perspective vis-à-vis the five-factor model of personality. The essence of this approach centres on the issue of establishing if EI represents some distinctive mental capacity, personality dimension or ability. As early as 1998, Davies *et al.* compared a range of EI measures with a range of instruments designed to elucidate cognitive aptitudes, verbal abilities, social functioning and personality variables. After extensive analysis, Davies and her colleagues raised serious questions as to whether emotional intelligence is indeed a distinctive mental aptitude (Davies *et al.* 1998). At the same time, the emergence of an array of more sophisticated psychometric measures in the interim suggests that further assessment is needed around reliability and validity of measures designed to isolate and measure EI as a distinct construct.

More recently, Matthews *et al.*, in an exhaustive and scholarly study of the subject, observe that both the mixed and ability approaches to EI 'appear to lack a firm foundation in the existing extensive research literature on both intelligence and emotion' (Matthews *et al.* 2002: 514). Noting that the perceived malleability of emotional intelligence has attractiveness for employers, trainers and educators in social, employment and indeed clinical settings (p. 514) has led to claims that these authors suggest are both 'extravagant and hyperbolic' (p. 466). The fact that a major disjunction exists between theorists and the absence of any general agreement regarding the specification of the construct and its ultimate scientific significance among those publishing in peer-reviewed journals provides a sobering message.

The critical issue to emerge from the Matthews *et al.* review is that there does not appear to be any general agreement regarding how EI is aligned with broader conceptions of personality and intelligence or whether EI exists as a distinct theoretical and psychometric construct. Nonetheless, these authors are not ultimately dismissive of attempts to unravel the potential offered by research in this area and observe that 'the benefits of EI appear to reside in raising awareness of emotional issues and motivating educators and managers to take emotional issues seriously' (p. 543). So while popular conceptions and the urgings of a discrete group of organizational consultants posit emotional intelligence as a contemporary panacea for organization and personal development, scholarly endeavours are bound up with struggles regarding the existence of the construct and potential implications of research findings for advances in personality, intelligence and competency development.

The journey to discover the essence of emotional intelligence may ultimately lead to significant discoveries in the field of social and personality psychology, and may at the very least allow for the more detailed mapping of a 'minor province of terrain already charted' (Matthews *et al.* 2002: 545).

See also: **leadership definition**, **leadership development**

Further reading: Fineman 2000; Fredrickson 1998, 2001; Fredrickson and Losada 2005; Lord *et al.* 2002

EMPOWERMENT

Richard A. Couto

Like so many other concepts of leadership, empowerment assumes different meanings in different contexts. For example, empowerment means very different things in formal organizations of hierarchical control and in informal networks that make up a movement for social change. Within any context, however, genuine forms of empowerment require some degree of direct socio-political representation in which people act on their own behalf or as authorized and delegated by those with more **power** and decison-making **authority**. In order to distinguish empowerment from **delegation**, we may want to consider various forms of representation and participation in specific contexts. Likewise, we should distinguish instrumental empowerment, provided by those in position and authority for their purposes or that of their organization, and constitutive empowerment, acquired by those without position or authority, by their own effort, for their own purpose, and expressive of some enhanced capability of adaptive work. As we shall see, even constitutive forms of empowerment may vary from psycho-symbolic to psycho-political.

A. Alexander Chauncey (1967) suggested three types of representation – technical, modal and socio-political – that begin our delineation of empowerment. The first two are indirect forms of representation: technical, enacted by an expert with knowledge about a group, and modal, expressed by individuals who share demographic or other characteristics of a group. These are most often invited forms of representation extended by those with more **power** and decison-making authority within a context.

The social movements of the 1960s inspired models that juxtapose representation and participation. Sherry R. Arnstein (1969) prepared a ladder of participation (Table 1) that extended from citizen control, at the top, down to manipulation. In between were degrees of effective and ineffective participation. The ladder image of various levels of participation, when combined with forms of direct and indirect representation, differentiates degrees of **influence** and power or measures of genuine empowerment. As represented in Table 1, the three top rungs of participation entail degrees of power and the next three entail degrees of recognition that imply some power. The last two rungs, therapy and manipulation, are forms of control by those in authority and of nonparticipation by those served by programmes. Forms of representation vary with forms of participation.

The three degrees of effective participation – control, partnership and delegation – coincide with direct forms of socio-political representation. The latter may include modal and technical representatives, but only if they are selected by the group they represent and have accountability to them. The false promise of partnership that ends up on the ineffective participation rungs of the ladder – placation, consulting and informing – involve indirect representation or even cooptation of modal or technical representatives. The means of selection on these rungs is less important because there is very little power sharing. There is even less on the two lowest rungs of participation – therapy and manipulation – or what Joanne Ciulla (1996) calls 'bogus empowerment'. Claims of empowerment at this level of participation are purely symbolic and most often intended to avoid any of the forms of empowerment higher up the ladder.

The most complete form of empowerment involves a group taking control of some aspects of decision-making, implementation, planning or production, or entering partnership with those previously in complete authority. This form of participation would also involve direct representation of the group through people they elect and may hold accountable to their purposes. We may call this psycho-political empowerment because all empowerment has the psychological intent to increase the sense of agency of a group, but empowerment with direct representation and full participation entails a political change in the control of authority and resources.

The shallower forms of empowerment entail indirect modal or technical representatives of a group, selected or appointed by those with authority, with no accountability to the group they represent.

Table 1 Comparison of models of participation, representation and forms of empowerment

Ladder of participation	Forms of representation	Forms of empowerment
Full participation Control Delegated power Partnership	*Direct* Sociopolitical Delegated (Elected modal and technical representatives)	*Psycho-political* Changed relations among actors and new allocation of resources. Individual and group changes. New forms of decision making. Acquired or provided additional information and new knowledge to increased and improve participation.
Partial participation Placation Consultation Informing	*Indirect* Modal Technical (Appointed or elected modal and technical representatives)	*Psycho-symbolic* Changes in individual and group attitudes, but relationships of power or authority, within an unchanged system of decision making and resource allocation, e.g. coping, stress management. News forms of expressing concern for conditions without action to change them. Some blaming the victim may be implied.
Non-participation Therapy Manipulation	*Indirect-coopted* Modal Technical (Appointed modal and technical representatives)	

There is a psychological intent to these forms of representation and participation to give group members symbols of concern but not shared authority.

In hierarchical and authoritative contexts, in which leadership and management share blurred boundaries, empowerment is most likely to be psycho-symbolic and always instrumental. In these settings, as Lynn Offermann (2004a) explains, empowerment most often comes down to hierarchical authorities delegating some authority and decison-making and thus expanding the boundaries of discretion and autonomy of **followers**. The psychological benefit of such delegation depends on the meaningfulness of delegated tasks; the degree of discretionary judgement; self-efficacy of the follower; and belief in the prospect of significant impact on the work of the group. Offermann explains this form of delegation as instrumental in the sense that it may represent adjustment to the increased capabilities and expectations of followers and may extricate those in authority from management tasks to more genuine leadership tasks (Offermann 2004a).

Gary Yukl discusses empowerment within the organizational trend to use teams, especially self-managed teams. He describes them as 'small task groups in which members have a common purpose, interdependent roles, complementary skills, and considerable discretion about how to do their work' (Yukl 1998: 351). Again, this form of empowerment is clearly but not exclusively instrumental. It is a means to further the goals of an organization and to achieve them more effectively. The increased sense of agency and satisfaction among followers is a positive externality, but not sufficient to continue this or other forms of empowerment if they proved ineffective in promoting organizational goals.

In the context of social movements, we find the fullest and least instrumental forms of empowerment (Zimmerman 1990a, b; Zimmerman and Rappaport 1988; Price 1990). Indeed, hierarchical relationships and authority become problematic in this context; empowerment may mean breaking dependence and **trust** in leaders (Zola 1987; Rappaport 1985). Charles Kieffer (1984) identifies three elements of empowerment in a context of profound change: the development of a more positive self-concept; the development of more critical or analytical understanding of a political or social environment; and the development of collective resources for social and political action. Similarly, Ann Bookman and Sandra Morgen emphasize empowerment as a process of increased sense of self-efficacy and incompatible goals with authority. 'Empowerment begins when they [the women of their study] change their ideas about the causes of their powerlessness, when they recognize the systemic forces that oppress them, and when they act to change the conditions of their lives' (Bookman and Morgen 1988: 4). These assessments stress empowerment as a combination of psychological and political factors, as Table 1 depicted, with the corollaries of participatory forms of control and partnership and direct socio-political forms of representation.

The empowerment of social movements expands the boundaries for action immensely and people who had been 'followers' may begin to see themselves as agents of history, self-empowered to take collective action for the benefit of ordinarily unthinkable social change. The 'YES' Campaign in Northern Ireland expresses this sense of empowerment. Within an incredibly short time, leaders of the voluntary sector of Northern Ireland banded together in a 1998 campaign to gain a 60 per cent margin of endorsement of the Good Friday Peace Accord (Mitchell 1999). 'YES' offered the opportunity to some citizens to influence and participate in the referendum by more than voting. It ran a 'people's' campaign in view of the inability of the political parties to mount a cross-party campaign (Oliver 1998). Participants are very clear about the empowerment they felt in their renewed sense of agency to make history. Diane Greer, one of the coordinating board members, recalls:

> It was almost like a sixth sense, [I knew] that if I did not get together with other individuals and act at that time, we were going to lose the moment, something of great value. And yet I did not know what that thing was. But I did know it was an opportunity for change. Those are the only words I can put on it – it was an opportunity for change. And I knew that I had a part to play in that.
>
> (Greer 1999: np)

This dramatic sense of the chance to change politics and history exceeds the psychological benefit of this form of empowerment, however great, precisely because this empowerment is not instrumental to existing institutions, organizations or their goals but to their transformation. Paul Nolan (1999) remembers the sense of possibility; the incredible rush of events, both supportive and unhelpful, the intoxicating quality of the whole event, and judges 'I never felt so alive'. Thus he offers the psychological benefit of this form of self-empowerment as a positive externality. He and 'YES' empowered themselves to be an instrument for the purposes and goals that made new historical and political goals, not organizational ones, possible.

See also: **authority, ethics, delegation, leader–follower relations, participatory leadership, power**

Further reading: Bookman and Morgen 1988; Ciulla 1996; Couto 1993; Kieffer 1984; Offermann 2004a; Zimmerman 1990a, b

ETHICS

Joanne B. Ciulla

'Leadership ethics' emerged as a distinct area of applied ethics in 1995 (Ciulla 1995). Like other areas of applied ethics, it consists of a distinctive set of ethical challenges related to a person's occupation or role. However, unlike other areas of professional ethics, leaders face additional challenges because the work of a leader is not as well defined as the job of a doctor or lawyer.

Leadership scholars have often disagreed on the definition of leadership (Rost 1991), not about what leaders *are*, but rather what leaders *ought to be*. The question 'What is a leader?' was really the question 'What is a good leader?' Joanne B. Ciulla argued that what she called the 'Hitler problem' illustrates this point. The Hitler problem is about how you would answer the question 'Was Hitler a good leader?' The answer to this question hinges on whether the word 'good' refers to the ethics of Hitler's leadership or his competence as a leader. The answer is unsatisfactory if it only applies to his competence or to his ethics. Hence, the overarching question of leadership ethics is 'What is the relationship of ethics to effectiveness in leadership?' (Ciulla 2004).

A number of things about being a leader make it difficult to be ethical and effective. We hold leaders responsible for their actions and for things over which they have no control. Some leaders are neither ethical nor effective, but we think that they are because they are lucky. Leaders have moral luck when events outside of their control conspire to make them appear to be good leaders (Williams 1981). Unlucky leaders may be moral and competent but have their carefully planned initiatives destroyed by matters of fate.

There are three moral facets to the ethics of leaders.

1   The ethics of leaders themselves – the intentions of leaders and the personal ethics of leaders. These we cannot always know.
2   The ethics of how a leader leads or the process of leadership. This includes the means that a leader uses to get things done. It also includes the relationship between leaders and all those affected by their actions.
3   The ethics of what a leader does or the ends of a leader's actions.

In short, an ethical and effective leader is someone who does the right thing, the right way, for the right reasons. Some leaders only get it morally right in one or two of the three areas. Niccolo Machiavelli is best known for arguing that the ends of a leader's actions justify the means (Machiavelli 1532/1991). Leaders sometimes face the problem of 'dirty hands', where they must choose to use unsavory means to prevent an imminent disaster. What is morally important in such cases is that leaders feel bad about making this sort of choice and try to avoid it in the future (Temes 2005).

Power is the most obvious distinguishing characteristic of **leader–follower relations**. Whatever the source of power, leaders who appeal to **followers**' emotions can be very dangerous. As Robert C. Solomon argues, the most important emotional relationship between leaders and followers should centre on the emotions related to **trust** (Solomon 2004).

The more power leaders have, the greater their **responsibility** for what they do and do not do. The empirical evidence for moral problems of power is quite old and documented in history books, religious texts, literature and newspapers. For example, Plato's 'Ring of Gyges' is the story of a shepherd boy who discovers a ring that makes him invisible (Plato 1992). The story raises the question: would you be moral if no one were watching? Leadership is like having the ring of Gyges. Without checks and balances, leaders can do what they want and conceal what they do. Since there are no leaders without followers, followers have **influence** over their leaders. Followers enable leaders to do good things and bad things. Hence to varying degrees, followers share responsibility for the actions of their leaders, which is why people sometimes get the leaders they deserve.

Success may also be morally dangerous to leaders. When leaders are successful, they can become overly confident or inattentive. Such leaders can fall prey to the 'Bathsheba Syndrome' (Ludwig and Longnecker 1993). Leaders who have this lose strategic focus, overestimate their ability to control outcomes and abuse their power to cover their misdeeds. The longer leaders stay in office, the more difficult it is for them to maintain their moral standards and those of their associates.

Leaders need more self-knowledge and discipline than others to exercise power ethically. Confucius focused on the importance of duty and self-control. He stated: 'If a man (the ruler) can for one day master himself and return to propriety, all under heaven will return to humanity. To practice humanity depends on oneself' (Confucius 1963: 38). Confucius connects self-mastery to **effectiveness**. He observes: 'If a ruler sets himself right, he will be followed without his command. If he does not set himself right, even his commands will not be obeyed' (p. 38).

We often give leaders special privileges, which may make them feel that they are above others and not subject to the same rules. These privileges may include everything from a large salary, private jets, to special access to information and resources, or exceptional privileges vis-à-vis rules and regulations. Terry Price argues that when followers grant privileges to leaders, they make it easier for leaders to believe that they are outside of the scope of common morality. Leaders make moral mistakes because they do not think that certain rules apply to them or they are ignorant of what is right (Price 2006). This is why ancient Eastern and Western traditions identify reverence as the key virtue for leaders. Reverence is the virtue that reminds leaders that they are part of a larger whole. It is the virtue that keeps them from trying to act like they are gods (Woodruff 2001).

The people leaders choose to include and exclude in their moral obligations is also a key issue in leadership ethics. Leaders often have to put the interests of people they don't know before the interests of those they do know. Yet history is littered with leaders who serve the interests of themselves, their families, cronies, ethnic or religious groups, over the needs of, or to the detriment of, the rest of their constituents. Such behaviour may be functional insofar as it brings support, but is clearly open to charges of being unethical. On this point, ethics and effectiveness converge. The job of a leader is to take care of his or her constituents. In this respect the definition of a leader is inherently utilitarian (Mill 1987).

The notion of looking after a constituency is inherent in leadership. The things leaders have to do to become leaders and stay in power can conflict with the interests of their constituents. This is one of the most common conflicts of interest, especially in political leadership. Some scholars believe that leaders are effective only when their actions are altruistic (Kanungo and Mendonca 1996). Altruism is behaviour that benefits others at a cost to oneself. Altruism is a motive for acting, but it is not in and of itself a normative principle – i.e. a terrorist suicide bomber may be altruistic, but not ethical.

In contemporary leadership theory, **servant leadership** attempts to capture the altruistic aspects of leadership and the need for leaders to keep their egos in check. The idea of servant leadership comes from ancient Eastern and Western religious texts. It was made popular in the twentieth century by the novel *Journey to the East*, by Hermann Hesse (1991) and then by Robert Greenleaf (1977b). The servant leader leads because he or she wants to serve others. Greenleaf says a servant leader must pass this test: 'Do those served grow as persons? Do they *while being served* become healthier, wiser, freer, more autonomous, more likely themselves to become servants?' (pp. 13–14).

One reason why James MacGregor Burns's (1978) theory of transforming leadership is the most prominent leadership theory is because it accounts for both ethics and effectiveness. Burns distinguishes between transforming and **transactional leadership**. Transactional leadership rests on the values found in the means of an act. These are called modal values, which include responsibility, fairness, honesty and promise keeping, etc. Transactional leadership helps leaders and followers reach their own goals by supplying lower level wants and needs so that they can move up to higher needs. Transforming leadership is when leaders and followers morally elevate each other to various stages of morality and need. Through this process, leaders empower their followers to become leaders. Burns's theory describes effective leadership as the ability to bring about change. Ethical leadership is based on leader–follower relations that consist of an ongoing dialogue about values. Transforming leadership is also concerned with end-values. The quality of all aspects of leadership rests on how well they promote the end values of liberty, justice, equality and happiness (Burns 2003). These are lofty moral standards, but the relationship between what leaders are and what they should be is the main point of studying leadership ethics.

See also: **cross-cultural leadership, derailment, effectiveness, leader–follower relations, leadership definition, transactional leadership, transformational leadership**

Further reading: Burns 1984; Ciulla 2004, 2005; Price 2003, 2005

FOLLOWERS

Cynthia J. Bean

Followers are essential to the construct known as leadership, especially given the widely accepted perspective of leadership as understood to be an **influence** relationship (Fiedler 1993; Rost 1991). After all, if a leader looks around and finds no followers, is he/she truly leading?

One insightful view provided by Gardner identifies 'four factors crucial to the practice of effective leadership' (Gardner with Laskin 1995: 36), with each factor calling attention to the importance of followers in the development and identification of leaders. The first factor is a tie to the community or audience, described as ongoing intercourse with members of one of more groups. The second factor is a rhythm that oscillates between isolation and immersion with followers; a balance between time spent alone in reflection (for the purpose of knowing one's own mind) and time spent amidst those one desires to lead. The third factor Gardner lists is the alignment of a leader's words and deeds, specifically noting stories must match embodiments so that the influence of leaders on followers is enacted through portrayal of a particular self as well as through the statements, accounts and interpretations offered by a leader in discourse. The final factor Gardner identifies is the centrality of choice on behalf of followers. He focuses his study on leaders that have attained some stability in a situation because followers have chosen to heed the leader's influence; thereby omitting dictators and others who rely upon force or solely upon **authority** as influence mechanisms. Leaders, in Gardners' view, may be direct (interacting with followers to influence thoughts and actions) or indirect (influencing through dissemination of ideas and display of artifacts (e.g. scholars and artists) that influence others).

Expressing much the same notion as Gardner's four factors detail, Fiedler (1993) noted that leadership involves leaders, followers and situations – making leadership a highly contextualized concept. Even earlier, Burns' (1978) definition of **transformational leadership** notes that leader and follower act as a system.

Given the increasing focus on leadership as an influence relationship, it comes as no surprise that research seeking to improve and define better understanding of followers and followership is needed. Leadership, understood as a relationship, is dependent upon followership (Kelley 1992). Conger (1998) recognizes the persuading or influencing relationship of leaders with and among followers, highlighting communication aspects, such as negotiating, as well as leader and group developmental processes, such as learning. Understanding how meaning is created intersubjectively among leaders and followers and examining how agreement is attained, and action fostered, in **leader–follower relations** is increasingly seen as central to understanding leadership (Smircich and Morgan 1982). Rost's (1991) definition of leadership as an influence relationship – a multidirectional relationship highlighting interaction – frames this perspective. Harkins notes 'the echoes of his or her voice throughout the organization' (1999: 149) signifies leadership.

While influence and control are often separated, it is worth noting that Daft (2005) provides a continuum of leader–follower relations defined by where in the relationship control is situated. From this perspective, when the leader maintains control, the follower is an obedient subordinate, while the opposite extreme is **servant leadership** wherein control is centred in the follower. In between, the participative leader shares some control with followers, and the empowering leader shares more control with followers, moving along the continuum toward servant leadership. Bass (2000) and Kelley (1995) both note that servant-leadership focuses intently on followers, and is key to the success of post-industrial organizations.

Much of what is written about followers and followership, however, maintains a leader-centric tone, but not all. Kelley (1988) does not define followers, but tells us that to be an effective follower one must manage oneself well, be committed to the organization or purpose – or a principle or purpose outside him or herself – be courageous and honest, competent and credible, and focus his or her efforts towards goal attainment. Chaleff (1995) takes the position that followers can enhance leaders' abilities and strengths or emphasize leaders' shortcomings.

While scant research exists that places followers centre-stage, there is increasing agreement that followers and leaders are active partners (Densten and Gray 2001). With that in mind, a definition of followers is offered here:

> Followers may be defined as those individuals and groups interacting with a leader or leaders' ideas to achieve a purpose or goal that is aligned with the purpose or goal the leader pursues. This notion incorporates possibilities of subscribing or adhering to ideas, teachings or methods. It might also include the options of serving or subordinating oneself (one's goals) to another (other goals). Furthermore, followership might imply enthusiasm, mimicry or fandom. There is often an inference as regards to sequence and/or direction of energy that implies the leader takes action to move or motivate the follower, rather than the follower acting with intent to move or motivate the leader. The implication is that the leader either moves first or exerts energy, whilst the follower is likely to await the leaders' direction and/or respond to a leaders' stance.

Aligning with Gardner's (1995) notion of direct and indirect leadership, followers may directly or indirectly interact with a leader. Direct followership involves interaction such as face-to-face communication in small groups or communities, or organizational interaction through permanent or temporary hierarchical structures (Nahavandi 2005). Indirect followership involves pursuing a goal or purpose with a leader by engaging that common purpose, but without interaction with the leader, such as Christian religious groups or impressionist artists.

A poem titled 'Follower' penned by Seamus Justin Heaney, an Irish poet and Nobel laureate, captures a particular sense of followership. The poem expresses the feelings of a boy admiring and following his father, while at the same time being carried (as a burden) by his father. Yet this same boy, as an adult finds himself ahead (in the lead) and sensing obligation to the father, as in a duty of care, or burden. The essence of shifting from the role of follower to the role of leader carries with it a shift in terms of who bears the yoke of **responsibility**.

Leaders and followers thus may be seen to be complicit in defining one another by intersubjectively creating meaning in context, especially as regards to assignment of responsibility towards one-another in a relationship.

See also: **influence, leader–follower relations, leadership definition, participatory leadership, servant leadership**

Further reading: Fairhurst and Sarr 1996; Hamilton and Bean 2005; Smircich and Morgan 1982; Tichey and Cohen 1997; Weick 2001

GENDER AND LEADERSHIP

Donna Ladkin

Although they would purport to be gender neutral, when scrutinized, many of the prototypical images of leadership would appear to be gender linked. Ely (2003) quoting Hiefetz (1994) writes that 'Leadership, as we know it, is steeped in idealised masculine images, our collective fantasy sees leaders as "big, colourful, fast, and assertive"'. Women attempting to enact this image find themselves caught in a 'double bind' – if they act like men, they are rejected for being 'unfeminine', but if they act like women, they couldn't possibly be a leader. What's a woman to do?

This piece briefly considers four frames for understanding gender differences associated with leadership, before turning to consider the role post-heroic models of leadership might have in opening up the territory for more varied and diverse enactments of leadership.

Although the actual differences between male and female ways of enacting leadership could be debated (is there really a difference, if so, to what could that difference be attributed?) the fact remains that women occupy far fewer formal positions of senior leadership within businesses, government, education, NGOs or health provision than do men. This is particularly startling in sectors such as health care provision, wherein the majority of lower ranks are dominated by women, but whose senior cadres are overwhelmingly male. Vinnicombe and Singh's (2005) report of FTSE 500 companies reveals a worrying trend; numbers of women Board Directors seemed on the rise during the 1990s, but have since fallen to levels commensurate with the 1960s.

Ely (2003) offers four frames for interpreting the dearth of women leaders in senior organizational roles, summarized below.

1 According to the first frame, sex role socialization has made women less skilled than men to compete in business. The solution to this is to 'fix the women' – remedy the situation by developing women's skills of assertiveness, logical thinking and task focus in order to minimize the effect of their socialization.

2 The second approach suggests that women and men are different, and organizations should celebrate this difference in order to gain the most benefit from the unique capabilities, such as empathy, relational understanding and care which women offer.

3 The third way of understanding disparities in gender representation suggests that organizational structures, including hiring procedures, promotional routes, the very working hours required in order to demonstrate organizational 'commitment', are what hold women back. These structures contribute to the 'glass ceiling' experienced by aspiring women.

4 Proponents of the fourth frame, according to Ely, 'reject the assumption of sex-linked skills and traits and move away from their under-representation as a problem to focus on'. Instead, they use the under-representation of women to pose the question 'Who else is missing from leadership roles?' (2003: 156)

This fourth frame provides the starting point for a discussion of post-heroic leadership and how it might contribute to the realization of larger numbers of women in senior formal positions. As summarized by Fletcher (2003), the rhetoric of post-heroic leadership includes:

- Questioning the concept of the autonomous self and the possibility of individual achievement.
- Challenging static, command and control images of leadership, proposing ideas of **servant leadership** or **distributed leadership** instead.
- Questioning the assumed goal of good leadership and the skills it requires.

From a post-heroic frame, 'leaders are expected to create conditions under which collective leading and continuous improvement can occur' (Fletcher 2003: 205). Rather than an omnipotent, directive role, creating such conditions requires relational skills, empathy – those capabilities associated with **emotional intelligence**, and from a gendered perspective, those stereotypically associated with women, rather than men.

Given that organizations throughout the West are recognizing the benefits of such capabilities in our fast-changing and complex world, Fletcher questions why we are not seeing a commensurate rise in numbers of women in senior roles? One answer she proposes relates to the 'separate sphere' phenomenon. This theory argues that the relational behaviours and capabilities called for by post-heroic leadership are those associated with the personal domain, a domain which is seen as unskilled, passive and inherently lacking in **power**. Suggesting that women, as supposedly more naturally bestowed with these capabilities, will be easily accepted as leaders in this new, post-heroic era denies many of the power issues, as well as the psychological dynamics inherent in **leader–follower relations**.

Whereas Fletcher concludes her argument rather bleakly, returning to the fourth frame for understanding the disparities in gender representation within senior leadership roles seems to offer more promising possibilities. This would involve questioning how the under-representation of women in leading roles might bring insight into leadership and how it is constructed. Sinclair (2004) argues that it is the image of leadership which makes it difficult for women to lead, not the fact that they are inherently less assertive, individualistic or task-focused than their male counterparts. In fact, the prevalent image of leaders similarly hinders males with more relational tendencies. From this frame, we can ask: 'what are we missing from leadership by constructing it in the way that we do – and how is this construction limiting **creativity** and innovation in our leadership approaches?' Such a question could helpfully contribute to the discourse around post-heroic approaches and aid the construction, rather than the deconstruction, of a notion of leadership which is more aligned to the requirements of our times and the great diversity of human beings involved in all aspects of organizational and community life.

See also: **distributed leadership**, **emotional intelligence**, **great man theory**, **heroic leadership**, **servant leadership**

Further reading: Ely 2003; Ely *et al.* 2003; Fletcher 2003; Sinclair 2004

GREAT MAN THEORY

Nathan Harter

Ancient history records the virtue and exploits of great men – prophets and philosophers, commanders and kings. A popular interest in the rich and powerful continues to this day. In the study of human organization, one finds considerable attention paid to leaders. Out of this persisting tendency to notice remarkable individuals arose an attempt in the West to understand leadership as the activity of great men. We know this attempt by the name of the great man theory of leadership, in which scholars tried to uncover what makes leaders – presumed at the time to be male – distinct.

Human beings are indisputably different from each other, and at certain activities, these differences determine whether one person is better than another – including activities commonly regarded as leadership. One can find Plato and Aristotle, for example, making such claims about the unique excellence of the philosopher-king or mature man. About 500 BCE, the philosopher Heraclitus observed that 'the many are worthless, good men are few. . . . One man is ten thousand, if he is the best' (Fragments LIXb and LXIII; Heraclitus 1979).

Human difference has frequently justified leadership. Something about a man apparently identified him for prominence and **power**. In cosmological empires, such as ancient Egypt, that special something would derive from his lineage, as an heir of royal blood, frequently traced to a divine forbearer. In the Greek tradition, it would have been more about the man's constellation of virtues. In the Hebrew tradition, it would have been divine anointing. (For a historical analysis, see generally Voegelin 1956, 1957.) Similar claims of preeminence have been made for centuries on behalf of the elder, the father, the master, the conqueror, the saint, the superior race, corporate management, intellectuals generally, and elites of all sorts. Only infrequently were women similarly acknowledged.

Historians are interested in leaders not so much for who they were, but rather for what they precipitated – a distinction emphasized by Sidney Hook (1943). Leadership matters to those who believe that individuals do make a difference as causal agents. It has been widely assumed for centuries that, whatever their particular merits, certain people had a disproportionate impact on events. We want to be able to credit or blame someone for the past. For that reason alone, they believed great individuals deserve study. Even then, the question arose about what it was about certain individuals that had such disproportionate impact. (The field of study known as psychohistory responds to this particular question. See generally Mazlish 1990, Chap. 9.)

It was Isaiah Berlin who explained that the underlying assumption in all of these early approaches to understanding leadership was that there is an abiding, transcendent order represented by exemplary individuals. Representation of an unseen order qualifies the leader. It is in the interest of everyone else to attune themselves to that unseen order. Groups, organizations and empires are ultimately called to align and thereby fulfil their transcendent purpose. Ordinary people were advised to defer to the right leaders, leaders who prove their worth by somehow being great.

This assumption about leaders who shape their communities according to an 'unseen order' started to collapse in Europe with the Renaissance and Reformation, twin assaults on the existing regime. Many brilliant thinkers at the time rejected the unifying vision of medieval Roman Catholicism, yet they still sought an immanent order, a true cosmos. They hoped to discover it, and with it, the persons best suited to achieve it. After the collapse of the medieval social order, without another comprehending social order determining the right way to live and the right person to follow, it became even more important to discern a prospective leader's worthiness to lead.

At about this time, Niccoló Machiavelli emphasized that leadership depends not so much on one's qualities as on the *perception* of those qualities, such that leadership depends to an extent on image or what came to be known as **impression management** (1532/1991). One must seem to be great. John Keegan, in a study of military leaders, put it this way: 'The exceptional are both shown to and hidden from the mass of humankind, revealed by artifice, presented by theatre' (1987: 11). This insight tended to detach leadership from any unseen order, so long as the leader convinced a gullible community that still believed in such a thing.

Mostly in response to the assumption of an order that is given and needing to be found, a number of writers preferred a romantic ideal in which human beings are free to imagine their own order, so that according to this ideal, pre-eminent figures are creative, unbound by circumstance, overcoming the present in order to build a better future (Berlin 1994: 168–93). They are heroes. As heroes, they qualify to lead.

An era of hero-worship ensued. Influential authors such as Thomas Carlyle and Ralph Waldo Emerson recognized the importance of self-transcending characters, larger than life, whether by virtue of their intuition, daring or artistic sensibility, until Friedrich Nietzsche depicted the embodiment of their ideal as the *Übermensch* (Superman). By living only in accordance with some internal, impossibly mystical standard, like a knight's code or quest, the hero develops in contradis-tinction to the rest of the world and through suffering imposes an order that otherwise would not have existed. Furthermore, the hero inspires subsequent generations to exceed them (Jennings 1960; Bentley 1944). One might imagine hero-worship as the romance of merit.

Hero-worship influenced ambitious men such as Adolph Hitler to cultivate the appearance of heroism, relying on propaganda to achieve pre-eminence (Keegan 1987: 305). In the popular imagination, these efforts at projecting greatness occasionally succeeded. When the human sciences coalesced at the turn of the twentieth century, hero-worship found expression in early theories. For instance, sociologist Max Weber composed a classic account of leadership based on a critique of **charisma**, which subsequently influenced theories of **transformational leadership**. Weber embedded his study into a broader inquiry about the basis of leadership, i.e. what it is that legitimizes domination (Weber 1947, §III). The great man theory holds that legitimacy resides in the greatness of the man, in his being great.

The first half of the twentieth century renewed interest in the study of great men such as Winston Churchill, Franklin Roosevelt and Josef Stalin. Political scientists examined leadership as part of the historical process, considering the impact of distinctive characters on the ordering of society (Rustow 1970: 5). What, they ask, can we attribute to a Gandhi, Nkrumah, de Gaulle or Bismarck? In more recent years, popular authors have seen fit to publish the leadership secrets of a number of supposedly great men, on the presupposition that one can learn leadership partly from the example of others. Rudy Giuliani, former mayor of New York City, wrote his own book titled *Leadership* (2002), in which he asserts the following: 'All leaders are influenced by those they admire. Reading about them and studying their development inevitably allows an aspiring leader to grow his own leadership traits' (p. xiv). The study of greatness inspires greatness in us.

Not everyone agrees. Michael McGill and John Slocum (1997) doubt that most people can identify with great leaders and their outsized predicaments. Great leaders are largely irrelevant to their daily plight.

When subjected to closer scrutiny, hero-worship faltered. Key terms such as 'hero' and 'great' are vague. The origins of greatness, however we define it, are nearly impossible to trace, echoing today in debates over whether leaders are born or made. The most sympathetic writers, such as William James, had to concede that leadership arises from the conjunction of the right actor with the right circumstances. Nobody does it alone (Harter 2003). And even the most rigorous attempts to isolate traits associated with leadership, when it *does* happen, failed to deliver a satisfactory theory.

E.E. Jennings (1960) adds that this elitarian understanding of social change and differentiation appears to collide with democratic values. McGill and Slocum (1997) argue that leadership does not have to be great to be useful anyway. The sheer scale of greatness – great crises, great men, great accomplishments – is actually unhelpful to ordinary leaders with modest ambitions.

The most vivid rebuke of the great man theory comes in the form of any woman who leads, since one of the most widespread assumptions had been that certainly the leader would be male, and this is just not always so.

Vestiges of the great man theory remain. In 2005, the Center for Public Leadership at Harvard University's John F. Kennedy School of Government convened 35 experts to choose America's 25 best leaders, hoping to identify those who are good and worthy. Director of the center David Gergen declared: 'Whether America moves forward will hinge in significant degree upon the quality and number of those who lead' (2005: 91).

Occasionally, enthusiasts lapse into hero-worship, if not outright cults of personality, but leadership studies seeks to validate what it can and largely repudiate the rest as naïve, unhelpful and vaguely pernicious – without altogether ignoring its place in history. Like so many before and since, the great man theory both helped and hindered our understanding of the phenomenon.

See also: **charisma**, **gender and leadership**, **heroic leadership**, **philosophical approaches to leadership**, **transformational leadership**

Further reading: Bentley 1944; Harter 2003; Hook 1943; Jennings 1960; McGill and Slocum 1997

GROUP DYNAMICS

Donelson R. Forsyth

Group dynamics are the influential actions, processes and changes that take place in groups. Much of the world's work is accomplished by people working with others in groups, and the processes that take place within these groups – the continual vying for social status, the give-and-take collaboration between members, the pressure of the group on the atypical individual, and the eruption of conflict and discord that can shatter the group – significantly shape members' experiences as well as their accomplishments. It was the eminent social scientist Kurt Lewin (1951) who used the term 'group dynamics' to describe the powerful and complex social processes that emerge in groups.

Neither leaders nor their **followers** go uninfluenced by these group processes. Although trait-level analyses of the unique personal qualities of leaders and the close connection between these traits and followers' outcomes often ignore where leadership occurs, when leadership is viewed as a social process involving leaders and their followers then the interpersonal context of leadership must be considered. Because groups are the context for these interpersonal processes, a complete analysis of leadership requires a thorough understanding of group dynamics.

The connection of group dynamics to leadership processes is a reciprocal one: the way the leader organizes, directs, coordinates, supports and motivates others in the pursuit of shared goals influences the group and its dynamics, but the leader's own actions and reactions are shaped by the group as well. Lewin *et al.* (1939) were among the first researchers to affirm this close connection between leadership and group dynamics empirically. They studied boys working in small groups on hobby projects. A young man was appointed the leader of each group, and this leader was trained to adopt one of three different styles of leadership. The autocratic leader made all the decisions for the group without consulting the boys. He gave the boys orders, criticized them and remained aloof from the group. The participatory, democratic leader explained long-term goals and steps to be taken to reach the goals and rarely gave the groups orders. The laissez-faire leader provided information on demand, but he did not offer advice, criticism or guidance spontaneously.

These different methods of leading significantly influenced the groups' dynamics. Groups with autocratic, directive leaders spent more time working than did the other groups – particularly those with the laissez-faire leader. This productivity, however, dropped precipitously when the autocratic leader left the room, whereas those groups with a participative leader worked diligently even when the leader was not present. The groups with an autocratic leader also displayed higher levels of conflict and hostility, as well as demands for attention, more destructiveness and a greater tendency to scapegoat one or more members.

The basic implications of these findings – that leadership processes substantially **influence** a wide range of group processes – forms the basis of most theories of leadership and has been reaffirmed in both applied and basic studies of laboratory and bona fide groups. Although some have questioned the impact of leaders on their followers, leaders influence the processes that occur in groups just as surely as Lewin's three kinds of leaders changed the way the groups of boys worked together and related to each other (Forsyth 2006). Groups of individuals, when they face an emergency, often fail to respond; but if a leader is present in the group this bystander effect becomes less likely (Baumeister *et al.* 1988). Groups, when discussing solutions to problems, tend to spend too much time discussing information shared by many members – unless a leader is present in the group who controls the group's tendency to focus on shared information (Larson *et al.* 1996). Groups seeking creative solutions to problems tend to perform less effectively than individuals working alone, but not if a leader is present in the group who pushes the group to reach higher standards of performance (Offner *et al.* 1996). Groups get more done when a leader is present, due to reductions in social loafing and increased member–member coordination (Karau and Williams 1993).

But the direction of influence goes both ways. Just as leaders shape group processes, so many core group-level processes significantly influence leadership. Fiedler's (1978) contingency theory, for example, assumes that the favourability of the leadership situation is determined by the type of task the group faces and leaders' position **power**, but it is the group's acceptance of the leader's influence that is the key factor determining the success of a leader who focuses primarily on the task compared with one focusing primarily on relationships. Not only are situations that differ in favourability more propitious for one style of leadership than another, but in many cases skilled leaders will change their basic style of leadership depending on the group situation (Hersey and Blanchard 1982). Leaders may also change their approaches to leading unintentionally, as they respond to the subtle pressures of the group's dynamics. Janis's (1982) theory of groupthink, for example, describes the close association between group processes and leadership in disrupting the flow of information within groups seeking solutions in highly stressful situations. Groupthink occurs when a group becomes highly cohesive, and as a result fails to provide the leader with accurate feedback about his or her initiatives. Leaders, when working in such supportive, closeknit groups, often respond by becoming even more directive and closed to input, with the result that the group makes critical errors that are not corrected through dissent and deliberation.

Conceptualizations of leadership emergence also note that who becomes the leader of a group depends both on the qualities of the leader and the status-confirming processes of the group. For example, Berger and Zelditch (1998), in their work on status differentiation, confirmed that leaders emerge in groups through a status-organizing process as members accept influence from some members but refuse to be influenced by others. The emergence process is also influenced by leaders' ability to build coalitions among followers, but their failure often results when a revolutionary coalition of members forms that demands change within the group (Lawler 1975). Studies of social **identity** suggest that the tendency to identify with a group and to take on the qualities of that group as one's own also determine who will be accepted as the leader of that group: the individual who best matches the shared prototype of the group will likely lead it (Fielding and Hogg 1997).

In sum, groups are dynamic: powerful rather than weak, active rather than passive, fluid rather than static, and catalysing rather than reifying. Because leadership, in most cases, occurs in a group context, these dynamic processes determine how leaders lead groups and organizations, but these processes are themselves influenced by leaders. In consequence, leadership and group dynamics combine to determine a wide range of interpersonal outcomes.

See also: **behavioural theories of leadership, contingency theories, identity, leader–follower relations, trait theory**

Further reading: Avolio *et al.* 2003; Chemers 2000; Forsyth 2006; Hackman and Wageman 2005; Hogan and Kaiser 2005

HEROIC LEADERSHIP

Stephanie Jones

The concept of 'heroic leadership' has emerged in several leadership studies. Where does it come from, and what does it mean? On one level, 'hero', a Greek word, refers to a person of superhuman strength, fearlessness and integrity, gifts that showed he or she was favoured by the gods. The leader as hero or great man (or woman) is one 'who exhibits extraordinary courage, firmness or greatness of soul, in the course of some journey or enterprise. We, as humans, have a tendency to admire and venerate them for their achievements and noble qualities', explains John Adair (1989) in his study *Great Leaders*.

Adair went on to add, by way of warning, that

admiration can become inordinate and they come to worship the hero or great man. They can even make a fairly ordinary leader into a hero simply because they need a hero to worship. An ambitious and unscrupulous leader, who discovers that he or she has some magnetic power, can capitalize on this aspect of human nature.

(Adair 1989: 227)

The concept was more recently discussed in a *Harvard Business Review* article (Gosling and Mintzberg 2003), including a comparison between 'heroic management, based on self' and 'engaging management, based on collaboration'. This takes a sceptical view, contrasting 'Heroic Management' as 'thrust upon those who thrust their will upon others' with 'Engaging Management' where 'leadership is a sacred trust earned through the respect of others'.

In spite of these critical views of 'heroic leadership' as a concept, it is still very much with us. The topic has maintained its popularity with the continued celebration of heroic leaders, both historical and contemporary, in books which attract attention in popular literature and continue to occupy the coffee tables and bedsides of leaders at all levels. A Google search for 'heroic leadership' produced 5,630,000 references that, discounting huge duplication and irrelevancies, are still impressive. Searches on Amazon were similarly productive.

A sample of these references shows that not only is 'heroic leadership' still popular, but the concept of 'post-heroic leadership' has also caught on (Jones and Eicher 1999a, b, c), as well as that of the Heroic Follower (Palestini 2006). The debate continues with articles on heroic leadership and the role of gender (Fletcher 2003), suggesting that heroic leadership is masculine and post-heroic leadership emphasizes feminine values and approaches; and **quiet leadership**, sometimes seen as the opposite of heroic leadership, which plays a part in the concept of moral leadership (Badaracco 2002b, 2004).

However, in his popular 'Moral Leader' class at Harvard, Badaracco

discovered that students like their leaders cut from heroic cloth; that is, with high principles, noble behaviour, and acts of self-sacrifice that inspire a legion of followers . . . even today, through its stories of human triumph and tragedy, the [heroic leadership] model provides people with momentary escape from the routines of everyday life and, on occasion, the inspiration necessary to transcend circumstances and perform unexpected acts of greatness

(Badaracco 2004)

Here, moral leadership can include heroic leadership – depending on its direction, focus and circumstances. Thus Mahatma Gandhi, Martin

Luther King and Mother Teresa are at the top of the pyramid for Badaracco's students – but it can be argued that they are both moral and heroic leaders.

References to 'heroic leadership' in Google and Amazon are inevitably about famous individuals, such as studies of politicians including Churchill (Gilbert 2004), American presidents (Roper 2001), Blair (Seldon 2005), Giuliani (2002), and captains of industry like Jack Welch of GE (Slater 2000), Lou Gerstner of IBM (2003), Warren Buffett (O'Loughlin 2004), Roberto Goizueta of Coke (Greising 1999) and David Jones of NEXT (2005).

Historical biographies with specific leadership lessons have emerged, of which an early instance was of Shackleton (Morrell and Capparell 2001). Another example is of the famous British Admiral, Lord Nelson, whose bicentennial was celebrated in 2005. Of the more than 30 books on his life published to celebrate the event, one in particular focused on the leadership lessons suggested by Nelson's career and the relevance to modern-day leaders (Jones and Gosling 2005).

Admiral Nelson can be seen as an archetypal heroic leader, who committed to heroism as a teenager: 'I will be a hero, and confiding in providence, I will brave every danger' (Jones and Gosling 2005: 13). Heroism was the way that Nelson defined leadership, as a 'transcendent sense of purpose and a level of ambition that can only be described as obsessive' (Jones and Gosling 2005: 16). If you want to be a heroic leader, the authors ask: 'have you got the energy and commitment for it?' They also suggest that you should 'spread the word about your achievements with stories that will be repeated, to inspire others and remind them of the values they most admire' (Jones and Gosling 2005: 20). As UK leadership guru Sir John Harvey-Jones argued, 'the lessons from Nelson's leadership are even more appropriate today than they were two centuries ago' and 'people want leaders they can respect, on whom they can model themselves. Heroes are examples from whom you can go on learning' (Jones and Gosling 2005: 195).

In a more wide-reaching historical survey, Keegan (1987) argues that heroism was a necessary quality of military leaders when they were required to literally lead their troops into battle; but with the development of the rifle and new ballistic missiles, commanders stay entirely invisible and personal heroism plays a far less tangible role in their effective **authority**. Comparing Alexander the Great, the Duke of Wellington, Ulysses Grant and Hitler, he concludes that modern leaders, with their fingers on the nuclear button (or the equivalent in asymmetrical conflict) may need moral courage, but this hardly qualifies as heroism in the classical sense. However, heroism may still be a valid concept in describing the individuals and small bands of so-called insurgents who resist force; certainly the image of a frail individual facing the tanks of an occupying force carries with it the echoes of heroic struggles of classical times. Thus, we come to a crucial point about heroism – it marks out the individual, the focus of greatness, agency and moral conviction, against the indistinct mass of ordinariness. It is inevitably a romantic concept, and one that denies the subtleties of systemic interdependencies; and yet it is as powerful as the search for **identity** and meaning.

Thus 'heroic leadership' can encompass many concepts. It includes the leader as hero, embodying courage, strength, firmness and greatness of soul, and thus as a role model. It also features the pull-factor – addressing the need for hero-worship on the part of the populace. Then there is the anti-hero, the manipulative and unscrupulous leader who can pull the strings for good or evil, given the need for heroes and the lack of discernment on the part of the populace. 'Heroic Management' refers to style rather than qualities, where strategy and decision-making is passed down from on-high to unconsulted and largely resisting workers below. 'Post-heroic leadership' tends to argue for the reverse, leaders and managers seeking engagement and collaboration, seen by some as a form of '**quiet leadership**'. Yet 'heroic leadership' is also seen as playing a part in 'moral leadership', but in a selective way. Finally, 'heroic leadership' stays with us through the heroes around us, both historical and contemporary, which suit this early twenty-first century celebrity-watching age we live in.

See also: **charisma**, **ethics**, **gender and leadership**, **great man theory**, **quiet leadership**

Further reading: Badaracco 2004; Fletcher 2003; Gosling and Mintzberg 2003; Jones and Eicher 1999a, b, c; Jones and Gosling 2005; Keegan 1987

HIERARCHY

Nathan Harter

Students of leadership frequently encounter issues of hierarchy. For one reason, leadership takes place within or against hierarchies; they are the structures within which leadership takes place. Hierarchy is part of the context. For another reason, leadership *implies* hierarchy, a kind of relationship that is itself a hierarchy or could very easily transform into hierarchy. It is not uncommon for critics of hierarchy to be wary of leadership for this reason.

What then does 'hierarchy' mean? The word combines two images. The portion 'hier-' refers to a spatial relation denoting above and below, originally in the Greek conveying a separation according to that which is holy or set apart, almost detached. The portion '-archy' means a structure of **authority**, as in monarchy or oligarchy. Thus, the word once conveyed the image of those who preside from lofty positions over sacred rites.

The word has since found secular uses, representing organizational structure in which certain positions rank higher than others, as in the stereotypical chain of command. The *Oxford English Dictionary Online* defines 'hierarchy' as '[a] body of persons . . . ranked in grades, orders, or classes, one above another'. In ordinary usage, the term depicts a formal relationship where one person is in some important respect superior to the other.

The spatial imagery of being above and below one another occurs regularly in the English language. Probably the most obvious example would be the role of overseer or supervisor, as one who views from above. Organizational charts traditionally show gradations in a pyramid, so that the higher the position, the greater the status and authority (Morgan 1986, Chap. 2). For that reason we say that managers 'climb the corporate ladder'. As they thrive, they can be said to 'rise' as they 'move up' in the world. Even the very words 'superior' and 'subordinate' derive from prefixes ('super-' and 'sub-') intended to show being positioned up or down.

In his seminal work on types of authority, Max Weber included in his list of fundamental categories of bureaucracy 'the principle of hierarchy; that is, each lower office is under the control and supervision of a higher one' (1947: 331). Subsequent writers identified principles of management theory that illustrate hierarchy, such as the centralization of authority as part of the division of work, so that only a portion of workers exercise authority. They become the organization's managers. In order to reflect this division, writers show the division vertically, creating a scalar chain with cascading spans of control (Morgan 1986, exhibit 2.2). Once divided, the organization seeks to coordinate vertically through policies, rules, planning and control (Bolman and Deal 1991: 57).

The relative positions in any hierarchy are abstractions, conceptual, occupied in reality by individual human beings who then play a role more or less consistent with a differential of authority. Hierarchy refers not to the people involved, nor even to their specific behaviour, but to the form of their relationship, such that one person tends to defer to the other. The relationship is also likely part of a larger structure, such as a family, community or business.

The persons who occupy relative positions in a hierarchy are unique individuals distinct from the relationship. For instance, the employer and employee during the day might reverse their roles in a service club or simply go their separate ways at the end of the day. They are partly oriented to each other according to their relationship and partly oriented away from the relationship, so that they can look at it, think about it, and possibly alter it to suit their changing needs – if not walk away completely. Hierarchy does not in and of itself define a person. Nevertheless, we know that relationships do shape who we are, so that to some extent a hierarchy with its implied attributions of rank and class may **influence** personality. In other words, despite our independence from social roles, we often do adapt ourselves to them (see, for example, Hummel 1994: 8). Hierarchy is but one example of this.

Hierarchy is an archetypal depiction of organizational structure. Leadership occurs within the context of organizational structure, whether to advance the purposes of the organization or to work at cross-purposes. In either case, leadership must be understood as taking place in response to what Amitai Etzioni (1961: 89) calls the power structure. Those we identify as 'leaders' possess **power** relative to the structure within which they operate. John Gardner, for example, wrote that 'the authority stemming from the leader's hierarchical position is a potent weapon, always there, even if the leader chooses to use it with a light hand' (1990: 98).

Leadership itself connotes hierarchy between the leader and the led, a differential of authority. Joseph Rost insists that in leadership the 'relationship is inherently unequal because the influence patterns are unequal' (1991: 112). That differential can become formal, solidified by practice over time, in a process studied by sociologists under **elite theory**. Leaders can be tempted to consolidate power. Terry Price (2006) critiques this tendency of leaders to abuse their status or position of leadership by creating a more permanent separation of themselves from their **followers**, but it does not have to be objectionable for leadership to congeal.

A number of theorists oppose hierarchy, for a variety of reasons. (a) Some object to the injustice of differentiation by rank and pernicious inequalities (Harter *et al.* 2006). Hierarchy can appear incompatible with equality. (b) Some theorists object to hierarchy as a practical impediment to organizational success. Hierarchy might be well and good in certain circumstances, they admit, but it also has its limitations (Morgan 1986: 34–8). (c) Some object that hierarchy is an inadequate representation of reality. Mary Parker Follett favoured images of process and flow, dynamic representations rather than static ones. Her characterization 'does away with hierarchy. . . . There is no above and below. We cannot schematize men as space objects' (1919: 582–3).

Richard Weaver disagreed. He wrote: 'If society is something which can be understood, it must have structure; if it has structure, it must have hierarchy' (1948: 35).

See also: **authority, ethics, leadership definition, organizational culture, power**

Further reading: Bolman and Deal 1991; Follett 1919; Harter *et al.* 2006; Morgan 1986; Weber 1947

IDENTITY

Mats Alvesson

Identity is an increasingly commonly used term that refers to different levels and entities. We can talk about the identity of Europe, corporate identity, the identity of a profession and about personal identity (often called self-identity). Identity is sometimes viewed as a matter of the characteristics (essence), the coherence and the distinctiveness of an individual or a collective (Albert and Whetten 1985). Frequently when identity is addressed, it is in the context of some uncertainty, questioning or unclearness of what may be coherent and distinct, such as the characteristics of an occupation, a company or a person. In dynamic contexts – like many parts of contemporary social and working life – identities are changing, making it more reasonable to talk about temporary forms of coherence rather than something fixed and stable.

Identity refers to subjective meaning and experience. 'Who am I (or we) and – by implication – how should I (we) act?' These are questions answered by the constructions of identity. A particular personal identity implies a certain form of subjectivity, and thereby 'ties' a person's feelings, thinking and valuing in a particular direction. Decisions are often affected by the logic inherent in a specific self-image. If one defines oneself as primarily a professional working in a specific company or as an organizational member doing a particular job, these mean rather different identities even though the 'objective' work situation is the same. The 'professional' may be somewhat less inclined to follow instructions of management when conflicting with what is seen as key characteristics of the profession, while the organizational member may be more inclined to try to take the firm's best interests into account.

Role and identity are terms sometimes used as synonyms (when individuals are referred to), but a richer understanding calls for distinctions. Role is perhaps better used to refer mainly to external expectations and the position taken in relationship to others. Roles are complementary. Identity refers to a person's view of him/herself, it is an experience and goes deeper than a role. A role is the position I take in interaction with others, identity is how I see myself. One may take a role and act smoothly in it, but also feel that 'this is not me', just something I am doing temporarily, and distance oneself from the role. It is not possible to distance oneself from one's own identity construction – although one may resist the efforts of others to define or regulate one's identity.

There are various theoretical approaches to identity, e.g. psychoanalytic, symbolic interactionist, narrative, discursivist, poststructuralist. One influential version is proposed by Giddens, who defines self-identity, saying: 'it is the self as reflexively understood by the person . . . self-identity is continuity (across time and space) as interpreted reflexively by the agent' (1991: 53).

Many argue today that identity is best understood as constructed, multiple and varying, rather than something fixed, monolithic and robust. This reflects the increasing influence of narrative, discourse and poststructuralist thinking. Identity is – as social life in general – constructed, e.g. it is not a reflection of a psychological or social 'objective reality'. Identity is about how an individual or a group of people understand and define themselves individually and collectively. Constructions involve an element of invention and the use of a vocabulary that creates a particular version of reality. Identity is constituted through comparisons and interactions with other people and groups. A person seeing herself as a consultant does so because there are clients and client personnel confirming the consultant's position. And she is viewing herself as a particular kind of consultant – temporary extra worker, professional expert, sparring-partner – partly contingent upon the negotiations of meaning around the relations and work involved. Similarly, a manager calls for someone to manage – or at least people seen as not having managerial responsibilities or a managerial position.

Within the contemporary studies on identity it is thus increasingly common not to look for some essential traits or stable characteristics of self-definitions, but to acknowledge the process-based nature of identity. People in organizations routinely engage in *identity work*, aiming to achieve a feeling of a coherent and strong self as well as a basis for social relations, which is necessary for coping with work tasks and social interactions (Alvesson and Willmott 2002). Identities are constituted, negotiated, reproduced and threatened in social interaction, in the form of narratives, and also in material practices. Identities are, at least partly, developed in the context of power relations. The exercise of **power** is then about the development of subjects tied to particular identities regarding how one should feel, think and act. Through defining who a person is – or how he/she should be like – and indicating deviations from the ideal, the person is regulated and the thinking and feeling become effects of the exercise of power. It is, of course, dependent upon the person being regulated accepting the definition and the norms involved.

Organizations are significant sites for various forms of identity work; arenas for on-going and dynamic negotiations in the creation of a sense of self, and in providing temporary answers to the questions 'who am I (we)?' and 'who might I (we) become?' Individuals associate themselves with their organizations and sometimes define themselves as organizational members. In identifying with – and sometimes against – the organization, individuals not only create a sense of self, they also construct the organization's identity and, in defining whether and how they fit into an organization, individuals develop particular constructions of what they believe the organization to be. For managers, identity issues are viewed as significant due to their exposure to an increasingly destabilized working world. Managers are frequently affected by a multitude of expectations, demands, incoherent discourses and ethical problems. In contemporary business and public sector life, social contexts are frequently portrayed as unstable, ambiguous and sometimes contradictory, making managerial life complicated and difficult: conflicting expectations and demands, ethical problems, worries, stress, a sense of lack of meaning, and being victims of time and place are not uncommon (Sveningsson and Alvesson 2003).

In the organizational and work context it is often *social*, rather than highly individualized, identities that are of greatest relevance, even when it is a matter of understanding individuals. A social identity refers to the group category that the individual identifies with: company, division, occupation, gender, nationality, ethnicity, age (Ashforth and Mael 1989; Turner 1984). An important aspect is organizational identification, often defined as 'the degree to which a member defines him- or herself by the same attributes that he or she believes define the organization' (Dutton *et al.* 1994: 239). Social identity is not the same as internalization of values and norms and commitment to a certain issue. Social identity refers to self-categorizations as a point of departure for thinking and relating. It does not necessarily imply a set of sentiments and should not be equated with corporate culture (or any other culture). One may feel as a corporate member, a woman or a Frenchman without necessarily internalizing all or most of the values and meanings assumed to be typical for the category. As experiments have shown, people may adopt a particular social identity without any distinctive ideas, values or emotions being involved (Turner 1984). Two groups may have similar values and beliefs but still perceive differences and exaggerate their distinctiveness. Often, however, a specific social identity increases the likelihood that certain ideas, values and norms associated with the group or company concerned are internalized. The opposite is also common: if the values of a group are appealing, one tends to identify with the group.

See also: **cross-cultural leadership**, **group dynamics**, **organizational culture**, **power**, **process theory**

Further reading: Alvesson and Willmott 2002; Ashforth and Mael 1989; Dutton *et al.* 1994; Sveningsson and Alvesson 2003; Turner 1984

IMPRESSION MANAGEMENT

Nathan Harter

One of the central lines of inquiry in leadership studies asks how the person we refer to as the leader influences others to follow: what are the causal mechanisms?

We have known throughout history that human beings respond to the impressions they have of notable individuals. People bear images of each other. We rely on this knowledge during ordinary interactions, such as job interviews and courtship, when we take actions specifically in order to **influence** the impression others would have of us. To quote B.R. Schlenker, we do things 'to create and maintain desired impressions in others about ourselves' (1980: 41).

During the twentieth century, a range of popular books on social success in the West depended on the same assumption. Probably foremost among these is Dale Carnegie's 1936 bestseller *How to Win*

Friends and Influence People. Over the years, readers were advised to dress for success, put their best foot forward, offer a firm handshake and make a good first impression – 'riding on a smile and a shoeshine', as the playwright Arthur Miller put it in *Death of a Salesman* (1949).

We each build an image we want the other person to regard as our **identity**; we are taking steps to form an identity that will serve our interests. That identity forms in the imaginations of other people. To the extent that we attempt to shape that identity, therefore, we can be said to engage in impression management or IM. 'When a person deliberately sets out to establish a particular identity in the eyes of others we speak of impression management or self-presentation' (Tedeschi and Melburg 1984: 52; on the subject of self-presentation generally, see Mead 1934/1962: part II; Goffman 1959).

Jerald Greenberg (1996: 107) notes that the dramaturgical perspective and IM in particular 'has a rich tradition in the social sciences' such as sociology, social psychology and organizational psychology. Specifically with regard to leadership studies, it has proven to be an effective line of inquiry. Bruce Mazlish, for example, once wrote that 'image . . . is a vital part of the [leadership] relationship [because i]t is the image . . . that leads followers' (1990: 256). Leary *et al.* (1986) put it this way:

> [P]eople who wish to become or remain a leader must continually affirm to those they want to lead that they possess the characteristics that qualify them for the leader role. One way in which they may do this is through their self-presentation to group members.
>
> (p. 742)

Three years later, Leary went so far as to claim that IM is a determinant of who becomes a leader and how successful they are (1989: 364).

Mazlish (1990) wrote from a historian's perspective about the importance of a leader's image. John Keegan – also a historian – devoted a long study to what he referred to as *The Mask of Command*, in which he stated:

> The leader of men in warfare can show himself to his followers only through a mask, a mask that he must make for himself, but a mask made in such form as will mark him to men of his time and place as the leader they want and need.
>
> (1987: 11)

Historians more interested in politics directly also find it useful to examine a ruler's efforts at image-building. Several centuries ago, Niccoló Machiavelli had observed that rulers are evaluated by the virtues and vices they are perceived to have. He wrote, 'Everyone can see what you appear to be, whereas few have direct experience of what you really are. . . . For the common people are impressed by appearances and results' (1532/1991: Chap. XIII). For this reason, he advised the prince to gain an advantageous reputation (e.g. 1532/1991: Chap. XXI).

As a technical matter, an impression involves the direct experience one person has of another, at least in part by means of sensation. Eric Voegelin once referred to these as primal images. These experiences include stimuli from paramount reality. Thought images – as opposed to primal images – are conceptions, constructs with a less direct attachment to sensation. They emerge in more reflective moments, connecting memories of primal images with current sensations and with inferences to form a more comprehending schema (Harter 2006: Chap. 4). According to this way of understanding, identity is a thought image, influenced by impressions. Much of impression management therefore implicates how one sounds and looks, as that pertains to creating a favourable identity, which is why scholars of leadership consider the effects of gestures, facial expressions, language, attire, use of space and the like.

While scientists study how IM works, others debate its **ethics**. IM can appear to be manipulation, based on a divergence between who they are and who they want others to believe that they are. Such behaviour is not 'authentic'. Greenberg notes that managers find it more important to seem fair than in actual fact to be fair toward their subordinates (1996, part II). By this line of reasoning, follower perception is the relevant reality. IM is ubiquitous, how things get done, even among those who **trust** each other most (Wayne and Green 1993: 1438). At the entrance to the Globe Theatre in London, these words appear: *Totus Mundus Agit Histrionem*, 'all the world's a stage' (Schlenker 1985: 21).

IM can be useful, even necessary. For example, leaders sometimes have to repair false impressions, set a good example and control their emotions. It is also conceivable in certain circumstances that **followers** will prefer a managed impression to freely expressed emotion (Leary *et al.* 1986: 742).

Aristotle found objectionable what we refer to as impression management, yet he wrote that 'the whole business of rhetoric being concerned with appearances, we must pay attention to the subject of delivery, unworthy though it is, because we cannot do without it' (*Rhetoric* III: 1 [1404a1] in Aristotle 1952). Leadership specifically occurs among the glassy surfaces of human interaction. Prudence suggests that prospective leaders and wary followers attend to that realization.

See also: **ethics, identity, influence, leader–follower relations, philosophical approaches to leadership**

Further reading: Goffman 1959; Leary 1989; Mazlish 1990; Schlenker 1980; Tedeschi and Melburg 1984

INFLUENCE

Joseph C. Rost

Influence is a very important concept to understanding and practising leadership. Why? Simply stated, leadership cannot be understood without knowing what influence is and leadership cannot be practised without using influence. In the ordinary course of human events, one cannot consistently practice something as complicated as influence without knowing what it is. One may use it by chance, luck or as an only viable option several times, but not consistently by deliberate choice. Thus, influence becomes a very key component for people who are operating from a leadership framework. *Influence* is the most frequently used word in the definitions of leadership written in books and serious articles about leadership beginning in the 1940s through the 1980s (Rost 1991: 79). I theorized in *Leadership for the Twenty-First Century* that the experience of raw, dictatorial **power** before and during World War II might have had something to do with the importance of influence to the practice of leadership. While that conclusion is impossible to prove, I think that significant background assumptions throughout society and the world tend to exert meaning into words such as *leadership*. An event as all-consuming as World War II could not help but develop assumptions about power and control of people and societies.

The concept of influence has continued to be vital to understanding leadership in the twenty-first century. While the great-person view of leadership maintains its strong hold on popular views of leadership, there is abundant evidence in the literature and in life experience that people associate leadership with great persons who use influence, that is, relational and cooperative/collaborative strategies in doing leadership rather than strategies that rely on overt **authority** and power-wielding.

Newer, postindustrial ideas about leadership have tended to put the locus of leadership activity in a relationship that involves small to large numbers of people as opposed to the activities of a single leader or an elite group of high-level executives in an organization. As a result, the meaning and practice of influence has become even more crucial to leadership studies and practice than it was when more traditional models of leadership were taken for granted. With that in mind, the following material is meant to clear the air about the nature and practice of influence.

The major issue that confronts leadership scholars and practitioners is distinguishing between authority, power and influence. The words are often used synonymously in books and articles about organizational dynamics and behaviours, and in the leadership literature.

First, authority, power and influence involve relationships. They are not activities that involve only one person: a single person cannot do them in isolation from other people. Bell (1979) exemplifies our understanding of authority, power and influence as relationships among people.

Second, authority, power and influence are not things. The use of things may be involved in the practice of all of them, but the things themselves are not the essence of authority, power or influence. A person's authority, power and influence are not quantifiable.

Authority is the easiest of the three to identify.

Authority is a relationship of human beings when one or more persons are authorized to command others regarding legitimate areas of social interaction. Thus, authority involves:

- A relationship wherein one or several persons have command over other persons.
- The authorization comes from another source, not one's self.
- The ability to command means that others are required to obey in order to stay in the authority relationship.
- Legitimate areas are those wherein the authorities are authorized to command. These areas are almost always spelled out in a contract or job/position responsibilities.

Some comments on authority are in order.

First, people in authority relationships have the ability to exit the relationship if they are adults. If that ability is not present, the relationship is something other than mere authority – for instance, a dictatorship or an abusive relationship. Second, people in authority relationships can refuse legitimate commands by resignation or attempting to convince the authorities that the legitimate command is not a wise course of action. Third, people who have authority in a relationship may choose not to use that authority. Fourth, conflicts can arise regarding the legitimacy of certain commands. Different methods are used to mediate or resolve such conflicts so that people in authority relationships may continue in the relationship while questioning the legitimacy of certain commands.

Delineating these elements of authority makes it clear that leadership is not an authority relationship.

French and Raven's (1960) description of power sources has been influential, but does not make distinctions among power, authority and influence, since authority and influence are power sources. They list five kinds of power: reward, coercive, legitimate, expert and referent. The first four are self-explanatory; the last has to do with role-model relationships.

The problem with such an understanding of power and the numerous models derived from the original article is that they are all-encompassing. Every social activity is power-oriented by this definition but if power is everything, we have no ability to choose other strategies that could be not power-oriented. If this conception of power is accurate, leadership has to be a power relationship, a concept that many people reject.

Burns developed a strong case in his book, *Leadership* (1984), for stating that leadership is a form of power. His understanding of power would include every human action that people normally use to establish organizational and societal control. But his discussion does illuminate three points: (1) power is a relationship, (2) power-wielding has one person or clique getting its way, but (3) in democratic institutions, power involves the motives and purposes of many people in the relationship, not just the power-wielder(s). Burns dispenses with influence as 'unnecessary and unparsimonious' (1984: 19), and declares that leadership is an 'aspect of power, but it is also a separate and vital process in itself' (p. 18).

Bell's (1979) understanding of power is more simple and straightforward. Power is a relationship in which some people use rewards or threaten to use sanctions to obtain desired behaviours from others in the relationship. Bell's definition of power is embodied in the 'paradigm' (to use his word), 'If you will do X, I will do Y' (1979: 20). His view of power is down-to-earth, easy to understand, and available to be used by everyone. And using Bell's definition of power, it is easy to see that leadership is not necessarily a power relationship.

Influence is most often confused with power, but in these modern times when managers suggest instead of command, the relationships of authority and influence are often blurred. But influence is quite easy to understand if one keeps two essential elements in mind.

First, influence is non-coercive, meaning that commands, rewards or punishments cannot be used in an influence relationship. Second, influence is multidirectional, meaning that people in social situations can influence from the bottom-up, sideways, diagonally, circularly and top-down.

Bell defines influence as 'a communication intended to affect the action of B in the absence of sanctions (i.e., threats or promises)' (1979: 23). He does this by introducing a second-person contingent statement: 'If you do X, you will do (feel, experience, etc.) Y' (p. 25).

Generalizing on Bell's ideas, influence can be defined as people using persuasion to have an impact on the thoughts and actions of other people in a relationship.

A good example of influence in modern life is the commercial or advertisement. The people who use commercials cannot command, reward or punish other people to use their products. The infomercials are an even better idea of influence. People talk to other people for a half-hour or more to persuade them to use their products. There is no possibility of using commands, rewards or punishments because the people listening would turn the infomercials off if they felt that kind of relationship. Most of us may not like commercials, in part because they interrupt some entertainment or enlightenment we may be seeking from the media with which we are interacting. But there is no doubt about the results that commercials have on us as individuals, on specific groups and communities as well as on our society and the world. And all of this is due to using influence.

Influence is the post-industrial understanding of how leadership works. Influence works when people get involved in a relationship to develop a project or solve a problem about which they are concerned or interested. It works because people are not coerced to think one way or do what another person commands, threatens or rewards, but because they believe that they can have an impact on the project or problem. Leadership in this kind of relationship becomes collaborative and the influence patterns are multidirectional. The motives and purposes of many people are influential, and the resulting decision or plan of action is a reflection of their joint or common purposes.

If significant decisions, especially those regarding changes, were made in organizations using leadership relationships that involve non-coercive and multidirectional influence, organizations and the people who inhabit them might be changed forever. Much of the hierarchical and bureaucratic dynamics in organizations that are now seriously dysfunctional would gradually disappear and those that were left would be directed at organizational **effectiveness** built on a community perspective that focuses on the common good.

People in organizations would become good at influence strategies and skills; they would care about what happens in their organizations because they have redefined the ownership of the organizations. They would develop attitudes and behaviours about belongingness and community participation that would reshape their assumptions about what organizations are and what their purpose is. Leadership thus becomes a way to influence decisions, a way of connecting to other people in our communities, locally and globally, a way of living our lives with purpose, imagination and **responsibility**. By using influence, the people in a leadership relationship forge new strategies and use different behaviours that foster **trust**, honesty, responsibility and integrity.

See also: **authority, ethics, great man theory, leader–follower relations, leadership definition, organizational culture, power**

Further reading: Bell 1979; Burns 1984; French and Raven 1960; Rost 1991

LEADER–FOLLOWER RELATIONS

Crystal L. Hoyt

A common theme across many definitions of leadership is that leadership involves interpersonal processes between individuals in a group working toward a common goal. Thus, relations between leaders and **followers** are integral to the understanding of leadership (for a comprehensive review see Hoyt *et al.* 2006). These leader–follower relations can be examined from a number of perspectives: leaders and followers interact in groups and are thus involved in many important group-level processes; at an interpersonal level, leader–follower relations are concerned with how individual group members **influence** and persuade one another; at the perceptual level, leader–follower relations involve followers' perceptions and expectations of leaders; finally, leader–follower relations are integral to many leadership theories, including style and **contingency theories** as well as theories concerning both tangible and psychological exchanges and motivational relationships.

Analysing leader–follower relations at the group level includes understanding how groups affect individual performance as well as group decision-making processes. The presence of others affects individuals, both leaders and followers, in a number of ways (Forsyth 2006). One group process of great concern to leaders of small groups is **motivation** loss and decreases in performance when individuals work collectively, or, social loafing. Interpersonal exchanges between leaders and followers play an important role in the social loafing process such that people are less likely to loaf when they have high-quality exchanges with their leader (Murphy *et al.* 2003). Contrary to popular belief, brainstorming groups are often plagued with social loafing, rendering them less effective than aggregates of individuals. In addition, a number of group processes can undermine a leader's ability to produce an effective group decision. For example, group members have a tendency to focus on shared information and ignore important information only known by a few members, they tend to make extreme decisions (group polarization), and they have a strong need for concurrence among group members that can result in catastrophic decisions (groupthink).

Leader–follower relations can also be examined at the interpersonal level of influence and persuasion. Generally speaking, social influence refers to the ability to affect another's behaviour or beliefs. Successful leaders are often masters of social influence tactics, successfully influencing followers to achieve the group objectives. One approach to thinking about social influence is social impact theory, which conceptualizes social influence as a function of the strength, immediacy and number of influencers (Latane 1981). For example, an employee would be more influenced in a meeting of board members than by a letter from his direct supervisor because in the boardroom there are more influencers (number), it is a face-to-face meeting (immediacy) and the board members have significant **power** (strength). People are particularly prone to obey strong **authority** figures as was clearly illustrated in Stanley Milgram's (1974) well-known shock experiments in which people willingly obeyed an authority requesting them to shock a helpless participant in an experiment, even when there was no pre-existing relationship between leader and follower.

The impact leaders have on group members can take on three forms: compliance, identification and internalization (Kelman 1958). With compliance, followers merely obey the leaders' orders but are not persuaded. This type of influence often isn't considered leadership, but rather the mere yielding to authority. Identification refers to a type of influence spawning from a follower's desire to be like or form a relationship with an attractive leader, whereas with internalization the follower integrates the leader's values into her or his value system. Lastly, the distinction between identification and internalization is similar to the distinction between central and peripheral routes to persuasion. With the central route, attitude change comes about from thoughtful deliberation on the part of the follower, whereas the peripheral route relies on signals or cues, such as the attractiveness of leaders or the number of bullet points in their presentation, distinct from the argument itself. Effective leaders must consider both the strength of their argument as well as other peripheral, yet influential, elements including factors related to themselves (e.g. appearance), the followers (e.g. mood) and the message delivery (e.g. uplifting or easy to remember).

Another important perspective on leader–follower relations is that of the followers' perceptions of the leader. Recent theorists argue that leadership stems from cognitive and attributional processes that lead people to perceive others as leaders (Lord and Maher 1991). People's preconceptions of leaders' traits, abilities and behaviours are referred to as implicit leadership theories (ILTs) and often include qualities such as dominance, determination, intelligence, honesty and humour. Unfortunately, these implicit leadership theories are often biased against certain individuals, including women and minorities (Eagly and Karau 2002). According to leader categorization theory (Lord *et al.* 1982), to the extent that a person matches one's implicit leadership theories, that person is considered a leader and the perception and evaluation of the leader is guided by these implicit theories. For example, if a person thinks intelligence is an important leader characteristic, she is likely to prefer an intelligent group member to lead her group and she is likely to evaluate the leader's actions as demonstrating intelligence. Another perception-based approach to leader–follower relations is the social **identity** theory of leadership (Hogg 2001) that maintains that leadership is a result of normal processes associated with group membership. According to this theory, the more strongly the group members identify with their group, the more they perceive and evaluate the leader based on how prototypical, or representative, of the group the leader is. Hence, in a group where ambition is highly valued, the more group members identify with the group, the more they will look to ambitious members for leadership.

Nearly all theories of leadership style, starting with the Ohio State and University of Michigan studies, assert that maintaining positive relations with and among followers is integral to the leadership process (Northouse 2004). These theories propose that leaders engage primarily in two types of behaviours: task behaviours and relationship behaviours. A number of contingency approaches to leadership, such as Path-Goal theory (House and Mitchell 1974), Hersey-Blanchard situational theory (Hersey and Blanchard 1993) and Vroom and Yetton's (1973) model, suggest that leaders need to focus more on relations in certain leadership situations than others. For example, in Fiedler's contingency theory (Fiedler and Chemers 1974), the extent to which a relationship-motivated leadership style is effective depends on the favourability of the leadership situation, which is most strongly determined by the quality of leader–member relations as well as task structure, and position power.

A number of leadership theories concentrate on the psychological and tangible exchanges between leaders and followers. Leader–member exchange theory makes the leader–member relationship the fundamental component of the leadership process and describes the importance of tacit exchanges and interactions between leaders and followers to many important personal and organizational outcomes (Graen and Uhl-Bien 1995). Hollander's (1993) social exchange theory maintains that as leaders bring rewards to the group, demonstrate competence and conform to group norms, they are granted 'idiosyncrasy credits' from followers. Leaders can then spend these credits when they deviate from the norm or are innovative or risk-taking. If their departure brings success, the leader builds up further credits. The social exchange model of leadership contends that beyond simple tangible exchanges, many important psychological exchanges occur between leaders and followers (Messick 2005). For example, leaders satisfy many needs of followers, including providing them direction, protection, achievement, a sense of belongingness and self-respect. In return, followers give leaders focus, gratitude, commitment, sacrifice, respect and legitimacy. Further, the relational model of authority in groups maintains that followers' perceptions of fairness are more important than their specific outcomes (Tyler and Lind 1992). To gain voluntary compliance and be perceived as legitimate, it is more important that leaders make decisions fairly (procedural justice) than distribute rewards fairly (distributive justice). That is, leaders must treat followers with respect and be unbiased and honest in their decison-making in order to develop a trusting relationship that will satisfy followers' needs to feel like valued members of the group.

Finally, theories of charismatic and **transformational leadership** highlight the important motivational relations leaders foster with their followers. Early conceptions of **charisma** (Weber 1947) regard it as a leader personality constructed from the collective perception of followers that a certain individual has extraordinary characteristics worthy of leadership. Newer conceptions of charisma focus on the behaviours and traits of charismatic leaders, including inspiration through a compelling vision, self-sacrifice, being responsive to followers' needs and being emotionally expressive with their followers (Conger and Kanungo 1998; Riggio 2004). Thus, charismatic leaders are thought to have important relationships with their followers; they yield significant influence through their commitment to the followers, their aura of competence, their inspiration and motivation and their emotional expressiveness. Burns' (1978) concept of transforming leadership also goes beyond simple social exchanges by demonstrating the pivotal role of the leader in cultivating a relationship with followers that increases both the leaders' and the followers' commitment, performance and morality. Building on Burns' transforming leadership, Bass (1998) highlights the importance of both transactional and transformational leadership. While **transactional leadership** represents the social exchange nature of leader–follower relations, transformational leadership provides a deeper level of connection with followers through the leader's ability to be a role model for the followers, inspire them through a vision, intellectually challenge them and demonstrate a genuine concern for the individual follower's well-being.

See also: **charisma, contingency theories, group dynamics, style theories, transactional leadership, transformational leadership**

Further reading: Burns 2003; Hogg 2001; Hoyt *et al.* 2006; Northouse 2004; Tyler and Lind 1992

LEADERSHIP DEFINITION

Joseph C. Rost

Definitions of leadership have been a source of controversy since leadership studies achieved some recognition as a legitimate field of inquiry. Studies in the early decades of the twentieth century did not generally define leadership as anything else but the activities of a leader. By the middle of the century, however, 'scholars viewed leadership as an influence process oriented toward achieving shared purposes' (Rost 1991: 53).

In the 1960s and 1970s, there was increasing evidence of more academics in various disciplines publishing studies on leadership. Leadership as an idea and a practice became very popular, and with that popularity came a wide variety of notions as to what leadership is. More often than not, even in scholarly studies, leadership was not defined precisely or at all. But a strand of definitions became widely accepted among both scholars and practitioners of leadership: Leadership is leaders influencing others to embrace goals that are widely shared among group or organization members. The claim is that the behaviours of the leaders widen the acceptance of the goals and increase the commitment of the members to them.

James MacGregor Burns changed the nature of leadership studies with the publication of his book *Leadership* in 1978. He insisted that leadership had to be defined if we are to understand and study it. His definition emphasized leadership as a process in which numerous people participate, not the activities of a single person – the leader. He introduced the idea of mutual goals as the gold standard for leadership, and he put forth a moral requirement in his framework of **transformational leadership** wherein 'one or more persons *engage* with others in such a way that leaders and followers raise one another to higher levels of motivation and morality' (Burns 1978: 20). The association between leadership and transforming change – i.e. real, significant and substantial, with moral ramifications – was central to Burns' book.

Burns' general definition of leadership is repeated several times in his massive volume, but it is perhaps best stated at the end of his book.

> Leadership is the reciprocal process of mobilizing, by persons with certain motives and values, various economic, political and other resources, in a context of competition and conflict, in order to realize goals independently or mutually held by both leaders and followers.
>
> (1978: 425)

Note that the general definition encompasses both transactional and transforming leadership. The definition is long and arguably has too many variables to be practically useful to either scholars or practitioners. But he crystallized several essential elements of the nature of leadership for those who came after him to synthesize more simply. These elements are: (1) reciprocal process, (2) mobilizing resources, (3) competition and conflict and (4) mutual goals or purposes.

The changing paradigm of leadership started slowly in the 1980s, since most writers and researchers accepted the traditional model of leadership as doing-the-leader's-wishes. But a few scholars attempted to use Burns' definition in some qualitative research studies with varying results. Some popular books about leadership included ideas about transformation, involvement and shared vision: Bennis and Nanus (1985), Kouzes and Posner (1987), Peters and Waterman (1982) and Tichy and Devanna (1986). Unfortunately, the practice of developing a straightforward definition of leadership was lacking in all of these books. Other scholarly books on leadership that were not as well known, such as Cleveland (1985), Foster (1986), Kellerman (1984), Schein (1985) and Smith and Peterson (1988) developed Burns' themes but also lacked clear definitions.

The 1990s witnessed a stronger movement towards a new paradigm of leadership, perhaps because the new century was looming. Armed with the notion that leadership is vested in a process, not a person, writers, researchers and commentators started thinking new thoughts about the nature of leadership and how to define it.

John Gardner began the last decade of the twentieth century by defining leadership as 'the process of persuasion or example by which an individual (or leadership team) induces a group to pursue objectives held by the leader or shared by the leader and his or her followers' (1990: 1). While a definition with three 'or' possibilities in it is clearly unacceptable, Gardner is strong on his emphasis that leadership is an interaction among leaders and constituents, which he called 'the heart of the matter', and the idea that leadership is dispersed throughout organizations.

Bolman and Deal (1991) introduced the notion of reframing leadership using four different frames (lenses): structural, human resources, political and symbolic. An integrated definition did not emerge, but the authors left little doubt that the traditional understanding of leadership was inadequate and that leadership had to be reframed sooner rather than later.

Joseph Rost (1991) explicated a postindustrial definition of leadership that was based on the emerging values of the twenty-first century. He argued for constructing a definition of leadership in order to distinguish leadership from management and other forms of governing or controlling people in a social setting. In later published works, he modified his definition and called it collaborative leadership (rather than postindustrial). 'Leadership is an influence relationship among leaders and collaborators who intend significant changes that reflect their mutual purposes' (Rost 1991: 102). This definition has four essential elements, all of which have to be present to label a series of activities leadership. They are: (1) influence relationship, (2) involving both leaders and collaborators, (3) intending significant changes and (4) mutual purposes.

Margaret Wheatley's (1992) *Leadership and the New Science* created a big stir, but in my opinion she seems to confuse leadership with management. Her last chapter is titled 'The New Scientific Management'! The ideas in the book are provocative, but we would need to ask why the word 'leadership' is in the title, and in my opinion there is no good answer.

Peter Block's (1996) *Stewardship* argued persuasively for replacing leadership, meaning **power** over and control, with stewardship, choosing service over self-interest. The book was very popular, but essentially Block criticized and then rejected the traditional notion of leadership instead of attempting to reconstruct the concept of leadership by integrating it with stewardship.

Chrislip and Larson (1994) did not offer a definition in *Collaborative Leadership*, but it is clear that they reject the traditional understanding for 'a new vision of leadership' (p. xx). This new vision requires (1) real collaboration among (2) leaders and citizens to (3) solve serious problems.

Heifetz, in *Leadership Without Easy Answers*, has an extended discussion of leadership theory and definitions. Debunking traditional views, Heifetz developed 'a prescriptive concept of leadership' (1994: 19). While no definition of leadership appears in the book, Heifetz's view of leadership is clear. Leadership is about doing adaptive work, which 'consists of the learning required to address conflicts in the values people hold, or to diminish the gap between the values people stand for and the reality they face' (p. 22). Thus, leadership is: (1) mobilizing activities (2) that bring about substantive changes (3) through adaptive work.

Kouzes and Posner included a definition of leadership in their revised book. Leadership is 'the art of mobilizing others to want to struggle for shared aspirations' (1995: 30).

Kevin and Jackie Freiberg stated that 'leadership is a dynamic relationship based on mutual influence and common purpose between leaders and collaborators in which both are moved to higher levels of motivation and moral development as they affect real, intended change' (1996: 298). Including a moral element as essential to leadership in a definition has been highly controversial because – among other reasons – it is difficult, if not impossible, in this pluralistic world to collectively decide what specific activities are moral or ethical. Burns got around this problem by developing two kinds of leadership, one of which has no moral element in it. So, his general definition quoted above logically contains no moral element.

Shriberg *et al.* define leadership as 'the process by which leaders and collaborators work together to achieve mutual goals' (1997: 6).

Bradford and Cohen (1998) in *Power Up* suggest that we transform organizations through shared leadership. After an extended critique of **heroic leadership**, they explicate a model of post-heroic leadership that emphasized (1) shared **responsibility** and (2) mutual **influence**. There is no definition of leadership, and for all the rhetoric of sharing the book is quite leader-centric, as the authors often suggest that the leader is the person who does the sharing.

Peter Senge went through a profound transformation in his definition of leadership from his famous 1990 book *The Fifth Discipline* to *The Dance of Change* in 1999. In the latter, Senge defined leadership as 'the capacity of a human community to shape its future, and specifically to sustain the significant processes of change required to do so' (Senge *et al.* 1999: 16). That definition has a number of twenty-first century elements in it.

Richard Barker (2002) wrote 139 pages *On the Nature of Leadership*, a meaty, challenging and very important book. At the end, he defined leadership as 'a process of transformative change where the ethics of individuals are integrated into the mores of a community as a means of evolutionary social development' (p. 106).

Sharon Daloz Parks (2005) updated Heifetz' understanding of leadership. She defines leadership as 'the activity of making progress on adaptive challenges' (p. 10).

This survey of leadership definitions may give a false impression that the majority of leadership scholars and commentators are moving away from the traditional heroic paradigm of leadership. That certainly is not true. The majority of leadership authors, both scholarly and practitioner-oriented, are ensconced in the industrial paradigm of leadership, which Rost defined as 'great men and women with certain preferred traits who influence followers to do what the leaders wish in order to achieve group/organizational goals' effectively (1991/1993: 95). Shortened up, leadership is 'good management' (p. 94).

The second false impression that the survey leaves is that most authors define leadership in clear, succinct terms. That again is not true. It is still rare to find a straightforward definition of leadership in articles and books about the subject.

The good news, however, is that there are many more people teaching and writing in leadership studies who are questioning the old paradigm and moving to a newer, twenty-first century view. The difference between 1978 and 2007 is remarkable. This is the rationale for emphasizing the emerging paradigm in this section on leadership definitions.

See also: **change and continuity**, **ethics**, **influence**, **participatory leadership**, **responsibility**, **servant leadership**, **transactional leadership**

Further reading: Barker 2002; Burns 1978; Gardner 1990; Heifetz 1994; Rost 1991

LEADERSHIP DEVELOPMENT

Scott J. Allen

Leadership development, its meaning and even its definition have long eluded philosophers, scholars and practitioners alike. The development of leadership can be traced back to Confucianism, the Egyptians and Plato. Today, corporations are spending millions (perhaps billions) (Dolezalek 2005; Delahoussaye 2001; Salas and Cannon-Bowers 2001; Vicere and Fulmer 1996) in an effort to build the leadership capacity of the workforce. However, the literature on leadership development is fragmented. Authors writing on the topic of leadership development hail primarily from two fields: business (e.g. Jay Conger, Alber Vicere and Robert Fulmer) and psychology (e.g. Bruce Avolio, David Day, Manuel London and Cynthia McCauley). To an extent, not-for-profit foundations, the training industry, consulting firms and the military have made contributions as well.

Unfortunately, not everyone agrees that money spent on leadership development is a solid investment. For example, an anonymous executive suggests: 'Probably at least half of every training dollar we spend is wasted – we just don't know which half' (Martocchio and Baldwin 1997: 15). Others well known in the field of leadership have concerns as well. For instance, Conger asserts: 'Most would agree that to seriously train individuals in the arts of leadership takes enormous time and resources – perhaps more than societies or organizations possess, and certainly more than they are willing to expend' (1992: 38–9). Although it is important to be aware of the inherent challenges faced by any architect of a leadership development initiative, this entry will focus on five critical components: leadership theory, linkage to business/organizational systems, adult learning and adult development theory, a combination of sound leadership sources of learning and evaluation.

A number of 'leadership' initiatives across the globe are one-quarter leadership and three-quarters management/job function training. If the objective of the training is to develop *leadership* capacity, it should rest on a foundation of leadership theory (e.g. Goleman *et al.* 2002; Popper and Lipshitz 1993; Vicere and Fulmer 1996). After all, the theory provides the roadmap for what leadership development architects are hoping to develop in others. A leadership development initiative not built on a theoretical foundation may teach concepts and topics having little to do with *leadership*, although it is also possible that designers seeking only to evaluate their theory may be blinded to informal or implicit aspects of development.

Along with a theoretical foundation, a number of authors have discussed the need for organizations to link development to the business systems. McCauley *et al.* assert that

> To be fully effective, a development system must be integrated with the organization's other processes: management planning, performance management, job selection, reward and recognition systems, and even mistake systems. The confluence of these processes determines the relative effectiveness of any one development activity.

(1998: 228–9)

According to the Center for Creative Leadership (CCL 1998) organizational systems may include: business context, target population, shared **responsibility** and supportive business systems. When 'supportive business systems' is examined, a number of topics emerge. These include: technology (e.g. Avolio 2005; Spreitzer 2003; Vicere and Fulmer 1996), personal development plans (e.g. McCauley 2001), reward systems (e.g. Bass 1990b), the immediate supervisor (e.g. Bass 1990b), hiring (e.g. Conger 1989), succession planning (e.g. McCauley 2001), career development (e.g. Yukl 2002) and performance management (e.g. Giber *et al.* 2000).

Failure to link the development initiative to the **organizational culture**, strategy and objectives will present a challenge for organizational architects as they examine 'transfer of training' when participants return to their job.

A major challenge of leadership development initiatives is a lack of *intentionally* incorporating adult learning theory. Some authors mention this notion in passing, but rarely expand (e.g. Avolio 1999; Conger and Benjamin 1999; Goleman *et al.* 2002; London 2002; Murphy and Riggio 2003; Wright *et al.* 2001). For instance, Goleman *et al.* suggest that leadership development initiatives should be 'based on the principles of adult learning and individual change' (2002: 234). However, the authors offer few suggestions.

Similarly, a leadership development initiative should incorporate principles of adult development theory. In the phrase *leadership development*, the word *development* connotes change. If initiative architects hope to *develop* leaders, they should realize that they are asking humans to change behaviour, which is no small task. Initiative architects are inviting leaders to expand their world view, become aware of biases, prejudices and perceptions, potentially to create new insights, to become more self-aware and change behaviour. Heifetz and Linsky suggest that 'To persuade people to give up the love they know for a love they've never experienced means convincing them to take a leap of faith in themselves and in life' (2002: 26). Incorporating adult development theory into the discussion of leadership development helps programme architects to create better development experiences. In his book *Learning to Lead*, Jay Conger (1992) sums it up well. He suggests:

> The development of leadership ability is a very complex process. It starts before birth, with a prerequisite of certain genes that favor intelligence, physical stamina, and perhaps other qualities. Family members, peers, education, sports, and other childhood experiences then influence the child's need for achievement, power, risk taking, and so on. Work experiences and mentors shape the raw leadership materials of childhood and early adulthood into actual leadership by providing essential knowledge and behavioural skills. Opportunity and luck are the final determinants of who gets a chance to lead.
>
> (1992: 33)

Another theme of the leadership development literature is the use of learning activities to accommodate different learning styles and objectives. For this entry, I call these *sources of learning*. Sources of learning take on differing characteristics and are the primary methods for delivering leadership development learning activities before, during and after the leadership development initiative. At times, sources of learning are mixed and matched, depending upon the objectives of the initiative. At times, organizations use single sources of learning as *the* mechanism for leadership development. In reality, a combination of sources of learning, linked to organizational culture/business objectives, are likely to yield the best results (McCauley *et al.* 1998). It is important to note that sources of learning have benefits and drawbacks (depending upon the context) and each has its time and place in a leadership development initiative. Examples of sources of learning include: job rotation, job enlargement, developmental assignments, games, simulations, e-learning, 360-degree feedback, open space technology, assessment centres, instruments, hardships, personal development plans, action learning, coaching, outdoor education, classroom-based education and developmental relationships.

The evaluation of leadership development initiatives is a challenging endeavour, especially when utilizing a number of different tools to assist in development. However, when evaluating development programmes and whole systems of programmes, the real goal is to find a causal link between initiative objectives and behaviour change or 'development'. According to Avolio (2005), those interested will find that only 10 per cent of the leadership development interventions evaluate past Kirkpatrick's (1994) first level (reaction). Conger (1992) asserts that 'The value of leadership is difficult to measure. The answer is that you cannot. This dilemma makes it extremely difficult for companies to commit large sums of money to something from which they will see no immediate tangible results' (p. 190).

On the other hand, Avolio suggests that

> Evaluating leadership development programs is essentially testing the construct validity of the model that underlies leadership development. Taking the full range model as an example, there is an expectation that transformational leadership transforms followers into leaders. Having a valid theoretical model to guide leadership development efforts is fundamental to understanding how this 'black box' works.
>
> (2004: 93)

Regardless, the majority would agree that this issue is a challenge. Kirkpatrick's four levels (1994) have been around for years and bring the discussion to a certain point. However, the thinking of Kegan and Lahey (Subject-Object Interview), Michael Quinn Patton (User-Focused Theory of Action Approach) and Cascio (Costing Human Resources) may add to a difficult and challenging discussion.

Along with the five topics mentioned, scholars and practitioners have written on additional aspects of leadership development:

1 Leadership Development Defined (e.g. Allen 2006; Avolio 2004, Adair 2005).

2 Models of Leadership Development (e.g. Allen 2006; Klein and Ziegert 2004).

3 The Process of Leadership Development (e.g. Cacioppe 1998; London 2002).

4 Leadership Development and Race (e.g. Livers and Caver 2005).

5 Curriculum Content (e.g. Hunt 1991; London 2002; Popper and Lipshitz 1993).

6 Leadership Development and Technology (e.g. O'Neil and Fisher 2004).

7 Types of Leadership Development Programming (e.g. Conger 1992; Bolden 2006).

Many scholars, practitioners, military veterans, trainers and philosophers have worked at the puzzle of leadership development. The challenge is that we don't have all of the pieces out of the box yet and we may not even know what the end product is supposed to look like. However, research, dialogue, trial and error and luck have gotten us to our present state. Perhaps we are on the right path to find that anonymous executive's missing 50 cents . . .

See also: **change and continuity**, **cross-cultural leadership**, **organizational culture**, **philosophical approaches to leadership**

Further reading: Avolio 2005; Conger and Benjamin 1999; London 2002; McCauley *et al.* 1998; Vicere and Fulmer 1996

MEASUREMENT

Sen Sendjaya

A myriad of leadership measures are currently in existence and accessible to academics and practitioners. The burgeoning interest in developing and validating multidimensional measures of leadership can be understood in light of the fact that psychometrically sound measurement is a prerequisite of any theoretical advancement (Schwab 1980). Without carefully constructed and validated scales, it would not be possible for researchers to achieve any theoretical progress (Schriesheim *et al.* 1993; Schwab 1980). Schoenfeldt remarked that 'the legitimacy of organizational research as a scientific endeavour is dependent upon the psychometric properties of the measuring instrument' (1984: 78).

Closer examination of the existing leadership measures, however, reveals that many of them would not stand the rigour of scrutiny associated with the psychometric properties of a measure. To minimize the errors within a measurement instrument, the American Psychological Association established that sound scales must demonstrate internal consistency reliability, content-validity, criterion-related validity and construct validity (Hinkin 1995). These criteria determine the psychometric soundness of behavioural measures, which ensures that aspects of reliability and validity are well established.

The reliability of a scale refers to 'the proportion of variance attributable to the true score of the latent variable' (DeVellis 1991: 24). While reliability is necessary for validity, it is not sufficient by itself (Emory 1980). Validity examines 'the extent to which a test measures what we actually wish to measure' to ensure that there are no logical errors in drawing conclusions from the data which could undermine the meaningfulness of the research (Thorndike and Hagen 1969: 162). Validity is a critical issue in development of a scale since it determines whether 'the variable is the underlying cause of item covariation' (DeVellis 1991: 43). Most leadership measures employed multi-method research design involving qualitative and quantitative approaches to establish evidences of reliability and validity.

Content validity, or content adequacy, is a psychometric property that exists when the content of a measure contains 'an adequate and representative set of items that would tap the concept' (Sekaran 1992: 171). The purpose of assessing the content validity of an instrument lies in the following question: 'Is the substance . . . of this [measurement instrument] representative of the content or universe of content of the [construct] being measured?' (Kerlinger 1973: 458). As a prerequisite of construct validity, content adequacy must be established prior to examination of construct validity (Anastasi and Urbina 1997; Nunnally 1978; Schwab 1980).

Construct validity is established when an instrument which measures a certain theoretical construct behaves in a similar pattern of intercorrelation with other established measures (Sonquist and Dunkelberg 1977). Construct validation is central in the development of quality measures since measurement instruments must be valid representations of constructs before any inferences can be made (Stone-Romero *et al.* 1995). Construct validation has two aspects, one that requires agreement between scores obtained from instruments measuring the same construct, and disagreement between two instruments measuring different constructs (Kidder 1981). If there is an agreement or positive/negative correlation between scores from the two instruments measuring theoretically related constructs, then convergent validity is evident. On the contrary, if there is a disagreement or no correlation between scores from the two instruments measuring theoretically distinct constructs, then discriminant validity is established.

The development of a measurement instrument progressed through several stages. Schwab (1980) recommended that the development of measures should comprise three distinct elements: item development, scale development and scale evaluation. Echoing this view, Dawis (1987) provided a three-stage framework of scale construction: scale design, scale development and scale evaluation.

The primary purpose of the scale design stage is to generate a pool of items for a multidimensional rating scale. According to Hunt (1991), there are two fundamental approaches to item development: deductive or classification from above, and inductive or classification from below. The deductive approach is used when items are developed on the basis of the theoretical definition of the construct resulting from a thorough review of the literature. Alternatively, the inductive approach involves soliciting responses of individual respondents to identify constructs and identify measures as little theory has been established (Hinkin 1995). A good measure typically employs both deductive and inductive techniques, in that the items are generated from, for example, both the literature review and interview data.

The development of items is the most important element of establishing sound measures (Hinkin 1995). A review of nearly 300 scale development practices revealed that measures generally lack content validity in the item development stage (Hinkin 1995). Content validity must be embedded within the measure through the generation of items to ensure that the measure sufficiently captures the specific domain of interest and excludes irrelevant items. A second common problem with item development is that many items do not have strong and clear linkages with their theoretical domains. Regardless of whether they are deductively or inductively derived, items must have a clear association with the theoretical domains.

To establish content validity, scale developers must go through a rigorous process of domain identification, item generation and judgement-quantification or content expert validation (DeVellis 1991). Content expert validation is a method for ensuring the content validity of the measurement instrument (Grant and Davis 1997), and is essentially a sorting process which is used in this study to identify and delete theoretically incoherent items (Hinkin 1995). Following the suggestions of Grant and Davis (1997), content experts typically were asked to address three elements in examining the **servant leadership** instrument: representativeness, comprehensiveness and clarity. Representativeness in this study refers to the degree to which each item reflects and operationalizes its nominated domain. The second task was to evaluate the comprehensiveness of the entire instrument by identifying items which the expert panel members perceived to be incongruent with their nominated domain and, subsequently, assigning them to an alternative domain with which the items were better matched. Finally, the content experts were asked to identify the clarity of item construction and wording to ensure that there were no ambiguous and poorly expressed items.

The measurement items retained in the scale design stage should then be subjected to a number of statistical tests using data typically obtained through survey questionnaires. This involves pre-testing the scale to examine the extent to which the instrument performed as expected. Pre-tests are defined as 'trial runs with a group of respondents for the purpose of detecting problems in the questionnaire instructions and designs' (Zikmund 1991: 184).

Fowler (1993) suggested that the most effective way to pre-test a self-administered questionnaire is for the researcher to administer it in person with a group of potential respondents. This approach enables the researcher to find out the length of time required to complete a survey instrument, and identify ambiguous questions, unclear instructions and any problems in understanding the kind of answers that were expected. The questionnaire length, wording, format and sequence of items were revised and amended based on the recommendations by participants in the pre-test stage.

A survey design is a common data collection procedure used to obtain 'a quantitative or numeric description of trends, attitudes, or opinions of a population by studying a sample of that population' (Creswell 2003: 153). There are three general objectives of survey research: description, explanation and exploration (Babbie 1990). Survey data are used to explore the factor structure of the scale and establish the unidimensionality of the scale through specification, assessment of fit and respecification of the one-factor congeneric measurement models.

Churchill (1979) recommended that a minimum of two studies is necessary as a basis for developing a scale in order to establish good psychometric properties, noting that the second study should be considered as further scale refinement, and not to test hypotheses. Preliminary evidence of construct validity of a measure is established at the scale evaluation stage. To that end, competing model analyses and tests of convergent validity, discriminant validity and predictive validity are normally conducted. Competing model analyses provided further evidence of within-measure discriminant validity. Evidences of convergent and discriminant validity are established in relation with other similar and dissimilar measures, respectively. As for predictive validity, the test is conducted to examine the extent a new leadership measure predicts other variables such as **trust** or organizational commitment.

Finally, since most leadership measures are self-report measures, they are prone to methodological problems known as common method variance. Method variance in self-report measures occurs because of a number of different reasons such as respondent's consistency motifs, transient mood states, illusory correlations, item similarity, social desirability (Podsakoff and Organ 1986) and acquiescence (Spector 1987), as well as response styles, refusals and reactivity in the form of attitude crystallization, cuing and response sets (Williams and Brown 1994). Various statistical methods have been developed to address concerns surrounding common method variance in self-report data.

The development of an empirically validated measure of leadership is paramount and necessary for any theoretical advancement. However, building a sound leadership measure is a complex, challenging and lengthy process (Schmitt and Klimoski 1991), in particular its construct validity. Independent validation studies need to be conducted repeatedly for a newly developed measure in various settings and across different samples to establish the generalizability of the findings.

See also: **behavioural theories of leadership**, **leadership definition**, **leadership development**, **trait theory**

Further reading: Churchill 1979; DeVellis 1991; Hinkin 1995; Schwab 1980; Thorndike and Hagen 1969

MILITARY LEADERSHIP

Jeremy Black and John Jupp

Military leaders bestride the centuries capturing the attention of contemporaries and posterity. Names such as Caesar, Genghis Khan and Napoleon resound down the centuries. They indeed helped mould the contemporary world with their campaigns, but more than individual drive and ability were involved. In addition, it is necessary to see how the campaigns of leaders interacted with the circumstances in which they operated. This is crucial because military success is a matter not of battle waged against an opaque background, but, instead, of the ability to fulfil objectives. In short, a task-based account of military achievement is necessary. This is key whether the leadership considered is at the tactical, operational or strategic levels.

These three levels are worthy of consideration because they indicate the variety of types of military leadership, and because to be a military leader at the highest level it is necessary to first succeed at the tactical level. There are exceptions, which we will come to, but let us first consider the general case. Military service is hierarchical and in most systems it is not possible to rise to senior command positions unless one has been an effective leader at the junior level. This entails command of a relatively small number of men and a comparatively limited amount of military resources. These are used in combat to achieve tactical objectives. Thus, for example, the clearing of insurgents from a street, the capture in the field of a hill, the crossing of a river or securing of a flank are classic tactical goals. Commanders have to display leadership skills in terms of working out how best to achieve the goal, and then do so. Key skills include the inspirational leadership often required to help troops cross the killing ground produced by enemy fire, and the ability to sustain morale and unit cohesion in the resulting combat. Personal example can be very important in this, and thus the commander needs to be able to display bravery, while remembering that his death will create serious problems.

Responding to circumstances in a dynamic yet effective fashion crucially depends on the ability to gauge and overcome enemy moves. There is a need thus to direct the flow of the combat and also to do so in a fashion that permits successful exploitation of emerging opportunities. This is the type of command and leadership that is most common in combat. It is the level that it is easiest to train for and also the level above which most leaders do not rise.

In terms of campaigns, it is the operational level that commands most public attention. This level used to be termed strategy, with grand strategy reserved as a phrase now applied to strategy. The operational level addresses issues like how best for Grant to outmanoeuvre Confederate forces near Richmond in 1864–65 or how best to exploit the D-Day landings in Normandy in 1944. A lower level of operational command will relate to the movements of brigades, divisions and corps. Most of the skills required at the tactical level are necessary at the operational one, although physical bravery is not generally necessary, and concern for unit cohesion and morale are also less pronounced. In contrast, at the operational level, there is a need for wide-ranging command and communication skills as the battlefield and zone of operations that are to be known are more far-flung than at the tactical level. Thus the commander has to receive, interpret and reconcile information from across a broad front, and also to try to anticipate and determine the enemy response. Operational commanders face the need to provide appropriate instructions for lower-level officers and to know how best to respond if they find it difficult to achieve their goals. This suggests a tension around the appropriate level for taking independent initiative – a tension often characterized around the notions of 'command and control', more recently 'mission command', in which operational commanders make known their 'intent', but permit considerable autonomy at the front line. Operational commanders are thus supposed to implement instructions based on strategic conceptions that they may have played little or no role in formulating; mission command is a doctrine that seeks to recognize the strategic advantages that can be gained by tactical initiative taken at the front line. While apparently derived from the '*auftragstaktik*' of Von Moltke (to which this Prussian general credited his success in the Franco-Prussian war of 1870), similar conceptions can be found in Nelson's approach to naval command in the Nile and Baltic campaigns of 1798 and 1801, and in Dowding's command of the RAF in the Battle of Britain in 1940. Modern warfare has added another layer to this devolution or **empowerment**, by capitalizing on the capacity for higher level command to gather, edit and distribute real-time information throughout the battle space, giving rise to significant knowledge-management challenges, and a new acronym – NEW (Network Enabled Warfare).

This indeed is a crucial interface in the politics of command and one that directs attention to the third level, that of strategic command. At this level, leadership is not necessarily the monopoly of the military. Thus, for example, Churchill, Roosevelt, Stalin and Hitler were more properly the military leaders of their respective countries in World War II than figures such as Alan Brooke, Marshall and Halder. The same argument could be made about David Lloyd George, the British Prime Minister in 1916–18 and even of Lincoln in the American Civil War. In many respects, this was inevitable for major states waging war across many fronts. This distanced leadership from campaigning.

Such a situation, however, was not unique to the twentieth century. Philip II of Spain might plan the Armada launched against England in 1588, but he was not going to command it. To have done so would have compromised the multiple other military and political activities of the Spanish Crown. However, although this was true of other leaders, this did not prevent them from campaigning in what they saw as the crucial zone of operations, the zone, indeed, that could become crucial as a consequence of their presence. If Suleiman the Magnificent chose to campaign in Hungary, this helped make that more important than the Persian front.

The political importance of campaigning was even more the case because there was necessary contrast between what would subsequently be seen as civilian and military leadership. The two were fused in monarchs, whether Roman Emperors, Mongol clan leaders, Turkish Sultans or European monarchs. Kings of England/Britain continued to lead their armies into battle until 1743 when George II commanded at Dettingen. His second son, William, Duke of Cumberland, was in command three years later at Culloden, the key battle in the defeat of the Jacobite claim on the British throne. For most rulers, military success was a crucial source of prestige and this prestige helped ensure the respect and support of their subordinates and subjects. Victory thus was the lubricant of obedience, and this helped explain the great concern to ensure a favourable 'spin' on campaigns. Proclaiming victory and associating it with the leader was a central feature of politics, whether that of Julius Caesar or of Napoleon, and is clearly still the case.

At the strategic level, the key ability is that of defining realizable goals, ensuring the necessary domestic and international support, or at least acceptance, and distributing resources between different campaign fronts. These are complex and difficult tasks, and most commanders and politicians are not suited to them. Civilian politicians frequently do not understand the nature of risk that is inherent in military operations, and do not know how to manage it, while many military commanders are only suited to the operational level. They lack the skills of coalition maintenance required for alliance politics, including the 'alliances' within their own forces that have become increasingly important as a result of joint operations. Furthermore, the military mindset is frequently not suited to the ambiguities and difficulties bound up in the term realizable goals when realizable extends to domestic constituencies of support.

Once these points are appreciated, then it becomes difficult to decide how best to define the most impressive military leaders. Success would seem to be an obvious factor, but that would exclude such defeated figures as Napoleon and Lee. Napoleon indeed raises a number of key questions, as his campaign failures in 1812–15 were arguably operational consequences of his strategic overreach, and it is important to determine where the focus of attention should rest. To look at another dimension of strategic conception, did Julius Caesar conquer Gaul (France) and invade Britain (England) in part to win prestige in the competitive politics of the late Roman Republic, as well as to build up a loyal army for political ends? From this perspective is he to be seen as a success because he gained **power** or a failure because his reliance on force helped lead to the conspiracy that claimed his life?

Such points may seem a long way from the classic understanding of military leadership, but this political dimension, in fact, has always been central as it has been crucial in the framing of strategic goals, the maintenance of support and the aftermath. Grant and Eisenhower emerge as more successful figures than Cromwell because they gained and exercised power peacefully; although Cromwell also faced very difficult domestic circumstances.

These points need to be borne in mind when looking at the question, but they have to be complemented by an understanding of the factors that made for success in the field, including a ready ability to appreciate problems, to devise workable plans, to understand enemy objectives, to respond rapidly and effectively to events in order to gain the tempo that permits a management of these events, to prepare for successful exploitation, and to learn the lessons necessary to secure best practice and improved planning. These criteria can be expanded, but they help explain why different readers and scholars can propose their own list. This indicates not only the complexity of the subject but also the extent to which war and military command reach out to interact with so many key issues that have moulded world history.

See also: **empowerment**, **great man theory**, **group dynamics**, **heroic leadership**, **leadership definition**

Further reading: Bungay 2005; Dixon 1976; Jupp and Grint 2005; Keegan 1987; Van Creveld 1985

MOTIVATION

Thomas Mengel

Motivation addresses the initiation, intensity and persistence of human behaviour (Geen 1995). Understanding and being able to **influence** the factors that initiate, sustain and change human behaviour are crucial to leadership theory and practice.

Interestingly, Maslow's (1943) theory of motivation, although based on the often disputed psychodynamics introduced by Freud and Adler, still has a strong influence on leadership (Shriberg *et al.* 2005). Surprisingly, the importance of Frankl's (1959) research on 'Man's search for meaning', which led beyond Freud's and Adler's emphasis on pleasure and **power**, has not yet been fully recognized. Combined with the results of other approaches, the human 'Will to meaning', the centerpiece of Frankl's (1969) motivational theory, could help develop a more comprehensive theory of human motivation and leadership.

Maslow's (1943) 'hierarchy of basic needs' (physiological, safety, love, esteem and self-actualization needs) is often presented as a sequential pattern of need satisfaction. However, Maslow states the 'pre-potency' especially of the physiological and safety needs (i.e. the urge to first satisfy these needs and to ignore others) to be particularly significant in the state of severe deprivation; in times of relative health and wealth, the pre-potency weakens. Furthermore, Maslow emphasizes the existence of variations, whereby people prioritize the satisfaction of higher level needs in spite of lower level needs not being fully met. Also, any particular human behaviour can simultaneously serve the satisfaction of various needs from different levels. Finally, Maslow preferably interprets the sequential character of his **hierarchy** as stages of psychological development. As recently verified (Reiss and Haverkamp 2005), young people tend to focus on the lower levels of needs, whereas the need for esteem and self-actualization is prevalent within the group of mature adults. However, as to the most important motive of human behaviour, Maslow did agree with Frankl (1959) that 'man's primary concern is his will to meaning' (Maslow 1966: 107).

McGregor (1960) suggested a continuum of beliefs that managers may hold about the motivation of their employees, ranging from the assumption that people primarily aim for security, dislike work and avoid **responsibility** ('theory x'), to the idea that people enjoy working, exercise commitment and self-control, seek responsibility and enjoy decision-making ('theory y'). The placement of one's assumption within this continuum obviously has significant impact on one's leadership practice.

In his 'dual-factor theory', Herzberg (1966) identified 'hygiene factors' (e.g. job security, supervision, relationships, working conditions, salary) that lead to dissatisfaction if not sufficiently met. In contrast, 'motivational factors' (e.g. developmental opportunities, responsibility, challenge and recognition) positively impact job satisfaction.

McClelland (1975) differentiated three major needs that influence workplace behaviour: the drive for power, the achievement motivation and the need for affiliation.

Based on the theories of conditioning and learning, experience influences motivation and reinforces certain behaviour through rewards and punishments.

In his 'expectancy theory' of motivation, Vroom (1964) suggested that leaders can choose how to influence others based on their perception of their co-workers' goals, of the value the co-workers place on these goals and of the likelihood of success that co-workers associate with a certain path toward the achievement of these goals.

Furthermore, 'equity theory' (Adams 1963) has placed importance on the perceived fairness and equality of one's own rewards in relationship to one's efforts and in comparison to the rewards of others. As a result, the perceived equity of rewards needs to be taken into account by leaders when choosing their influential behaviour.

In analysis of the approach of Freud and Adler, Frankl (1959, 1969) has pointed out that focusing on the satisfaction of the will to pleasure or the will to power are the result of the frustration of man's primary 'will to meaning' and often lead to an 'existential vacuum'. While power can be a means to the end of finding meaning, and pleasure and happiness may ensue, humans primarily search for individual meaning based on their personal situation. In response to their challenges, they need to engage in creating or doing something meaningful, in having a valuable experience with someone or something, or to choose their attitude toward a given situation by interpreting it in a meaningful way. Frankl's motivational theory provides an anthropological basis for the importance of values in leadership processes and for the need to create meaningful work environments.

Within the concept of 'transforming' or '**transformational leadership**' (Bass 1985; Burns 1978), leaders help their **followers** to reach a higher level of moral responsibility and appeal to them to participate in the process of generating and maintaining a shared vision and to commit to the resulting organization.

Locke and Latham (1990, 2002) have found that specific and challenging goals, regular feedback on performance and various incentives have a strong impact on the motivational force of goal-setting.

Research has provided evidence for a positive relationship between visioning and values statements on one side and the setting and achievement of goals on the other (Christenson and Walker 2004; Kouzes and Posner 2003; Paine 2003; Yukl 2002). Cooperatively identifying and implementing shared values, goals and objectives, provide ample opportunities for discovering meaning and for creating a meaningful work environment (Mengel 2004; Yukl 2002).

Humans have needs and they set out to satisfy them, often demonstrating typical patterns of behaviour. Through experience, observation and reflection, they learn and understand which behaviour will most probably satisfy their needs. Understanding the needs as well as the way that experience and learning have shaped the resulting behaviour is one major achievement of the various approaches to motivational theory building.

Humans' primary motive is their will to meaning that can be fulfilled by discovering and implementing meaningful options and actualizing the corresponding values. These must be translated into goals and pursued through corresponding behaviour in order to find fulfilment of our primary motive rather than losing ourselves in secondary activities.

A comprehensive concept of motivation helps us understand the interplay of the various factors in initiating, shaping and changing our behaviour. Leaders and the leadership processes will become more effective by comprehensively understanding these motivational facets of our behaviour and by responsibly applying this knowledge when influencing the behaviour of others.

See also: **contingency theories, ethics, influence, situational leadership, transformational leadership**

Further reading: Frankl 1959; McClelland 1985; Mengel 2004; Petri and Govern 2004; Reiss and Haverkamp 2005

NEED FOR LEADERSHIP

Richard A. Couto

Our need for leadership varies with the purposes, from basic to sublime, for which humans organize, and our explanations for that need depend, in turn, on our theories of human nature. Between the poles of beast and angel, humans are social beings who organize and work together for common benefit. The different forms of human nature, from primate to poiesis, evoke different forms of leadership, dominance to **influence**, and different purposes – from subsistence and procreation to self-creation and social actualization. These forms are not stages of development through which people pass in sequence; we remain all of these at once.

As a primate, humans have basic needs such as food, nutrition, security, procreation and shelter. A purely zoological metaphor for human society might lead us to carry the analogy further. In meeting these needs, small groups of primates depend on the dominance of one member to keep order within the group and to hold off predators or other threats to the group. Citing research on bands of mountain gorillas in Central Africa, Ronald Heifetz concludes that the dominant male of the group 'serves as a control function, mediating aggression within the group and maintaining stability' (Heifetz 1994: 50–4). He cites additional research that the **hierarchy** of dominance permits every animal to know its exact place among the others and reduces dissention and strife.

As humans expand the size of their social units – organizations, towns, nation states – to gain some security for the provision of basic needs, and seek some expressive ones – education, work, recreation, health and other professional services – they also construct patterns of **authority** that have less appearance of dominance and control. Max Weber offers three sources – tradition, rational-legal systems and **charisma** – that humans use to socialize group members to obey authority and recognize its legitimacy, whether it is a country or a choir. Weber ascribes this need to justify and obey authority to motives of fear and hope; upon the primate's need for stability of basic resources; and the poet's need to imagine a condition better than their present. Lest there be any doubt of the links of authority to our primate nature, Weber calls these sources of authority '*legitimations* of domination' and defines the state as the human community that successfully 'claims the *monopoly of the legitimate use of physical force*' (Weber 1947: 78–9; author's emphases). Our ordinary need for leadership may be a silverback gorilla with the cultural trappings of authority – ceremony, titles and, of course, clothes. The greater our socialization and legitimation of authority, the less chest thumping and bellowing are needed. Physical coercion wanes and authoritative sanctions and rewards take their place.

Our need for authority and the apparent defences it provides us from the threat of social disorder is a long standing topic in discussions of leadership. Plato's philosopher-king's major task was to maintain the myth of inherent distinctions among humans and hence the legitimacy of caste inequality. Confucius's genuine man had the **wisdom** to bring the order of the universe to the relations among humans. Machiavelli based the conduct of an ideal prince on the need of humans for order. Much of the leadership-as-management research of the twentieth century assumes the need for authority as a shield from inefficiency and a lever for increased human productivity for corporate goals; an 'industrial paradigm' (Rost 1991: 27). Most recently, examinations of bad and **toxic leadership** trace their origins to the need of humans for external authority (Kellerman 2004a: 21–6; Lipman-Blumen 2005a: 29–48).

Weber also suggests that our obedience to authority springs from hope; specifically for a reward in this life or beyond. This hope is possible because humans, unlike other animals, have the ability to imagine conditions that are different from the present. Naturally, some groups may hope for domination of others and thus invoke the primate style of coercion. Other groups may hope for an end to domination and inequity and for bonds of respect and equity among different groups. This latter human hope calls for leadership separate from coercion and dominance and for new forms of authority based on mutual relations and reciprocal influence.

Two prominent studies in leadership, published within a year of each other, both claim their origin in expansive hope of self-creation and cited a need for new forms of leadership. Robert Greenleaf (1977b) wrote to counter the mediocrity of institutions and their failure to meet their higher social purposes. Greenleaf offered his model of **servant leadership** as the needed means to turn institutions towards legitimate – non-coercive – **power** and greatness. Like Greenleaf, James MacGregor Burns (1978) wrote with a sense of urgency and a belief that our institutions, primarily American national political organizations, were in a crisis of mediocrity. Our need for leadership, in his estimation, surpassed authority or heroism. He outlines his hope for relational and collective transforming leadership that purposefully uses power for significant change. The latter seems to be the removal of some caste-like conditions from a group. Leadership holds hope for innovations that challenge cultural practices and social limitations – for example, racism and androcentricity – that restrict human actualization.

Figure 1 illustrates our discussion of our various needs of leadership – dominance, authority and relationship; the primary tool of each form of leadership – coercion, authority and influence; as both are related to the forms of human nature – primate, social animal and poiesis.

Our need for leadership, especially that of silverbacks, has a serious downside. Cautions about charismatic leadership (Conger 1990) have to do with people as **followers** too quickly investing their hope for change in an external authority. Erich Fromm (1994) suggested that, in the case of the tragic horrors of Nazi Germany, 'followers' were far

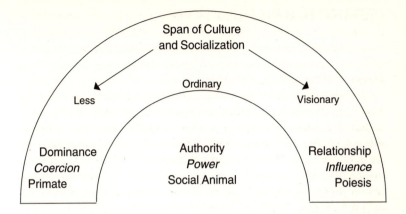

Figure 1   The span of human culture and socialization and the need for leadership

too ready to escape from their human freedom, poiesis, and not to think beyond primal needs. In experiments about obedience to authority, Stanley Milgram (1974) found that most people in his simulation experiments were willing to knowingly harm others, if they had the approval of a scientific authority.

Ronald Heifetz (1994, 2007) suggested the need for those in positions of power to separate authority from leadership. He explains leadership as the adaptive work of a group to bring their practices in line with their values and that the process of leadership entails giving that adaptive work back to all members of the group. Some needs for leadership require less authoritative, technical solutions without the involvement of the rest of the group; recognition that in many instances authority and coercion will not suffice; and acknowledgement that leadership may require sharing authority and power. This suggests a mutual relationship of influence and shared values and goals among those with and without authority. The need for this leadership emerges among those who value equality more than hierarchy and put less importance on expertise than on the contributory role everyone can play in imagining and creating the human condition without coercion and dominance.

See also: **authority, group dynamics, influence, philosophical approaches to leadership, servant leadership, toxic leadership**

Further reading: Heifetz 1994, 2007; Fromm 1994; Greenleaf 1996; Lipman-Blumen 2005a; Milgram 1974; Wheatley 2007

ORGANIZATIONAL CULTURE

Peter Case

Organizational culture can be defined as the institutionalizing processes which regulate cognitive, affective and self-presentational aspects of membership in an organization. These processes also govern the *means* by which thought, perception, feeling and expression are shaped and hence encompass various auditory, textual, symbolic, physical and narrative forms. Examples of such means would include: organizational modes of communication (memoranda, telephone, email, internet, meetings, etc.), rituals, ceremonies, stories, myths, jargon, gossip, jokes, physical architecture, office layout, decoration and prevailing modes of staff dress.

As one might infer from this definition, the concept of 'organizational culture' is somewhat nebulous. It can appear so vague and all-encompassing as to be meaningless or, at least, coterminous with the concept of 'human organization' itself (a problem that has dogged the field of social anthropology for many decades). Nonetheless, through the eyes of the beholder, it remains the case that organizations seem to vary in terms of the climate and 'feel' that pervades them and the kinds of 'signals' that they give off. To that extent, it can be useful to have recourse to a term – however provisional or unsatisfactory – for referring to this common experience of interpretative organizational difference.

The concept of culture has a long and rich tradition within social anthropology. Interestingly, its appropriation by management and organization theory is by no means a recent phenomenon. Several authors (Martin 2001; Parker 2000; Schwartzman 1993), for example, provide comprehensive accounts of the historical influence of social anthropology on the field. With regard to the Hawthorne Studies, so seminal to the human relations movement, Elton Mayo was personally acquainted with the anthropologists Malinowski and Radcliffe-Brown, whilst Roethlisberger and Dickson sought the direct assistance of W. Lloyd Warner in their interpretation of group behaviour. The Hawthorne Studies, which drew attention to the previously unrecognized importance of the informal workgroup, in turn, had a clear historical relationship with later and more explicit invocations of 'culture' in, for example, the writing of Eliot Jacques (1951). One of the earliest writers on culture in management studies, Jacques defined an organization's culture as its customary and traditional way of thinking and of doing things, which is shared to a greater or lesser degree by all members, and which the new members must learn and at least partially accept, in order to be accepted into the services of the firm.

(1951: 251)

Other lines of emergence may also be traced. The heritage of organizational culture was not solely anthropological. The psychological rendition of organizational culture provided by Harrison (1972), for instance, informed the widely cited fourfold functionalist typology offered by Charles Handy (1977), which classifies culture according to **power**, role, task and person.

The human relations thinking of the first half of the twentieth century was later inseminated by sixties humanist ideology to spawn a generation of managerial writings on organizational culture. Conditions were ripe for these ideas. Finding themselves economically threatened by Japanese competition, managers in the USA and Europe were about to make the ironic 'discovery' that the answers to their prayers for corporate control and competitive advantage lay latent in the very social fabric which they had taken for granted. Moreover, this dormant potential could be exploited with minimal capital outlay, and there was no shortage of evangelists available to make the revelation. Perhaps best known of these are Tom Peters and Robert Waterman, whose best-seller, *In Search of Excellence* (1982), became something of a bible to a generation of culturally inspired managers. According to Peters and Waterman (1982), successful companies possess 'strong cultures' in which employees are committed to a clear set of values that unite and motivate them. In their winning formula, 'Good managers make meanings for people, as well as money' (1982: 29). In other words, it is the manager's duty and prerogative to *persuade employees* of the imperative to buy into organizational values and to express a level of loyalty and commitment that will ensure business success. Similarly, Deal and Kennedy argue that companies with so-called strong cultures 'can gain as much as one or two hours productive work per employee per day' (1982: 15). They contend that managers can actively change organizational culture and bring about desired results through the manipulation of symbols, stories, myths, rituals, ceremonies and so on.

Models of 'cultural excellence' have, perhaps predictably, come under sustained attack from a number of detractors (see, *inter alia*, Kunda 1992; Parker 2000; Reed 1993; Willmott 1993; Wilson 1992) on a variety of grounds, including: (a) conceptual inadequacy; (b) questionable **ethics**; and (c) lack of feasibility. The managerial consumers of what Willmott (1993) disparagingly terms 'corporate culturism' are in the market for tools which promise to make their lives easier. So, correspondingly, a purveyor of 'culturism' will be obliged to couch his or her wares in the kind of functional language which mirrors such expectations. The cultural excellence literature is often characterized by a systems-orientated reification of 'culture' whereby organizational culture is seen as part of a set of contingencies that are open to simplistic managerial manipulation and control. 'Culture' is often listed alongside other 'variables', such as 'size', 'structure' and 'strategy'. Such reification has led to the vain search for ways in which 'organizational culture' might be operationalized and measured, giving rise to the search for a clear and unambiguous definition. Viewed from a more critical and interpretative standpoint, however, the problem is not simply one of definitional 'accuracy'. Rather, it resides in a mistaken logic of enquiry; a logic which implicitly or explicitly asserts that a performatively workable and accurate definition of 'culture' is, in principle, attainable.

Logical misconceptions, in turn, lead to the construction of spurious models of 'cultural change'. Organizational culture is generalized and reified to the point of meaninglessness, as pointed out by Reed, who offers the following caricature of functionalist prescriptions of the excellence literature:

(a) identify the corporate culture that your company has – preferably using a classification scheme (b) compare this to the ideal corporate culture for the company's particular strategic situation (c) change it or otherwise mould or shape it to optimize organizational effectiveness and (d) success will come your way.

(1993: 3)

The point is that each of the stages (a) to (c) is in itself extraordinarily problematic, if not unfeasible, *in practice*. Hence there cannot be a simple panacea for attaining the economic success promised in stage (d).

Kunda (1992), Parker (2000) and Willmott (1993) each attack corporatist conceptions of 'culture' on ethical grounds, challenging the assumed prerogative of executives to impose upon, manipulate and control the lives of others through normative means. Even granting the fact that symbols, ritual, meaning and value can be dictated, controlled or influenced by senior executives, what gives them the ethical privilege to do so and should it be done without the collaborative consent of those implicated in the change process?

A further challenge is posed by Wilson (1992: 72), who points to a series of theoretical and empirical grounds for rejecting the corporatist claims of the excellence literature. Perhaps most tellingly, he documents the fact that most of the companies identified as 'excellent' in the Peters and Waterman volume went on to significantly underperform financially when economic conditions changed.

It would be misleading to suggest that populist management writers and positivist academics hold a monopoly over the concept of organizational culture. Whilst relatively dominant, this corporatist line of thinking represents but one strand of development. Many writers in the organization studies field have extolled the virtues of an interpretative appreciation of organizational culture and symbolism (see Alvesson and Berg 1992; Linstead and Grafton-Small 1992; Kunda 1992; Martin 2001; Parker 2000). Commentators on the organizational culture literature have noted a broad structural dichotomy between practitioner orientation and academic analysis. Linstead and Grafton-Small (1992: 333), for instance, distinguish between 'Corporate culture [as a] term used for a culture devised by management and transmitted, marketed, sold or imposed on the rest of the organisation' and 'organisational culture [as] more organic, being the culture which grows or emerges within the organisation and which emphasises the creativity of organisational members as culture makers, perhaps resisting or ironically evaluating the dominant culture'. Similarly, Willmott (1993) distinguishes between protagonists of the deliberate imposition and manipulation of organizational ideology – what he terms 'culturism' – and 'purist' concerns with the study of organizational symbolism. Wilson and Rosenfeld (1998), in turn, couch this polarity in terms of 'applicable' versus 'analytical' approaches to culture in order to juxtapose managerial conceptions with more sociologically and anthropologically sensitive accounts of organizational culture.

What is variously presented as a dichotomy, however, might be more fruitfully conceived as a continuum between extremes: purist/analytical, at one end and practitioner/applicable at the other, with studies and accounts finding a location along an imaginary scale according to the degree to which they seek to engage with a managerial readership. Further dimensions representing other concerns, such as those of critical management scholars, might also be added. For example, Kirton and Greene (2000) identify a growing body of literature that criticizes studies of organizational culture for over-looking or marginalizing the diversity debate within organization studies. It is a criticism, moreover, that could be levelled in retrospect at both the applicable and analytical camps. The concern here is to acknowledge the manner in which discrimination on the basis of gender, race, age, disability and sexuality becomes institutionalized within organizations and the extent to which a deeper understanding of the ethics of managing diversity can be reflected in studies of organizational culture. In the hands of such critical authors, the study of organizational culture becomes a vehicle for sensitizing audiences to institutional discrimination and suggesting ways in which resulting inequities might be addressed.

See also: **change and continuity, cross-cultural leadership, ethics, identity, gender and leadership, process theory**

Further reading: Kunda 1992; Martin 2001; Parker 2000; Willmott 1993; Wilson 1992

PARTICIPATORY LEADERSHIP

Robin Ladkin

I imagine that the title of this piece immediately suggests participation as an active process in which leaders might engage others. Maybe a suggestion of participating in the decison-making process or other leadership activities might be advocated.

I want to take a different view, however, which is to discuss the possible implications of leadership as seen within a participatory paradigm or worldview. I am encouraged in this approach by the many authors who suggest particular consequences implied by this postmodern ontological perspective (amongst others, Barrett 2000; Drath and Palus 1994; Ladkin forthcoming; Senge *et al.* 1999).

My approach here is to offer a particular take on the idea of a participatory paradigm; to consider some likely consequences of such a perspective compared to a modernist view; and to illustrate these consequences through a number of particular notions in current discussion in the ever-expanding canon of leadership theory.

I draw on the ideas developed by Richard Tarnas (1991) in his thrilling history of western philosophy, *The Passion of the Western Mind*. The way he tells the story is of a series of fundamental shifts in the way we think about the world (paradigm shifts) and consequently the way we view knowledge and its acquisition.

Tarnas's view of the story has a particular quality I am keen to highlight, which is one of generative progression or evolution, rather than a stark negation of the 'modern' or enlightenment paradigm as so often suggested by a critical post modern argument.

> (This) participatory epistemology, developed in different ways by Goethe, Hegel, Steiner, and others, can be understood not as a regression to naïve participation mystique, but as the dialectical synthesis of the long evolution from the primordial undifferentiated consciousness through the dualistic alienation. It incorporates the post-modern understanding of knowledge and yet goes beyond it. The interpretive and constructive character of human cognition is fully acknowledged, but the intimate, interpenetrating and all-permeating relationship of nature to the human being and human mind allows the Kantian consequence of epistemological alienation to be entirely overcome.
>
> (Tarnas 1991: 434–5)

It seems to me that in offering us this generative or 're-constructed' as opposed to 'de-constructed' post-modern conception, Tarnas (along with other colleagues from the California Institute of Integral Studies (CIIS) and elsewhere) suggests a different order and direction for the **responsibility** of leadership. Rather than a concern for **effectiveness** in the way leaders might **influence** change in narrow organizational terms, Tarnas asks us to take a larger contextual view. And rather than sink into the depressing uncertainty and negation of instrumentality of much post-modern constructionist debate, Tarnas asks us to apply our full faculties to the way we choose to lead our lives.

He goes on to argue in this key passage,

> The human spirit does not merely prescribe nature's phenomenal order; rather the spirit of nature brings forth its own order through the human mind when that mind is employing its full complement of faculties – intellectual, volitional, emotional, sensory, imaginative, aesthetic, epiphanic. In such knowledge, the human mind 'lives into' the creative activity of nature.
>
> (Tarnas 1991: 434–5)

We have here, I believe, the basis for a way of viewing leadership as thoroughly relational, set surely in a complex context, fraught with uncertainty but likely to offer creative possibilities through a combination of due humility along with the exercise of all our marvellous human talents.

I want to suggest a number of consequences I have been led to in considering leadership from this particular participatory view.

One of my first moves in considering leadership as the exercise of natural talent is to notice carefully what leaders actually do in tangible terms. During a recent exercise with a group of military leaders, we were reduced to a starkly limited list, which included:

- speaking
- listening
- asking questions
- writing in various forms
- issuing information and instructions (often as a consequence of making a decision).

We were somewhat perplexed as to how these essentially ordinary acts of conversation could be invested with and interpreted as attempts to delegate, empower, coach, inspire and so on – a list of leadership characteristics you can soon turn up in so many texts.

So, if these ordinary acts of human interaction make up the 'what' of leadership behaviour, how are they so invested and interpreted? Clearly there is much skill in effective conversational acts, listening intently and empathically, speaking with passion and conviction, engaging in difficult and uncertain situations with good sense and fairness.

As we developed, in this and many similar conversations, skills and attributes of leadership, the thought begins to arise about the full complement of talents Tarnas refers to, both in terms of informing values and ideas and in forms of expression. As leaders we are fully bodied creatures of nature expressing through expression, motion, physical presence, the acts of leadership as well as the language of leadership. I am struck as I observe leaders working through their development in this tangible way by the notion of leadership as a craft. This thought leads me to a consideration of a number of 'ways of leading' suggested by colleagues equally engaged in this post-modern construction.

My first reference in this section is to Keith Grint's realization of leadership as an art. (We do not have space here for a reasoned debate about the competing claims of art and craft as informing notions.) Grint describes his painful conversion from seeing leadership in terms of empirical science to rather seeing it as an art, and suggests, in his re-framing, four aspects (or talents) (Grint 2000):

- Philosophical Arts – Identity (Who?)
- Fine Arts – Vision (What?)

- Martial Arts – Tactics (How?)
- Performing Arts – Communication (Why?)

Frank Barrett takes this line of argument further, especially in relation to leadership as performance. He likens leadership to the process of improvization in a jazz band. This offers brilliant insights into the balance of structure and uncertainty, which encourages innovation in a complexity view of leadership and suggests a number of implications familiar to current advocates of a quieter form of leadership (Barrett 2000):

- Minimal hierarchy.
- Dispersed decision-making.
- Designed for maximum flexibility and responsiveness.
- Minimal structure which guides what soloists can play.
- Mutual recognition of shared rules.

Donna Ladkin turns her philosophical gaze onto the specifically aesthetic aspects of leadership, a fascinating account of how spirit is manifested in the relational (erotic) acts identified as a stark and ordinary list above. We are here in the territory of how human talent converts the ordinary into the extraordinary (Ladkin forthcoming).

In their recent exploration of the leadership of change, Senge *et al.* (2004) express their dissatisfaction with their historical attempts to understand how change is led. They say

> we felt that what we had written in the past, at best, described the words but left the music largely in the background . . . as Otto puts it: 'this blind spot is not the what and how – not what leaders do and how they do it – but the who: who we are and the inner place from which we operate, both individually and collectively'.
>
> (Senge *et al.* 2004: 5)

The story of these four experienced practitioners in the field of organizational change leads to a thought which sounds remarkably like the description of participation from Tarnas with which I began.

> I think our culture's dominant story is a kind of prison. It's a story of separation – from one another, from nature, and ultimately even from ourselves. In extraordinary moments . . . we break out of the story. We encounter a world of being one with

ourselves, others, nature, and life in a very direct way. It's beautiful and awe-inspiring. It shifts our awareness of our world and ourselves in radical ways. It brings a great sense of hope and possibility but also great uncertainty. It can also be hard finding ourselves outside the story that has organized our life up to that point. It's wonderful to be free, but also terrifying.

(Tarnas 1991: 215–16)

This is a participatory 'who' from which I am suggesting the craft of leadership might emerge, talented and energetic, compassionate and committed, rooted in a thorough appreciation of context and self.

See also: **aesthetic leadership**, **cross-cultural leadership**, **philosophical approaches to leadership**, **quiet leadership**

Further reading: Grint 2000; Senge *et al*. 2004; Tarnas 1991

PHILOSOPHICAL APPROACHES TO LEADERSHIP

Terry L. Price

Perhaps the most important task of the philosopher is to bring conceptual clarity to topics of intellectual controversy. To achieve this task, the philosopher first aims at precision with respect to the terms involved. So a standard philosophical analysis of leadership would begin with questions about the definition of *leadership* (Ciulla 2004). For example, what does it mean to be a leader? Is being ethical a defining feature of leadership? Is leadership necessarily hierarchical and inegalitarian?

It is no wonder, then, that early philosophical accounts of leadership adopt a definitional approach. In Plato's *Republic* (1992), Socrates argues that the 'true leader' looks out for the interests of **followers**, not the leader's self-interest. Because leadership is a craft, and because crafts are complete and self-sufficient, leadership must focus its attention on the object of the craft – namely, followers. This feature of leadership, Socrates suggests, explains why leaders must ultimately be compensated for their efforts. Bad men lead for honour and money; good men become leaders because they cannot bear to be ruled by their inferiors. Aristotle (1981), Plato's most famous student, and Niccolò Machiavelli (1531/1992) similarly use concern for followers as a defining feature of leadership. The individual who rules for his own interest is no leader at all; he is a *tyrant*. In the twentieth century, political scientist James MacGregor Burns (1978) continues this tradition, distinguishing between leadership and mere 'power-wielding'. One criticism of this way of defining leadership, however, is that it assumes away important questions about leadership **ethics**. Unfortunately, making leadership moral by definition still leaves us with self-interested CEOs and power-wielding politicians (Price 2006).

A second candidate for a defining feature of leadership is **hierarchy** or inequality. Most obviously, leadership implies a **power** differential between leaders and followers. The job of the philosopher, then, is to determine whether these inequalities are justified. Here again, Plato's *Republic* is instructive. One way of understanding this work is to see it as a defence of the claim that there is a naturally superior class of individuals who are best suited to ruling. These 'philosopher-kings', as Plato calls them, are relevantly different from other individuals in the state, especially with respect to knowledge. In fact, so close was the connection between knowledge and leadership for Plato that a case can be made that his Academy was a model for modern-day schools of leadership. It is also worth noting that Plato had significant opportunities for the real-world application of his ideas on leadership in his work with Dionysius I and Dionysius II. His efforts in both cases, as it turns out, were unsuccessful. Aristotle, who famously tutored Alexander the Great, had similar opportunities. At the very least, we can say that the ancient Greek philosophy of leadership is the intellectual ancestor of *trait theories of leadership* in the social sciences (Price 2004).

We can likewise trace contemporary *social exchange views of leadership* to the development of social contact theory in the history of philosophy (Price 2004). Social contract theorists use the notion of agreement to justify necessary inequalities between leaders and followers. For instance, Thomas Hobbes is known for his defence of absolute sovereignty in his *Leviathan* (1651/1991). According to Hobbes, parties to the social contract give complete power to the ruler in order that they might be protected from the dangers of the state of nature. In conditions of equality, no one has sufficient power to resolve disputes. As a consequence, the state of nature is a war 'of every man against every man'. Society needs an all-powerful leader – one who is not subject to the rules and, thus, who can do no wrong – to put an end to conflict. As Randy Barnett characterizes the present-day Hobbesian, '[T]here's got to be the boss' (1998: 240). John Locke (1690/1988) also offers a contractarian justification of leadership, though his account ultimately makes leaders much more accountable to the people.

Eighteenth-century philosopher Jean-Jacques Rousseau (1755/ 1973) paints an alternative picture of how inequalities in status evolved. According to Rousseau, differences in talent became apparent when people first lived together in communities. Unlike advocates of **trait theory**, however, Rousseau denies that these differences are morally relevant to political status. Rousseau also denies the contractarian claim that inequality is the outcome of genuine agreement. Institutions such as private property are instead the result of what is essentially a trick to get citizens to treat natural differences as though they have political importance. Political inequality is tolerated even by those individuals oppressed by the system because they live in the hope that they will someday be able to exercise power over others. Still, according to Rousseau, political inequality need not be understood as a defining feature of leadership. A return to political equality requires a transformation of the citizen. Self-interest must be replaced by a concern for the common good, as this good is reflected in the 'general will'. If ancient Greek philosophy is the ancestor of trait theories of leadership, and if the social contract tradition represents the historical version of social exchange theories of leadership, then Rousseau's political philosophy is a precursor to James MacGregor Burns's theory of transforming leadership (Price 2004). (See the entry on **transformational leadership** for a discussion of Burns's theory.)

Philosophical approaches to leadership do much more, then, than simply get us to think carefully about what leadership is. These approaches tell us something about ideal relations between leaders and followers – for example, whether inequality can be justified and, if so, under what conditions. Conceptual precision about the nature of the relationship is necessary to identify the source of these controversies. But moral analysis must be brought to bear if we are to have any chance of resolving them. (See the entry on **ethics**.)

See also: **ethics, hierarchy, leadership definition, situational leadership, trait theory, transformational leadership**

Further reading: Hobbes 1651/1991; Locke 1690/1988; Machiavelli 1531/1992; Plato 1992; Rousseau 1755/1973

POWER

Elaine Dunn

At first sight the relationship between leadership and power appears obvious and uncomplicated. Powerful people **influence** others who follow them, perhaps in search of new lands or new ideas, perhaps in the name of social change or simply to satisfy the latest organizational objectives. This view suggests that power is located in individuals, that some people have it while others don't and that leadership is about exercising power. Conversely, others have argued that good leaders don't need to use power, thus implying that power is a negative concept associated with force or coercion. So what is the relationship between leadership and power?

The concepts of leadership and power are both multi-faceted. Each defies singular definition and the relationships between them are multiple and complex. Therefore it is essential to develop some definitional clarity if we are to progress beyond common usage. Power operates at three fundamental levels, these being interpersonal, organizational and societal (Watson 2002). These three levels are always interrelated, but their common feature is the capacity to affect outcomes.

> Power is the potential ability to influence behaviour, to change the course of events, to overcome resistance, and to get people to do things that they would not otherwise do.
>
> (Pfeffer 1994: 30)

Societal power relates to the relationships and understandings which give legitimacy to certain practices (Watson 2002). Organizational power is associated with rules, **hierarchy** and cultural norms which influence behaviour (ibid.). It is often complex, invisible, pervasive, unpredictable and produces unintentional effects rather than being consciously mobilized (Foucault 1977, 1980). However, this piece focuses on interpersonal power, which operates between one person and another and which is closely related to leadership.

Leadership has been described as a process whereby intentional influence is exerted by one person over another (Yukl 2002). So, while power can be defined in terms of an individual's or a group's *potential ability* to influence behaviour (Pfeffer 1994), or the *capacity* of an individual or group to influence outcomes (Watson 2002), leadership can be defined as an influencing *process*. When individuals seek to influence others, this might result in outcomes described as commitment, compliance or resistance (Yukl 2002). Resistance might manifest itself in pretence, delays, excuses or blatant refusal to carry out a request. Compliance appears as agreement, but is followed by the minimum possible effort. However, commitment is quite different, because it means that the individual not only agrees with the person or group influencing them, they also feel a sense of internal agreement. This might arise from alignment between their personal values, beliefs or interests and those of the influencing party. As a result, they not only comply with the request, they are emotionally involved and hence strive to achieve the associated outcomes regardless of the difficulties or personal sacrifices.

So what are the influence outcomes associated with leadership? Numerous definitions suggest that leadership produces more than compliance. For example, leadership has been described as the art of mobilizing others to want to struggle for shared aspirations (Kouzes and Posner 2003). Notice the words 'want to', which indicate that leadership is an influencing process which creates commitment (Yukl 2002). So if power is the potential of one person to influence the behaviour of another, and if personal commitment is the outcome of the influencing process, then leadership appears to be the word which we use to describe this process.

Interpersonal power is most commonly classified according to source and is based on the perception that one individual has of another (French and Raven 1959). Power is thus entrenched in the relationship between people rather than being an attribute of an individual. For example, if I perceive that you have expert knowledge relevant to the task, regardless of whether this is actually the case, then you will have *expert* power and hence the capacity to influence me (ibid.). Similarly, if I identify with you and desire to be like you in some way, then you will have *referent* power (ibid.). If I feel you are able to reward or punish me, then you will have *reward* and *coercive* power, and if I feel you have a legitimate right to order me to do something, then I am granting you *legitimate* power (ibid.). Legitimate, reward and coercive sources of power have been classified as *positional power*, while expert and referent sources have been called *personal power* (Bass 1960). Notice that perception is everything and that in the short term various sources of power might be perceived where none is deserved.

French and Raven's (1959) taxonomy highlights one of the difficulties we face, this being the paucity of the English language in relation to the notion of power. In contrast, classical Latin has three terms, namely *auctoritas*, *potestas* and *potentia*, with quite distinct meanings (Hopfl 1999). *Auctoritas* is the capacity to initiate and to inspire respect based on experience, knowledge or skill and is therefore similar to expert and referent power. *Potestas* is the right to command and to expect others to obey based on the position one holds, broadly equivalent to legitimate power. Thus the wise willingly comply with *aucto-*

ritas, the dutiful comply with *potestas* and those who are neither dutiful nor wise can be persuaded to comply by individuals who control incentives and sanctions (those with *potentia*). Understood in these terms, it is perhaps not surprising that research findings have associated certain combinations of interpersonal power with effective leadership (Yukl 2002). For example, an influencing process which involves legitimate power on its own (*potestas*) or a combination of reward and coercive power (*potentia*) is said to produce compliance, rather than commitment, and is unlikely to be described as leadership (ibid.). In contrast, when expert and referent power are combined (*auctoritas*), then research suggests that they produce subordinate satisfaction and performance, and when legitimate power is also added then this is reported to result in attitudinal commitment, highlighted earlier as a defining characteristic of leadership (ibid.).

When people or groups compete within organizations for access to scarce and valued resources, then they are consciously mobilizing their sources of power. This might be achieved via *instrumental* mobilization of power (Lukes 1974; Hardy 1995) through which dominant individuals secure outcomes in their favour in the face of competition and conflict, typically by controlling decison-making processes. Thus powerful actors (e.g. managers/leaders) can enforce their desired outcomes regardless of how others feel about it. However, power is most insidious when people remain unaware of its influence, such as when language is used to shape perceptions. For example, accusing an enemy of 'slaughtering civilians' while claiming that our own military only caused 'collateral damage'. This is known as *symbolic* mobilization of power to shape perceptions, cognitions and preferences in order to prevent conflict and thereby create legitimacy for decisions and actions (ibid.). Symbolic mobilization of power can be used on its own to remove opposition or in combination with instrumental mobilization of power to produce favourable feelings towards an outcome. In an organizational context, symbolic power is closely related to leadership because it influences perceptions and attitudes (Grint 2004).

The analysis of power outlined here indicates the need for greater clarity of language and the importance of understanding power as a fundamental concept in the study of leadership. On the one hand, the exercise of power might not necessarily have anything to do with leadership. For example, if I simply pay you a salary and demand that you obey my orders then I am likely to secure compliance rather than commitment and I doubt you would describe this as leadership! Perhaps you would refer to it as *management*, but that is a different debate which is not the focus here. However, using the concepts and definitions outlined in this piece, it is possible to conclude that leadership necessarily involves power. Leadership is an influencing process and power is the capacity to influence, hence some form of power is necessarily exercised when leadership takes place. However, what is particular interesting is the nature of power associated with leadership because it is potentially hidden. This is because the forms most closely related to leadership are the *symbolic* mobilization of power by an individual who is perceived to have *auctoritas*, or *auctoritas* and *potestas*. From the follower's perspective, this influencing process is likely to be regarded as an eminently sensible proposal from someone who is well respected, who is thought to know best and who might also (but not necessarily) hold an influential appointment. Thus the follower will willingly do something they would not otherwise do, whilst remaining unaware that their perceptions have been shaped in order to produce such positive feelings. Perhaps this begins to explain why some people associated power with force and coercion rather than with leadership. Those who believe that 'good leaders don't need to use power' might think again!

See also: **authority**, **cross-cultural leadership**, **effectiveness**, **empowerment**, **heroic leadership**, **influence**

Further reading: Clegg 1989; Hardy 1996; Jackson and Carter 2000; Salaman 2004; Turner 2005

PROCESS THEORY

Martin Wood

It has become fashionable in the field of leadership and management studies to emphasize the relational nature of leading and managing. Rather than focusing on 'leaders' and 'managers' as clear and firmly fixed economic entities, leadership is understood as a *process* rather than a property or *thing*. As a consequence, there has been a growing interest in research that helps explain rigorously both the phenomenon of leadership and explicates imaginatively particular leadership problems.

Process philosophy, or process thought, is a distinctive sector of philosophical tradition. Drawing on the pre-Socratic cosmology of Heraclitus, whose basic principle was that 'everything flows', the process approach puts processes (becoming) before distinct things or substances (being). For process thinkers, the actual facts of our experience are not 'things' but 'events'. *What* reality *is*, is change (process) itself. This kind of *ontology* is logically opposed to the static system of Parmenides, which views nature as permanent and unchanging, '*here, now, immediate,* and *discrete*' (Whitehead 1933: 180, original emphasis). In recent times, process thought has become identified most closely with the British mathematical physicist turned philosopher Alfred North Whitehead and the French radical phenomenologist Henri Bergson. Other intellectual associates include James, Leibniz and the twentieth-century philosophers Hartshorne and Deleuze.

The clearest expression of Whitehead's process philosophy can be found in his assertion that the 'passage of nature' (Whitehead 1920a: 54) or, in other words, its 'creative advance' (Whitehead 1978: 314), is a fundamental characteristic of experience. In this continuous advance, or universal becoming, every occasion of actual experience is the outcome of its predecessors. Actual occasions of experience or 'actual entities' have a certain duration during which they arise, reach satisfaction and perish. Nonetheless, they do not simply disappear without trace but always leave behind consequences that have the potential for entering into other passing moments of experience. So, at each step sense-making is no longer of things simply as they appear *to be* at any given moment: they are also what they were, even a fraction of a second ago and what they can become.

Following Whitehead, the experience of the immediate world around us does not obtain in the simple facets of things – for example, managers, leaders, **followers** and even organizations. This simple location, though handy, definite and manageable, is an error of mistaking abstract constructions for substantial processes – *the fallacy of misplaced concreteness*. This abstraction from an actual occasion of experience only arrives at traditional concepts of a 'here' and a 'now', as durationless instants without passage. But each actual occasion of experience is alive, it 'arises as the bringing together into one real context of diverse perceptions, diverse feelings, diverse purposes, and other diverse activities' (Whitehead 1920b: 9). It includes the perception and conceptualization of a situation whose actuality only exists at that moment: its permanence is constituted in its passage. The first two lines of a popular Christian hymn, 'Abide with me; Fast falls the eventide' (Whitehead 1978: 209), characterize this nexus. Here, the perceptual permanence of 'abide' and 'me' in the first line is matched by the perpetual passage of 'fast' and 'falls' in the second line, to create a new immanent synthesis (passage *and* permanence; perishing *and* everlastingness).

Bergson's contribution to process thought, like Whitehead's, is ontological. Like Whitehead, he suggests life and nature are not distinct things or substances, but rather sensations, feelings and ideas seized from an original process. Both writers assert evolutionary advance as a continuous creation – nature's *élan vital*. They recognize that life is *not* the thing, but the living of life *is* the thing. Living *is* changing, it is inventing, a creative advance into novelty. Unlike Whitehead, however, Bergson (1912: 44) argues the corresponding process of isolating, immobilizing or securing actual forms from the limitless flow of 'virtual' possibilities is an 'imitation', which, although useful for the apprehension of life, is 'a counterfeit of real movement'.

In doing so, Bergson enumerates two opposing tendencies for apprehending reality. The first is the logic (epistemology) of the *intellect*, which apprehends the world as an already determined series of solids. It forces on us a static conception of the real, which, if taken too far, cannot/does not embrace the continuity of flow itself (ontology). The second is the process of *intuition*, whereby we plunge into the very life of something and identify ourselves with it by a kind of indwelling. Here reality is expressed as 'fluid concepts', quite different from the static abstractions of traditional logic. On its own the intellect's 'spatial' abstraction of things is too deterministic. However, the flow of the actual world without a corresponding logic is too indiscernible, too 'inaudible'. Life is realized by infusing the intellect with intuition and not simply by reducing the intellect to intuition.

Bergson is primarily a philosopher of time, which he considers eludes our intellectual spatialization of things: 'In short, the qualities of matter are so many stable views that we take of its instability' (Bergson 1983: 302). In other words, we conceive immobility to be as real as movement and then mistake one for the other – the fallacy of misplaced concreteness. Nonetheless, time is always going on, it never completes: it is something lived and not merely thought. This is not to deny that time cannot be thought. Clearly it can. Bergson's point is simply that our conception of time as a series of positions, one then the other, and so on, is a matter of abstractive thinking and *not* a property of concrete (living) time itself. Simply located positions are surface effects we employ to give substantiality to our experience, but under whose supposed 'naturalness' the fluxing nature of reality is neglected. For us to grasp this principle, Bergson (1983: 237) argues, we must reverse our mental habits to see that mobility is the only actual reality. We must detach ourselves from the intellectual force of the 'already made' and attend to the instinctual force of the 'being made'.

Contemporary leadership research has now begun to pay attention to the *process* of leadership *being made*, rather than place value on the end *result* or a priori *thing already made* (see, for example, Barker 2001;

Gemmill and Oakley 1992; Grint 2005; Gronn 2002a; Hosking 1988; Yukl 1999). The most recent of these, Grint (2005), argues perceptively that understanding leadership as a relational process can add to our understanding of how it came into being in the first place. Nonetheless, whilst Grint's contribution adds very positively to the recent leadership literature, it does not move beyond the common-sense recognition of relational process as something to be entered into as an *exogenous* relation, between leaders and followers, or subordinates, whose 'here now' individualism is taken for granted – already taken to *be*. The ramifications of the insight that leadership is a relational process will be more sufficiently developed only if 'calls for a greater attention to process lead to a consistent reversal of the ontological priority' (Tsoukas and Chia 2002: 570; see also Hosking's work in a relational perspective).

The potential dissonance between some idealized concept of the attitudes and behaviours required of leaders and our 'lived' experience of leadership requires new insight and different options. New insight and a different option are far removed from leadership studies' preoccupation with individual functioning. To say that leadership is a relational process within terms, actors, identities, themselves (Wood 2005), is to invoke *interdependence* more at the level of an a priori characteristic and to accept becoming as ontologically preceding being. Leadership is not a function, characteristic or property of a taken-for-granted individual, nor something to be entered into as an exogenous relation between social actors, whose individuality can exist without the relation. Rather, leadership actually has two dimensions, each deferring as well as referring to the other, consistently. Leadership can be grasped only in terms of this immanent process of *difference-in-itself* (Deleuze 1994).

Finally, of course, there remain many dilemmas, challenges and debates surrounding the uses of process thought in leadership and management studies. One 'hot topic' relates to the different views scholars hold about whether leadership and management consist of things *or* processes, or whether these are complimentary ways of viewing entity *and* flux. A second topical issue of concern is the difference between process theorists purporting to explain organizational phenomena by making expedient use of longitudinal case studies (see, for example, Langley 1999; Ropo *et al.* 1997; Van de Ven and Poole 1995) and those accepting the metaphysical centrality of a process-relational outlook (Chia 1999; Wood 2005), but as yet unable/unwilling to fix 'gangways' to practice or only now beginning to fabricate methodological 'railings' that respond to the perceived demand of leadership and management studies (Tsoukas and Chia 2002; Van de Ven and Poole 2005; Wood and Ferlie 2003). Then again, perhaps these different views are problems only if we place more value in them as end results rather than how they came into being in the first place? Thus – by my reading at any rate – spoke Zarathustra (Nietzsche 1969: 219): 'O my brothers, is everything not *now in flux*? Have not all railings and gangways fallen into the water and come to nothing? Who can still *cling to* "good" and "evil"'?

See also: **change and continuity**, **creativity**, **leadership definition**, **organizational culture**, **philosophical approaches to leadership**

Further reading: Dibben and Cobb 2003; Dibben and Kelly 2007; Rescher 1996; Whitehead 1925, 1938

QUIET LEADERSHIP

Jonathan Gosling

Leading is not all about being up-front and visible. Making decisions, clarifying one's own thoughts, persuading others, projecting a sense of confidence are often better done away from the limelight. Negotiating big deals is usually best done without publicity, as is resolving differences amongst powerful colleagues. Of course, some situations call for a highly visible kind of leadership – battlefield operations, public meetings and rituals are all examples. But these are only a small part of effective leadership, which depends on the much less obvious work of building **trust**, mutual respect for skills and insights, enabling others to make their own contributions. Admiral Nelson provides a wonderful example of this range: he loved to be at the head of a boarding party, setting the example in courage and determination, and took great care that his exploits would be recognized, both for his own glory and to represent the kind of pro-active approach necessary for a battle fleet. But much more of his time was spent in quiet administrative work, setting standards for seamanship, systems for supply of his fleet, settling disputes and ensuring fair process in the organization of the work (Gosling 2006; Jones and Gosling 2005).

This theme has been picked up by a number of prominent theorists. Henry Mintzberg referred to 'covert leadership' by an orchestra conductor, by which he means 'managing with a sense of nuances, constraints, and limitations' (1998: 140). He coined the term 'quiet management', which is echoed in Joseph Badaracco's 'quiet leadership' (2001, 2002b). The latter suggests 'four basic rules in meeting ethical challenges and making decisions':

> The first rule is 'Put things off till tomorrow.' The passage of time allows turbulent waters to calm and lets leaders' moral instincts emerge. 'Pick your battles' means that quiet leaders don't waste political capital on fights they can't win; they save it for occasions when they really want to fight. 'Bend the rules, don't break them' sounds easier than it is – bending the rules in order to resolve a complicated situation requires imagination, discipline, restraint, flexibility, and entrepreneurship. The fourth rule, 'Find a compromise', reflects the author's finding that quiet leaders try not to see situations as polarized tests of ethical principles. These individuals work hard to craft compromises that are 'good enough' – responsible and workable enough – to satisfy themselves, their companies, and their customers.
>
> (Badaracco 2001: 120)

There are two converging themes in the work of these and related authors – distaste for the cult of the individual leader, often portrayed as the sole architect and agent of organizational effort and success; and appreciation of the craft-like skills required to sustain commitment and cohesion, especially in organizations of autonomous professionals and communities characterized by pluralistic values. Closely related to this is the idea of **servant leadership**, recognizing the idealism or altruism implicit in the **motivation** and style of many leaders (Greenleaf 1977b). In this quietist tradition, leadership is approached as something of a spiritual discipline in which 'care of the self' is interpreted in terms similar to Reinhold Niebuhr's famous prayer:

> God, grant me the serenity to accept the things I cannot change, the courage to change the things I can, and the wisdom to know the difference.

That is, quietness is a necessary corollary of careful attention to one's own actions. Self-control is strongly rooted in Western concepts of **wisdom**, which is itself intimately connected to notions of good action and responsible leadership (Case and Gosling 2007; Hadot 1995). A mindful approach to action is even more strongly represented in many strands of Buddhism, and Daoism is in many ways a philosophy of action-in-non-action (wu-wei) exemplified by the many oft-quoted aphorisms from the Tao Te Ching, such as

> Governing a large country
> is like frying small fish.
> Too much poking spoils the meat.
> (Macdonald 1996: 60)

It is worth noting, however, that all these approaches focus on individual leaders, and largely on how they conduct themselves. One criticism might be that leaders are far more dependent on social and political processes, and that their loudness or quietness should be understood as political rhetoric. Those of us who observe leaders may be more or less persuaded by them – and this is at least partly an aesthetic judgement based on the kinds of conduct and presentation that we find attractive and appropriate. Quietness has certain culturally nuanced aesthetic qualities that we may value; but there may also be ethical implications. If we associate 'loud' leadership with the cult of the personality, charismatic enthusiasm and tyranny, we could claim that democracy is an institutional way of ensuring that no single source of loudness dominates for too long. It would be hard to argue that democracy promotes quietness – but it may permit it, and the socially beneficial application of its fruits. However we would be wise to avoid romanticizing quietness. Tyrants and dictators impose their will through rigorous control of expression and by stealthily 'silencing' opposition. Quiet leadership may have its sinister side.

Another perspective is offered by psychoanalytic and group relations perspectives. Leadership can be an effect of unconscious processes (of splitting, projection, identification) that provoke people to invest hope and trust in leaders. **Authority**, autonomy and dependency are inter-related factors that come into play as we seek ways of coping with the anxiety as well as the opportunities posed by living and working with others. Sometimes the emotional energy propels groups, organizations or whole societies into followership relations with prominent 'charismatic' leaders. Although the leader might be anything other than 'quiet', this is all underpinned by unspoken but mass enthusiasm that is seldom exposed to critique at the time (Freud 1923; Bion 1961; Rice 1967; Miller 1993). Although rooted in Freudian psychology, this approach to understanding the legitimization of authority is now strongly represented in the social identity approach (SIA) to social psychology (Haslam 2004).

See also: **cross-cultural leadership**, **charisma**, **organizational culture**, **self-awareness**, **servant leadership**

Further reading: Badaracco 2001, 2002a; Gosling 2006; Greenleaf 1977b; Mintzberg 1998

RELIGIOUS MEANING

Tim Harle

'Man's search for meaning is the primary motivation in his life' (Frankl 1959: 105). Frankl approvingly quotes Nietzsche: 'He who has a *why* to live for can bear almost any *how*' (1959: 109). The search for meaning is not limited to existentialists and nihilists: finding meaning in work as a sign of divine approval formed a constituent element in the Weber-Tawney 'Protestant ethic' thesis that can be used both to explain, and to critique, the capitalist project. Although explicit allusion to religion is rare in the leadership discourse, influential thinkers – Drucker from North America and Handy from Europe may be offered as representative examples – are informed by faith traditions.

Before addressing issues of leadership, it is important to note the significance of worldview, *Weltanschauung*, offered by different religions. One of the ironies, and challenges, of contemporary debate is that different religious traditions can be perceived as either bringing a consistent worldview to all of life, or representing difference. Examples might include Puritanism and the *sharia* code. In sociological terms, religions of difference are often associated with dualism: seeing the divine as transcendent can promote a distinction between the sacred and secular (see e.g. Nash and McLennan 2001). Yet there are perennial calls for a more holistic approach, whether in liberation theologies emphasizing divine immanence or the rediscovery of Judeo-Christian mysticism, or Eastern traditions such as Buddhism promoting an inner search for meaning. Religious approaches can also have a distinctive contribution to debates about corporate social **responsibility** and business **ethics**, e.g. Islamic banking codes with their challenge to prevailing views on risk and relationship.

Religious traditions inform the leadership debate by providing both analogies (Green and Cooper 1998) and exemplars of leaders; Adair (2001) has looked at a number of figures in the Judaeo-Christian tradition. Certain twentieth-century figures – Gandhi (a noted secularist), Martin Luther King, Mother Theresa – are referred to in the literature. The use of religious language and concepts should also be noted. In addition to the widely used 'charismatic', examples include reference to 'corporate saviors' (Khurana 2002), while Case (1999) refers to 'managerial salvation devices', 'sacred motifs', 'absolution of the collective guilt' and 'attempts to acquire secular converts'. In a highly suggestive passage towards the end of a ground-breaking book, Wheatley offers a '*very* partial list of new metaphors to describe leaders: gardeners, midwives, stewards, servants, missionaries, facilitators, convenors' (1999: 165, original emphasis). Several have a religious association: the most widely used to date being 'servant' (Greenleaf 1977b), a term stretching back at least to the sixth century BCE, where an enigmatic figure in the book of Isaiah is variously seen as an individual and a community.

This introduces a key topic: whether the locus of meaning is found in the individual or the group. Descartes' *cogito ergo sum* has a number of contemporary challengers, e.g. the Sanskrit dictum, *so hum*: you are therefore I am (Kumar 2002); Kumar's subtitle, *A Declaration of Dependence* presents a challenge to those who expect omnicompetence in leaders. Buber's *I and Thou* (Buber 1970) has had a profound influence on concepts of reciprocity and relationship, but the prevailing trend in Western culture remains focused on the individual, with the associated risk of narcissism (Maccoby 2000). The influence can even be seen in authors who plead for a radical shift from the prevailing paradigm: 'if enough of us change ourselves, we can thereby change the world' (Zohar and Marshall 2004: x).

Change, at a corporate or personal level, is a topic which religions address. Paradoxically, religious traditions that claim to promote transformation are often perceived as among the most resistant institutions (the Vatican being one of many examples). Several faith communities speak of conversion: a multivalent word, whose richness of meaning is diminished if it is applied in too narrow a context. One of the Greek words it translates, *metanoia*, covers an interplay between process, event and attitudinal change: it can now be found in the leadership literature, describing a 'fundamental shift of mind' (Jaworski 1998: 94). The paradox that security can promote change is well captured by Benedictine monastic communities with their vows of stability and conversion of life. A book exploring the relevance of the Benedictine tradition to business sums up the leadership challenge: 'The call to conversion of life is in effect a vow to change, to never remain still either in self-satisfied fulfilment or self-denying despair' (Dollard *et al.* 2002: 201).

Note must also be made of the growing references to spirituality in work contexts (Mitroff and Denton 1999; Howard and Welbourn 2004). It would be hard to disagree with a dictionary entry: 'Spirituality is difficult to define' (Kroll in Carr 2002: 356f.), or with the observation that 'Spirituality has become a growth industry' (ibid.). The relation of spirituality to religion is a hotly debated topic (Carrette and King 2004). Many proponents of spirituality call for a rigid distinction from organized religion, though this approach has been criticized by Hicks (2003), who calls for a 'respectful pluralism', rather than the minimizing of differences. Block describes spirituality as 'living out a set of deeply held personal values, of honoring forces or a presence greater than ourselves. It expresses our desire to find meaning in, and to treat as an offering, what we do' (1996: 48). A theme of much writing relates to interconnectedness: a typical four-fold framework is offered by Howard and Welbourn (2004): self, nature, others and higher power. Links with new paradigms in science, especially complexity and chaos theory, can also be noted.

Others offer trenchant criticism. Two representatives may be quoted, applying respectively at a corporate and individual level. Roberts (2002) criticizes managerialism and a too easy acceptance of a consumer society: the 'commodification of the soul'. Tourish (2005b) warns against the perils of 'coercive persuasion' among leaders advocating spirituality in the workplace.

In summary, two key themes may be identified where religious approaches contribute to the search for meaning in the context of leadership. First, our interconnectedness: leaders exist within communities. Second, attitudes to change: the paradox that stability promotes change.

See also: **change and continuity**, **charisma**, **organizational culture**, **responsibility**, **servant leadership**

Further reading: Adair 2001; Henry 2002; Hicks 2003; Howard and Welbourn 2004; Wheatley 2005

RESPONSIBILITY

Terry L. Price

The concept of *responsibility* has two common meanings in leadership studies. The first meaning, which is the more general of the two, refers to the idea of behaving morally or ethically. To say that a leader or follower is responsible in this sense means that he did the morally or ethically correct action. This sense of the concept is also employed in discussions about corporate social responsibility. But *responsibility* has a second meaning. To say that a leader or follower is responsible can mean that he is accountable for his behaviour, regardless of whether it is right or wrong. Responsibility for morally or ethically correct action would imply praiseworthiness, and responsibility for immoral or unethical action would imply blameworthiness. The present entry focuses exclusively on the second meaning of *responsibility*. (See the entry on **ethics** for a discussion of the first meaning.)

Two general conditions must be met for a justified attribution of responsibility. First, the actor's behaviour must be within her control. Philosophers refer to this requirement as the *control condition*. If she is the victim of coercion or her behaviour is the result of an epileptic seizure or drugging, then it does not make sense to blame her when she does the wrong thing. The fact that she was made to do it gives her an excuse for her behaviour. We might even hesitate to say that she *engaged* in the prohibited behaviour, given that her agency was bypassed. Second, a responsible person's behaviour cannot be the result of mistaken belief. We can refer to this requirement as the *belief condition*. If a person mistakenly believes that she is doing something other than what she is in fact doing, then we should say that she has an excuse for her behaviour. Here, with respect to both conditions, an important caveat is in order: It must be the case that the person in question is not responsible for lacking control of her behaviour or for holding mistaken beliefs. If it turns out that the incapacity can be traced to negligence or recklessness, then an attribution of responsibility may be in order.

Justified attributions of responsibility can differ radically from the attributions of responsibility people actually make. Psychologists claim, for instance, that observers of behaviour are inclined to make 'the fundamental attribution error' (Nisbett and Ross 1980: 31). This kind of attributional mistake gives too much weight to an individual's personal characteristics and ignores important features of the situation in which he acts. Philosophers point to studies in psychology such as the Milgram (1974) experiments to show that situations, not traits, explain behaviour (Doris 2005; Harman 1999). In this particular experiment, subjects were willing to obey the experimenter's instructions to shock a 'learner'. Indeed, some subjects were willing to apply the shocks at what they took to be dangerously high levels. An example of the fundamental attribution error, then, would be to explain the subjects' behaviour in terms of personal characteristics, not the situation. Studies on these and other phenomena suggest that the theory of responsibility should attend to findings that support the *situationist* perspective in social psychology.

One situational feature of leadership raises particularly difficult questions about whether the control condition is met for **followers** in leadership contexts. Leadership is typically characterized by a **power** differential between leaders and followers. For example, French and Raven (1959) identify *coercive power* as one kind of power that leaders have at their disposal. Coercive power is the capacity to impose negative sanctions on followers who fail to behave as leaders would have them behave. The power that leaders have can thus cause us to wonder whether followers have any choice but to obey the directives of leaders. Disobedience can result in termination of employment or, in some leadership contexts, imprisonment and even death.

In general, however, obedience to orders does not constitute an excuse for wrongdoing. From the fact that it is hard for a follower to do the right thing, it does not follow that it was impossible, or even unreasonably difficult, for him to do so (Price 2006). As a consequence, followers can be held responsible when they are subject to the weaker forms of coercion that scholars such as French and Raven have in mind. This conclusion parallels the decisions in the Nuremburg trials and the trial of Adolf Eichmann, the so-called 'architect of the final solution'. In these trials, representatives of the Nazi Regime were unsuccessful in their claims that they were simply following orders.

More controversial are questions about whether the 'belief condition' on responsibility is satisfied for leaders who hold mistaken beliefs about morality. Philosophers such as Susan Wolf (1990) argue that a leader's inability to differentiate right from wrong makes an attribution of responsibility to the leader unjustified. This line of argument has important implications for any effort to assess the responsibility of dictators such as Adolf Hitler. If Hitler genuinely believed that persecution of the Jews was morally permissible, then Wolf's argument would seem to make an excuse readily available to him. But critics of Wolf's argument follow Aristotle in claiming that moral ignorance is no excuse (Moody-Adams 1994). Here, the idea is that all adults have the ability to tell right from wrong. Ultimately, this question is empirical in nature. The burden of proof is on the advocate of the view that some leaders are faultlessly mistaken about morality and, as a result, excused for their behaviour.

See also: **advice and dissent, cross–cultural leadership, ethics, power, situational leadership**

Further reading: Aristotle 1985; Doris 2005; Jones 1999; Nisbett and Ross 1980; Wolf 1990

SELF-AWARENESS

Donna Ladkin

Embedded within the term 'self-awareness' is the assumption that there exists a coherent self of which one can be aware. This in itself is perhaps a problematic and questionable idea, and one that is at the heart of the way in which I will introduce this term and its importance to leadership.

The concept of the 'self' as a relatively immutable, contained, individualistic entity has its roots in a modernist paradigm. In Classical times, the conception of the self was rooted in the community; the self was only the self in relation to the others with whom one lived. In Western cultures, it has only been since the Enlightenment that the individualized self has arisen as a viable concept, strengthened by the advance and general acceptance of psychological theories.

In a modernist sense, the self is linked particularly with ideas of authenticity and values. To be 'self aware' is to be aware of one's values, the relatively unchanging preferences at the core of our being, and to act on them in a consistent way. However, we are all too aware of the many times in which our 'theories in use', to use Argyris and Schön's (1978) term, will contradict those theories which we espouse. The frequency of such contradictions could cause us to question the notion of such a unified self as being a normative possibility.

A more post-modern rendering would see the self as 'constructed', the product of the many different roles we play and in a state of flux influenced by the people and events with which we engage. Such a conceptualization of the self suggests the self can be (to some extent) choicefully created. The implications for self-awareness of such an evolving self would involve awareness of the particular choices one is making in a given moment, and how those cohere with the kind of self one wants to construct.

Of course, this implies that 'choosing' is a rational and straightforward process. The reality is that in any given situation, a variety of factors, both conscious and unconscious, will **influence** what we perceive as the range of available choices available to us, as well as the behaviours we subsequently enact. These might be described as levels of self-awareness.

At a surface level, a person can be aware of his or her outward behaviours and acts. However, the benefit of this level of awareness only comes from knowing how these behaviours are perceived by others. The 'blind spot' identified by Luft and Ingham (1955) in their Johari Window Model refers to just this area of awareness, those aspects of the self – such as the way one is perceived – which are known to others but not to the self, except through eliciting feedback. This is a particularly important area for leaders, who will be carefully watched by their **followers**. Also important at this level of awareness is understanding the symbolic impact of their behaviours as well as their literal meanings. For instance, the action of a leader who raises her eyebrow during a meeting while a subordinate is making a case will be interpreted very differently from the raised eyebrows of a newly appointed junior manager.

It is impossible to always know how one is being interpreted, but this information can be even more difficult for leaders to ascertain, given that followers will understand it is not in their best interests to reveal their truthful reactions to a leader (especially if those reactions are not favourable). This produces a key difficulty for leaders who wish to become more aware of the impact of their actions on others. Organizational mechanisms, such as 360 degree feedback exercises, can help to provide leaders with this vital information. On an informal level, inquiring about others' perceptions, and being open to criticism can foster the sort of **organizational culture** in which constructive feedback can be more readily available to leaders who pursue this knowledge.

A 'middle' layer of self-awareness concerns being aware of one's emotional reactions and responses and how one handles them. In fact, some of the literature about self-awareness focuses on this aspect alone. The whole area of **emotional intelligence** is aimed at people developing a greater ease with their own and others' emotional responses. This is covered in greater depth on the entry on emotional intelligence.

However, there is an aspect of the self which often fuels the emotional self and contains the possibility of a deeper level of self-awareness. Within the unconscious reside motives and drives which can play a key role in influencing one's behaviour and reactions. In particular, the way one reacts to anxiety will often be rooted in unconscious levels of awareness. A leader (or his followers) may notice he is acting in a way which does not seem rationally connected to the present moment. He may be over-reacting, or finding himself trying to blame others or feeling unaccountably uncomfortable. Such reactions can indicate unconscious processes are at play. Frequently, deep-seated anxieties might have been triggered, and the leader is acting in ways aimed at protecting his sense of self. Becoming aware of these unconscious drivers for behaviour can be a challenging process, and is certainly an ongoing one. It is also a very important one for the leader, whose position of relative **power** provides the opportunity to act out unconscious motives in very unhelpful and destructive ways. In the worst possible scenarios, such unbridled reactions can result in the despotism witnessed in leaders such as Stalin, Hitler or Shaka Zulu (see Kets de Vries 2004b, for instance).

In some ways, the leadership role itself mitigates against self-awareness. The reluctance of followers to tell their leader the truth about the impact the leader creates is a major factor here. Furthermore, cultural norms and fantasies about effective leadership (being decisive, unwavering, unquestioning) contradict the more inquiring and tentative mindset that often accompanies the quest for greater self-awareness.

However, because of the power inherent in the leadership role, being aware of one's impact is crucial. So how can a leader foster a greater degree of self-awareness?

First, the leader can work to uncover the choices she makes about how she constructs the leadership self. This would include reflective work to understand the fantasies and assumptions which inform that construction and critical assessment of their utility.

Developing a circle of 'critical friends' with whom one can check is a second vital step one can take to develop self-awareness. The popularity of executive coaches speaks to this need. The challenge for the leader is to ensure that the coach actively challenges, rather than colludes with an idealized sense of self.

Finally, the leader might attend closely to hints of uncertainty or lack of clarity which could hold additional information about a given situation. Taking the time to reflect, to consider the possibility of alternative constructions of how the self might be, could both foster greater self-awareness, but also greater **effectiveness** in the leadership role.

See also: **cross-cultural leadership**, **effectiveness**, **emotional intelligence**, **power**, **process theory**

Further reading: Argyris 1999; Argyris and Schön 1978; Kets de Vries 2004b; Luft and Ingham 1955

SERVANT LEADERSHIP

Frank Hamilton

Robert Greenleaf first coined the term 'servant leadership' in his 1970 essay *The Servant as Leader*. Greenleaf first worked for 40 years in management and organizational development with AT&T. Then, after retiring, he spent 25 years as a consultant to numerous American corporations and universities, including the Mead Corporation, Ohio University, the Massachusetts Institute of Technology, the Ford Foundation, the Mellon Foundation and the Lilly Endowment Fund.

A self-described lifelong student of organizations and 'how things get done' (1977b: 336), Greenleaf compiled his observations on organizations and the individuals that they serve in a series of four essays intended to stimulate thought and develop a better, more caring society: *The Servant as Leader* (1970), *The Institution as Servant* (1977a), *Trustees as Servants* (1974) and *Teacher as Servant* (1979). In these essays, Greenleaf never formally defined servant-leadership, but he did define a leader as 'one who goes ahead to guide the way . . . maybe a mother in her home, any person who wields influence, or the head of a vast organization' (1996: 287). He also wrote: 'If one is a servant, one is always searching, listening, expecting that a better wheel for these times is in the making' (1977b: 9). In his view, servant-leadership 'begins with the natural feeling that one wants to serve, to serve first. Then a conscious choice brings one to aspire to lead' (1970: 13).

Throughout his writings, Greenleaf provided a model of servant-leadership and servant-leader development. In fact, he noted that there are no prescriptions for servant-leadership, only models (1970), and his model was based on behaviours. However, this model is atheoretical (Avolio and Gardner 2005) and only recently has empirical research provided support for it. Farling *et al.* (1999) noted that even though servant-leadership is becoming increasingly popular, the concept has been undefined and lacks empirical support. As the interest in servant-leadership has increased in both the popular press and the academic literature, others have attempted to define servant-leadership (Farling *et al.* 1999; Laub 1999; Page and Wong 2000; Sims 1997) and have developed new conceptual frameworks.

Sims distinguished servant-leadership as having the capacity 'to honor the personal dignity and worth of all who are led and to evoke as much as possible of their own innate creative power for leadership' (1997: 10–11). Laub (1999) delineated it as:

> an understanding and practice of leadership that places the good of those led over the self-interest of the leader. Servant-leadership promotes the valuing and development of people, the building of community, the practice of authenticity, the providing of leadership for the good of those led and the sharing

of power and status for the common good of each individual, the total organization and those served by the organization.

(p. 81)

Farling *et al.* (1999) used three parts of Greenleaf's definition presented above and compared them with Burn's definition of **transformational leadership**, in which the leader and follower act 'as a system to assist each other's improvement in all facets of life. The reward for this action is the other's gain' (1978: 50). Page and Wong stated: 'a servant-leader may be defined as a leader whose primary purpose for leading is to serve others by investing in their development and well being for the benefit of accomplishing tasks and goals for the common good' (2000: 70). These definitions share an 'other-focus' that accentuates the good of both individuals and the group, as well as those who come in contact with the organization. All of these definitions, as Farling *et al.* (1999) noted, have a transformational focus.

Servant-leadership has received significant attention in the popular press, but researchers have only begun to generate empirical findings that support a developmental model (e.g. Bass 2000; Barbuto and Wheeler 2006; Beazley forthcoming; Dennis and Bocarnea 2005; Dennis and Winston 2003; Farling *et al.* 1999; Humphreys 2005; Laub 1999; Page and Wong 2000; Sendjaya and Sarros 2002; Smith *et al.* 2004; Russell 2001; Russell and Stone 2002; Stone *et al.* 2004). Spears (1995) first identified what he considered the 10 critical characteristics of servant-leaders: listening, empathy, healing, awareness, persuasion, conceptualization, foresight, stewardship, commitment to the growth of people and building community. Russell and Stone (2002) have identified potential functional and accompanying attributes of servant-leaders (see Table 2) based on their conceptual model of servant-leadership.

The two categories of functional and accompanying attributes derived from an extensive review of the servant-leadership literature. Russell and Stone identified the functional attributes based on their repetitive appearance and prominence in previous research (2002: 146). The accompanying attributes, according to the researchers, supplement and augment the functional attributes. They stated: 'They are not secondary in nature: rather they are complementary and, in some cases, prerequisites to effective servant leadership' (2002: 147). These attributes have spawned several articles that have further clarified their roles in executing servant-leadership. Additionally, recent work on servant-leader assessment scales (Barbuto and Wheeler 2006; Dennis and Bocarnea 2005) has furthered the clarification of these

Table 2 Potential functional and accompanying attributes of servant-leaders

Functional attributes	Accompanying attributes
Vision	Communication
Honesty, integrity	Credibility
Trust	Competence
Service	Stewardship
Modelling	Visibility
Pioneering	Influence
	Persuasion
Appreciation of others	Listening
	Encouragement
Empowerment	Teaching
	Delegation

Source: from Russell and Stone (2002).

attributes and identified a new one: calling. Two additional streams of research have examined the values component of servant-leadership (Joseph and Winston 2005; Russell 2001) and the relation between transformation and servant-leadership (Humphreys 2005; Smith *et al.* 2004; Stone *et al.* 2004).

Servant-led organizations have been described as being values-based (Ciulla 1995; Graham 1991). The other-focus of these organizations has been linked to Gilligan's (1982) ethic of caring, an advanced stage of moral development. This relates back to Burn's (1978) original idea of transforming leadership, which he posited had a positive moral perspective.

Interestingly, although transformational leadership and servant-leadership share several similarities, transformational leaders tend to focus more on organizational objectives, while servant-leaders focus on **followers**' well-being (Stone *et al.* 2004). This again reflects servant-leadership's 'other-focus' in valuing the people in the organization rather than the organizational structure. This further clarifies servant-leadership, enabling researchers to explore and develop new constructs. Even though research has found that the servant-leader's focus is on the other and not on organizational outcomes, there are still beneficial organizational outcomes stemming from servant-leadership.

Greenleaf's essay *The Institution as Servant* (1977a) was aimed at organizations and the individuals who guided them. The question institutions need to ask is: 'who and how does it serve?' (1977a:

foreword). As noted earlier, Greenleaf only provided models for these organizations, not prescriptions. Research in this area is extremely limited.

According to Beazley (forthcoming), several outcomes are expected to derive from servant-led organizations. These included: mission and value focus, **creativity** and innovation, responsiveness and flexibility, a commitment to both internal and external service, a respect for employees, employee loyalty and a celebration of diversity. In sum, these outcomes indicate that all people that are touched by the institution are served, and they are neither used nor exploited.

As a transformational force, servant-leadership has the potential to move leaders and followers toward 'higher levels of motivation and morality' (Burns 1978: 20). Bass (2000), following Graham (1991), noted the parallels between transformational leadership and servant-leadership in both inspiration and individualized consideration. According to Bass (2000: 31), the strength of servant-leadership in encouraging followers' learning, growth and autonomy 'suggests that the untested theory will play a role in the future leadership of the learning organization'. The challenge for future organizations will be developing leaders who can both create adaptable systems and respect individuals' dignities. The paradox suggested by this challenge must address some traditional, underlying assumptions about organizing, human capability and individual contributions (Showkier 2002). Servant-led organizations require different practices and intentions to those led in more traditional ways which consolidate **power** in the hands of a few individuals and expect compliance from everyone else. Servant-leadership is an attitude and a number of practices that add up to an integrated way of serving all people involved with an organization. Servant-leaders, both today and in the future, face the challenge of integrating servant-leadership into a performance-oriented organizational paradigm.

See also: **empowerment**, **ethics**, **leadership development**, **transformational leadership**

Further reading: Autry 2001; Beazley *et al.* 2003; Greenleaf 1977b, 1998; Spears and Lawrence 2004

SITUATIONAL LEADERSHIP

Diane Boston and Jackie Hunt

Ken Blanchard described his Situational Leadership II model as outlining four different styles that a leader can adopt in his or her approach to the one-to-one management of a subordinate according to the situation or task. The leader moves between these styles depending on the development level of the subordinate, a combination of his or her levels of 'skill' (competence) and 'will' (commitment). The skill and will combinations are used to produce four possible follower development levels: D1 (low competence and high commitment); D2 (moderate competence and low commitment); D3 (moderate to high competence and variable commitment); and D4 (high competence and high commitment). To match the subordinate's development level, the leader has four styles to use: S1 Directing; S2 Coaching; S3 Supporting; and S4 Delegating. The leadership styles S1 to S4 are represented on the model as a bell curve, and can be used to chart the subordinate's progress through the development levels. In a 1996 article, written with his partner in the development of their Situational Leadership Theory, Paul Hersey, Blanchard named these four development levels as follows: Enthusiastic Beginner needing specific instruction; Disillusioned Learner needing feedback; Capable but Cautious Contributor needing recognition; and Self-reliant Achiever looking for their own rewards such as more autonomy or more thanks or training others.

After World War II there was an increase in interest in the possibility of a relationship between job performance, **motivation** and management style. For example, in 1966, Lawler had shown that high ability managers could make a significant difference to subordinates' job performance. In 1969 Hersey and Blanchard published their 'Life Cycle Theory of Leadership', which they renamed Situational Leadership in 1977. Their parameters were called Task behaviour and Relationship behaviour. They plotted follower 'maturity' as a curvilinear variable to show that leadership behaviour might be adjusted to the needs of subordinates or **followers**. Their thinking was influenced by a number of theorists, and in 1974 they acknowledged the work of Tannenbaum and Schmidt (1973 – Management Style Continuum), Korman (1974 – the identification of C and IS, see below), William J. Reddin (1967 – 3-D Management Style) and Blake and Mouton (1964 – the Managerial Grid). For some time Hersey and Blanchard have developed their model separately, during which time separate versions of the model have been copyrighted, and Ken Blanchard has developed the One Minute Manager series of books.

Korman (1974) summarized what had become a body of work on leadership, motivation and performance (although he did not include Hersey and Blanchard's work in this) as having identified two 'basic dimensions of leadership behaviour' (1974: 349). These are: consideration of subordinates' feelings (C); and goal attainment by subordinates and leader known as Initiating Structures (IS). Korman could not say if C and IS had predictive significance, but argued for more research into the 'situational variables which might be relevant and/or measured' (1974: 355).

Graeff (1983) described Hersey and Blanchard's Life Cycle Theory as building on Reddin's 3-D Leadership Framework (1967). He acknowledges the 'enormous popularity of the situational leadership theory' (1983: 285), but is unhappy with several aspects. In particular, he criticizes the possibility and nature of the 'curvilinear' relationship between the model's axes and other variables; the nature and definition of what they call follower 'maturity' and says the LEAD instrument they developed as a practical tool to identify leadership style is flawed in construction. He concluded 'situational leadership theory makes minor contributions to the leadership literature. Perhaps more important is their (Hersey and Blanchard's) focus on the truly situational nature of leadership'. Blank *et al.* agree that situational leadership is 'intuitively appealing and popular with practitioners' (1990: 579), but also criticize the definition of maturity and the idea of a curvilinear relationship, concluding 'the widespread acceptance and use of situational leadership theory indicate it deserves more empirical attention'.

The search for situational variables and their effects continues. Vecchio (2002) suggests the use of job level as a better predictor of performance than readiness/maturity of followers. Vecchio and Boatwright (2002) have been researching employee preferences for leadership style, making the link to the importance of employee expectations in leadership behaviour. Lee-Kelley (2002) has identified the importance of the situation in project management leadership. Yagil (2002) is interested in the **influence** on subordinate behaviour in flatter more self-managed organizations. She found that 'it might be concluded (that the leader's influence is) only similar to that of other major components of (subordinates') environment' (Yagil 2002: 397). Interestingly, Silverthorne and Ting-Hsin (2001) used the LEAD instrument in Taiwan and found it to be an apparently accurate predictor of adaptability for use in the high-tech industries of Taiwan.

In their 'Great Ideas Revisited' article Blanchard and Hersey (1996) restate that the model they developed is both simple and useful. This may well explain its popularity with practitioners who generally seek to help others make sense of their leadership experiences. In the intervening years they have reconsidered the concept of follower maturity and Blanchard now talks about working with the idea of followers becoming 'ready, willing and able' (Blanchard and Hersey 1996: 48). But together they agree that 'If either version of our model encourages you to be follower-driven, celebrate!' (Blanchard and Hersey 1996: 48). In the same vein, Vecchio (2002) quotes Yukl (1998: 108): 'Hersey and Blanchard's theory may be of greatest value to the extent that it reminds us that it is essential to treat individual subordinates differently as the situation changes.'

See also: **effectiveness, leader–follower relations, leadership development, motivation, style theories**

Further reading: Blanchard and Hersey 1996; Hersey and Blanchard 1974; Hersey *et al.* 2000; Zigarmi *et al.* 1985

STRATEGIC VISIONING

Kuldip S. Reyatt

Meaning and purpose are at the heart of leadership vision, which is the product of the visioning process. Kouzes and Posner highlight that 'One of *the* most important practices of leadership is giving life and work a sense of meaning and purpose by offering an exciting vision' (2003: 112). Consequently, leadership itself can be considered as the process of making meaning (Drath and Palus 1994). For Rost, leaders and **followers** developing mutual focus is a key aspect of the post-industrial leadership paradigm; he relates purpose to vision in that 'Purposes are broader, more holistic or integrated, more oriented to what people ordinarily think of as a vision' (1991/1993: 119).

Visioning is one of the key activities that distinguish leadership from management (Kotter 1999); also, in a recent leadership survey by The Gallup Organization, visioning is acknowledged as one of the key demands of effective leadership (Conchie 2004). Furthermore, scholars of leadership and other related disciplines assert that visioning is a critical aspect of the leadership process, organizational growth and success over the longer term (Baum *et al.* 1998; Collins and Porras 1997; Larwood *et al.* 1995; Lipton 2003).

Vision and visioning are central within several leadership theories, particularly Transformational (Bass 1985; Bass and Avolio 1993; Burns 1978), Visionary (Bennis and Nanus 1985; Nanus 1992; Westley and Mintzberg 1989) and Charismatic (Conger and Kanungo 1988; House 1977). These theories, classified as the *New Leadership* perspective (Boal and Hooijberg 2001), can be considered subsets of strategic leadership with particular features seen as delimiters. For instance, **charisma**-building characteristics (attribution or **impression management**) are noticeably differentiated from transformational processes (bonding of individual and collective interest). Strategic leadership is considered the least delimited and therefore broadest construct (Pawar and Eastman 1997).

Strategic leadership differs from other kinds of leadership in the magnitude of issues and the scale of complexity encountered (Adair 2002); it is concerned with the leadership *of* organizations, and should be conceptualized differently from leadership *in* organizations or lower level direct supervisory leadership (Hunt 2004). Finkelstein and Hambrick confirm that strategic leadership is leadership 'of an overall enterprise, not just a small unit; and it implies substantive decision-making responsibilities' (1996: 6).

Strategic leaders create meaning and purpose for the organization (House and Aditya 1997). Acting as pioneers, in their endeavours they have no maps or guidebooks to study, they can only imagine the possibilities; thus, strategic leaders are 'possibility thinkers, not proba-bility thinkers' (Kouzes and Posner 2003: 124). In effect, strategic leadership translates as those leaders responsible for considering possi-bilities and determining the future of the organization – they are the key actors in strategic visioning.

Strategic visioning is such an important aspect of strategic leader-ship that it should be well defined and agreed upon amongst scholars and practitioners. However, in their UK study of visioning practice, O'Brien and Meadows (2000) confirm that there is no clearly accepted definition of corporate (strategic) visioning. Nevertheless, at its core, the process of strategic visioning is about imagining *what is not present* and *what should be*. Strategic leaders need to consider not only the *What* – the content of strategic vision – but also the *Where*, *When* and *Why* it should be achieved (Grint 2000).

The reason for strategic visioning is that it clearly establishes both a direction and a destination; the process produces an artefact, which can take a variety of forms (vision statement, symbol, blueprint, etc.). However, it should be future-oriented, compelling, bold, aspiring and inspiring, yet believable and achievable (Levin 2000). Wilson integrates various definitions and perspectives in stating 'Strategic vision is a coherent and powerful statement of what the business can and should be (n) years hence' (1992: 18).

Practitioners often highlight the confusion between strategic visioning and strategy development processes. The emerging trend identifies strategic vision as independent of and preceding business strategy development, and an overarching concept under which a variety of other concepts are subsumed (Collins and Porras 1991). Strategic visioning is needed as 'the capstone and integrating mechanism for the elements of strategic planning – mission, philosophy, goals, objectives, strategy, action plans, organisation culture and structure' (Wilson 1992: 18).

Abell (2006) contends that there is increasing congruence between strategy and leadership in practice and that this will join the two fields in academia. Correspondingly, Westley and Mintzberg (1989) state that the strategic visioning process and contextual influences are intertwined; they highlight that concepts of strategy and leadership combine into that of strategic visioning, which is part style, process, content and context.

There is disagreement as to whether a strong charismatic or visionary leader is essential to becoming a visionary organization (Collins and Porras 1991). Additionally, Robbins and Duncan state that strategic vision is a negotiated reality 'arising from the political activity among members of the top management team' (1988: 229). Wilson (1992) concludes that strategic visioning is an activity that comes naturally to the born leader, but can be defined, laid out, learned and practised by others.

Ciulla highlights that 'Visions are not simple goals, but rather ways of seeing the future that implicitly or explicitly entail some notion of the good' (2005: 325); similarly, good leadership is not only effective but also ethical (Ciulla 2006). Hence, good strategic leadership is not just about occupying an executive position, but also about fulfilling strategic leadership responsibilities, which entail the provision of meaning and purpose for the organization through *good* strategic visioning.

Strategic visioning is a dynamic, multi-relational and highly context-sensitive strategic leadership group process for creating strategic vision, which provides meaning and purpose for *all* people within the organization. Strategic visioning is attributable to the leadership *of* organizations and entails balancing multifarious influences such as strategic leadership dynamics, stakeholder relationships and internal/external responsibilities. Encompassing more than an individual leader's vision and extending beyond **leader–follower**

relations, strategic visioning is a broader concept in scope than visioning related to other leadership theories. Affecting as it does the lives and livelihoods of so many people, the search for *good* strategic vision necessitates effective *and* ethical strategic visioning.

See also: **charisma**, **effectiveness**, **process theory**, **responsibility**, **style theories**, **transformational leadership**

Further reading: Boal and Hooijberg 2001; Collins and Porras 1997; Finkelstein and Hambrick 1996; Nanus 1992; Wilson 1992

STYLE THEORIES

Jon Aarum Andersen

Leadership theories can be grouped into three main categories (Andersen 2000): (i) leadership as personality, (ii) leadership as behaviour and action and (iii) leadership as a symbol (how the leaders or the actions of leaders are perceived).

Leadership style denotes the behaviour or behavioural pattern of leaders. Research based on the work, tasks, actions and behaviour or behavioural patterns of the leader tends towards an instrumental approach, focusing on what the leader *does*. Exploring the consequences of the behaviour of leaders is a more challenging research objective because of inherent difficulties in attributing causality to specific behaviours or styles. The research canon contains groups of theories concerning, for example: (1) leadership as function, (2) leadership as process, (3) leadership as behavioural pattern, (4) leadership as role, (5) leadership as work tasks and activities, and (6) leadership as skills. This entry deals with leadership as behaviour pattern, and especially with the theories using the term leadership style.

Theories which apply the term leadership style have the description of leader behaviour and behavioural pattern in common. This description does not cover what kinds of acts or work the leader is engaged in. Rather, leadership style describes what the leader emphasizes when acting in a leadership role. These observable actions are depicted as a behavioural pattern, from which it is possible, according to style theorists, to impute underlying preferences of 'style'. The term style is widely used, and sometimes only to denote leadership behaviour of any kind. However, the term leadership style is primarily reserved for theories describing behaviour, generally categorized according to the attention paid to the dimensions of task and relationships.

Leadership style theories are immensely popular (McCall 1976), and often go beyond a description of the behavioural pattern of leaders to offer explanations of the cause of the styles as well as their consequences in terms of **effectiveness** (Bass 1990b). The relationship between the leadership style and effectiveness is the main focus of the instrumental theories in general and for style theories in particular.

An extensive research programme was started in 1945 with the aim to describe the behaviour of managers. Leadership was tentatively defined as 'the behavior of an individual when he is directing the activities of a group towards a shared goal' (Hemphill and Coons 1957: 7). Using data collected by interviews, observations and questionnaires, two factors were found in the behaviour of all leaders investigated: 'Consideration' and 'Initiating Structure'. These dimensions were defined as follows:

Consideration. Reflects the extent to which an individual is likely to have job relationships characterized by mutual **trust**, respect for subordinates' ideas, and consideration of their feelings. A high score is indicative of a climate of good rapport and two-way communication. A low score indicates the superior is likely to be more impersonal in his relationships with group members.

Initiating Structure. Reflects the extent to which an individual is likely to define and structure his role and those of his subordinates toward goal attainment. A high score on this dimension characterizes individuals who play a more active role in directing the group activities through planning, communicating information, scheduling, trying out new ideas, etc.

(Fleishman and Harris 1962: 43f.)

The definitions of these dimensions led to the development and use of questionnaires (for measuring leadership style), making leadership research highly quantitative thereafter. Gibb (1969) pointed out the clear connection between these dimensions and the result emerging from other studies even when different methods were used. The dimensions of *consideration* and *structure* are theoretically meaningful and describe the behavioural patterns of leaders that can be easily identified, and are found simultaneously in all behaviours, but in varying degrees. Managers are not solely task-oriented, nor solely people-oriented. They are always both, but in varying degrees. This statement is arguably the most theoretically and empirically established of all in leadership research. Smith *et al.* (1989) investigated managers' behaviour in four continents and found the dimensions to be universal.

After the Ohio State Studies of leadership behaviour, a number of theories have been developed based on the same two dimensions. The terms used, however, have been given slightly different names: *concern for production* and *concern for people* (Blake and Mouton 1964), *task orientation* and *relationships orientation* (Reddin 1970), *task behaviour* and *relationship behaviour* (Hersey and Blanchard 1993). When Fiedler (1967) introduced the contingency theory of managerial effectiveness, he used the terms *task motivated leadership style* and *relationship motivated leadership style*. Recent research has come up with another dimension. *Change orientation* has been added to the task and relationship dimensions (Arvonen 2002; Ekvall and Arvonen 1991). According to Yukl, 'a three-dimensional taxonomy provides the most useful and parsimonious way to group behaviours of leaders into general categories' (2002: 64).

The causes of leadership style

Some differences are found in the style theories when explaining why leaders have different styles. Blake and Mouton (1985: 5) argue that assumptions regarding how to achieve results through other people guide their behaviour. Fiedler (1967: 29) claims that personality and **motivation** structure explain differences in behaviour. By doing so he is probably the only style theorist linking personality to behaviour, even though he refers to the shallower concept of attitudes. As a general statement, leadership style theories explain differences in style due to individuals holding different attitudes regarding the importance of achieving tasks and of taking care of relationships. Differences in attitude lead to different leadership styles.

When the Ohio State researchers managed to present a consistent definition of leadership style and its two dimensions partly based on the use of questionnaires, the road to quantitative, questionnaire-based research was laid bare. The first questionnaire was called the Leader Behaviour Description Questionnaire (LBDQ) (Hemphill and Coons 1957) and a number of revisions of this instrument followed and were applied in numerous studies on thousands of managers and their subordinates. Blake and Mouton (1964) also developed written instruments to measure leadership style (Blake and McCanse 1991). No other questionnaire has been subject to so much discussion and controversy as Fiedler's LPC instrument (Fiedler 1967). In fact, at times, there has been more on the qualities or lack of qualities of the LPC than on the theory itself. The MSDT instrument developed by Reddin (1970) has also been widely used, mostly in training programmes. The same goes for the LEAD questionnaire developed by Hersey and Blanchard (1993).

What insight do the instrumental theories give us into the relationship between leadership and effectiveness? For more than 30 years, Blake and Mouton (1964) have stubbornly claimed that there is one best leadership style (9,9 team management), advocating the universal approach (one best way to lead). Fiedler (1967) is the dominant advocate for the contingency model, claiming that leadership behaviour must be adjusted to the situation to create organizational effectiveness.

Several studies indicate that the impact of managerial behaviour on organizational effectiveness is probably weak and varies between companies and over time. A variety of circumstances within the company (situation) may determine how large the room for manoeuvre for the managers' behaviour to **influence** effectiveness. Given a specific room for manoeuvre in a specific organization, some studies indicate that the behavioural pattern which combines a high degree of task orientation with a high degree of relationship orientation does have some impact on effectiveness. This is especially so when the manager engages in a behaviour of influencing, controlling and assisting as well as a high degree of **responsibility** for others.

The contention that effective leadership is contingent on the situation is still only a weakly supported hypothesis. After more that 35 years of research – indeed intensive research – into **situational leadership**, we cannot claim that this research has given convincing or consistent answers as to what behavioural patterns or managerial types are effective in particular situations. It appears that over the last 20 years more and more theories imply a return to the universal argument (e.g. **transformational leadership** is better than **transactional leadership**). It is very difficult, however, to establish scientifically the importance of leadership for organizational effectiveness (Andersen 2006).

An instrumental view of leadership contains two components at least. There are tasks to be solved and people to solve them. This is the strength of the leadership style concept: it captures both the task orientation and the relationship aspect of behaviour at the same time.

See also: **behavioural theories of leadership, contingency theories, effectiveness**

Further reading: Arvonen 2002; Bass 1990b; Blake and Mouton 1964; Fiedler 1967; Yukl 2002

TOXIC LEADERSHIP

Michael Walton

Toxic Leadership is defined here as leadership behaviour which poisons, is disruptive, destructive, exploitive, dysfunctional and abusive. This covers workplace bullying and harassment in its various forms, deception and fraudulent dealings, forced imposition of unrealistic workloads, fostering disruptive internal competition, misinformation and misrepresentation, and aggressive interpersonal behaviour.

Toxic leadership highlights the deliberate destructive and self-servicing misuse of **power**; it describes a relationship which undermines the effective functioning of the organization and destabilizes sound working relationships. 'Corruption, hypocrisy, sabotage, and manipulation, as well as other assorted unethical, illegal, and criminal acts, are part of the poisonous repertoire of toxic leaders' is how Lipman-Blumen (2005a: 18) describes this concept, and describes leaders 'who, by virtue of their destructive behaviours and their dysfunctional personal qualities or characteristics, inflict serious and enduring harm on the individuals, groups, organisations, communities and even the nations that they lead' (2005b).

Such toxicity highlights what has been described as 'the dark side of leadership', a side which whilst always present has often remained in the shadows so far as much of the conventional training for leadership is concerned (Babiak 1995; Babiak and Hare 2006; Cavaiola and Lavender 2000; Conger 1990; Frost 2003; Furnham and Taylor 2004; Hogan and Hogan 2001; Kellerman 2004a, b; Kets de Vries 1985, 2001; Lipman-Blumen 2005a, b; Zaleznik and Kets de Vries 1985).

In spite of much of the 'positive' hype of the leadership industry, leaders are not, by definition, always good, ethical or correct in their behaviour, as has been evidenced in recent times by the deluge of material describing toxic leadership behaviour. High-profile toxic leadership within companies such as Enron and WorldCom reinforces the importance of addressing and examining such aspects of leadership (Anand *et al.* 2004; Frost 2003; Kellerman 2004a, b; Kramer 2002; Sankowsky 1995; Smith and Quirk 2004; Thomas and Hansen 2002; Wright and Smye 1996).

A major problem, however, is how to counter the pervasiveness of toxic leadership, as many of the attributes toxic leaders possess, when not used to excess or inappropriately, are the same as those exhibited by successful non-toxic leaders. The situation is further complicated as toxic behaviours may have previously been excused, denied or even encouraged, because of the results delivered and may have (i) reinforced and intensified toxic leadership behaviour, (ii) discouraged others from addressing the unacceptable behaviours experienced, and (iii) generated a groupthink and/or acceptant mentality within that setting (Harvey 1988a; Janis 1982; Milgram 1974; Zimbardo 1969).

Kellerman examines seven categories of bad leadership practices – incompetent, rigid, intemperate, callous, corrupt, insular and evil (Kellerman 2004a: 38), whereas Lipman-Blumen's primary focus concerns the *allure* of toxic leaders and on toxic *follower* behaviour (2005a; see also Janis 1982; Offermann 2004b; Stein 2005; Sulkowicz 2004); the focus for Frost (2003; Frost and Robinson 1999) is on 'toxic handlers'.

The Center for Creative Leadership's (CCL) research on executive **derailment** highlighted patterns of abrasive and abusive behaviour, insensitivity to the needs of others, distant, aloof and arrogant ways of behaving, unnecessary and intrusive micro-management, the manipulation of situations, and continuing self-serving behaviour – as significant contributors to an executive's derailment and demise. CCL's conclusions are backed up by the literature, which suggests that the most frequently reported disruptive executive behaviours are characterized by dramatic, histrionic, emotionally demanding, narcissistic, aggressive and somewhat grandiose leadership behaviours (Babiak 1995, 1996; Bendell 2002; Bernstein 2001; Conger 1990; Hogan and Hogan 2001; Kets de Vries 1979, 1985, 1989b; Khurana 2002; Levinson 1978; Lubit 2002; Maccoby 2000, 2004; Price 2000; Sankowsky 1995; Sperry 2002, amongst others).

The dangers of excessive **charisma** attract particular attention when thinking about toxic leadership and the self-aggrandizement that can accompany overly 'Heroic' and 'transformational' approaches to leadership (Kets de Vries 1991; Khurana 2002; Lubit 2002; Maccoby 2000; McFarlin and Sweeney 2000; Tourish 2005a; Waldroop and Butler 2000). McCall (1998) quotes Harry Levinson on the grandiose self-image which can develop as executives become more senior: 'They think they have the right to be condescending and contemptuous to people who serve them. They (executives) think they are entitled to privilege and the royal treatment'. McCall concludes: 'In summary, the development of arrogance is one of the most insidious of the derailment dynamics. It is a negative that grows from a positive, deriving as it does from actual talent and success' (1998: 46).

Toxic behaviours by leaders – and from **followers** – could be described as silent killers as they operate below the surface and sabotage, block and penalize those who raise issues for discussion (Beer and Eisenstat 2000). A combination of toxic leaders, vulnerable and demeaned followers, and conducive contexts results in an unhealthy 'toxic triangle' (Padilla *et al.* 2005; Paulhus and Williams 2002; Walton 2005a, b, in press). With such forces threatening an organization's success it remains surprising that a fuller exposition and exploration of the darker side of leadership, and the misuse of the power, is not at the top of the curricula for leadership studies (Dotlich and Cairo 2003; Kilburg 2000; Schell 1999).

The Hogan Development Survey (HDS), derived from the clinical personality disorders set out in DSM-IV (1994), assesses the potential for dysfunctional behaviour and identifies those which would put the respondent at risk of derailment. In addition, the B-Scan is a newly developed questionnaire which seeks to assess sociopathic potential within the leadership population (Hare and Babiak – in test phase). These instruments seek to identify a leader's potential for toxicity and can be used for diagnostic and developmental purposes. The 11 DSM-IV (1994) personality disorders can be categorized to describe different clusters of sub-clinical toxic leadership:

Cluster 'A'-leaders, who often appear odd or eccentric – executives in this category could be seen as imaginative, shrewd, independent-minded and rather challenging and sceptical

Cluster 'B'-leaders, who often appear dramatic, emotional or erratic – they are likely to come over as assured, competent and highly socially skilled; they will tend to adopt a high profile; image and **impression management** will be important to them, and

Cluster 'C'-leaders, who often appear anxious or fearful of others – individuals here will be concerned to get it 'right', be risk averse, hesitant and cautious in what they put their name to and sanction, to the extent that no action may be better than action in their mind.

Examining toxic leadership behaviour through a clinically oriented perspective opens up a broader and deeper insight into executive behaviour-in-context and reinforces the importance of assessing their psychological suitability as they progress, irrespective of the leadership styles or methodologies they espouse (Kets de Vries 2004a; Kets de

Vries and Balazs 2005; Lowman 1993; Oldham and Morris 1995; Quick and Tetrick 2003; Thomas and Hansen 2002).

Appointment to a position of formal leadership does not guarantee positive, constructive leadership behaviour. The leader as a person will remain susceptible to the full range of human strengths and vulnerabilities irrespective of their title, professional background and organizational context.

See also: **charisma, derailment, emotional intelligence, ethics, leader–follower relations, transformational leadership**

Further reading: Cavaiola and Lavender 2000; Finkelstein 2003; Kellerman 2004a, b; Kets de Vries 2001; Lipman-Blumen 2005a

TRAIT THEORY

Kenneth J. Levine

Trait theories of leadership are the basis of longstanding explanations of the phenomena of leadership. In its earliest form, trait theory provided an easy explanation for the complex set of individual characteristics that together form a leader. The origins of Trait theory are found in the writing of the English philosopher Thomas Carlyle (1969) and his **great man theory**. Carlyle believed that some people were born to be leaders, and it was this genetic heritage, or specific innate traits and characteristics, that made these people different from those that were **followers**. Carlyle, while ushering a new period of leadership enquiry, held strong to the European and Victorian ideal of the heroic individual possessing qualities of character that others would be unable to learn or acquire through experience.

The idea that leaders are 'born and not made' is no longer uncritically accepted. Further, the belief that there is only one set of traits that will guarantee leadership ability has also been dismissed through research. Trait theory research conducted in the 1940s found that 'a person does not become a leader by virtue of the possession of some combination of traits' (Stogdill 1948: 64), rather there are situational factors that are influential as well.

About 25 years ago the study of leadership traits regained popularity. A resurgence of research since 1980 has claimed that it is the leader's actions and reactions in specific situations that make a person a successful leader. While there is not one set of traits that guarantees an individual's ascension to leadership in any given situation, the possession of some will make it likely that a person will be granted or assigned a leadership position.

As it turns out, these characteristics have much in common with the qualities previously associated with great man theories. These include physical features (i.e. height); personality factors (i.e. extroverted); education and ability-related characteristics (i.e. speech fluency). This is hardly surprising: traditionally, members of the upper class were in leadership positions. With access to education, sanitation and nutrition, they and their offspring were typically healthier, taller and smarter than those of the lower classes.

Traits such as height, weight and physique are heavily dependent on heredity, whether genetic, social or a combination of the two, whereas others such as knowledge of the industry are contingent on experience and learning. Trait theory is now expanded to include this wider range of inherited and acquired qualities. Thus, leadership resides in and amongst people, and it is likely that leadership will only be effective when the position is held by people with these characteristics.

However, there is little consistency in the research as to how much of an influence these traits have on leadership and leadership ability. An analysis of 20 studies on leadership conducted during the 1940s revealed 79 unique traits; however, 65 of these 79 traits appeared in only one study, and only four (extroversion, humour, intelligence and initiative) appeared in five or more studies (Stogdill 1948). A further review by the Centre for Excellence in Management and Leadership (CEML 2002; Perren and Burgoyne 2001) listed over 1,000 traits, distilled to 83 more or less distinct attributes. While possession of some, many or all of these does not guarantee leadership success, there is evidence that effective leaders are different from other people in certain key respects. The current iteration of the Trait theory states that leaders share certain personality traits that differentiate them from followers. Depending on the research, these traits include:

achievement	honesty and integrity
alertness	humour
ambition	initiative
athletic ability	insight
cognitive ability	intelligence
cooperativeness	judgement
critical thinking	leadership motivation (*the desire*
emotional stability	*to lead but not to seek power*
energy	*as an end in itself*)

motivation	sociability
originality	social judgement drive
persistence	solution-construction skills
popularity	status
problem-solving skills	tenacity
responsibility	tolerance
self-confidence	verbal facility

Researchers have sought to categorize these traits to help understand and predict leadership ability; however, even when researchers agree on many of the above traits, the categorization of these traits into specific characteristics has proven difficult.

One such categorization found that the factors associated with leadership could be classified under six general headings: (1) capacity (intelligence, alertness, verbal facility, originality and judgement); (2) achievement (scholarship, knowledge and athletic accomplishment); (3) **responsibility** (dependability, initiative, persistence, aggressiveness, self-confidence and the desire to excel); (4) participation (activity, sociability, cooperation, adaptability and humour); (5) status (socioeconomic position and popularity); and (6) situation (status, skills, needs and interests of followers, objectives to be achieved) (Stodgill 1974).

Another categorization divided the above-mentioned traits into three general categories: (1) *Interpersonal* factors; (2) *Cognitive* factors and (3) *Administrative* factors (Boyatzis 1982).

Yet it is clear that traits alone are not sufficient to explain or to give rise to successful leadership. Rather traits are a precondition or precursor for action such as role modelling, formulating a vision and setting goals. Possessing certain traits only makes it more likely that the person will become a leader or be given leadership **authority**. However, it is by no means clear that these observable traits have any causal role in propelling people into leadership. More importantly, there is no agreement about what mix of traits really distinguishes leaders from others; and methodological doubts remain about attribution errors, suggesting that many of these traits are observed in leaders *because they are leaders*, and their apparent manifestation is consequent to the many other factors that constitute leadership.

There are both theoretical and methodological reasons for considering the link between the traits of potential leaders and their tendency to be perceived as leaders. A 1986 study focused on the question of how personality relates to leadership emergence. From the receiver's perspective, the assessment of leadership traits in others will create the perceptions of the other's leadership qualities. Hence, the traits of potential leaders need to correlate with the traits that the receiver/ followers both expect and view as important. This study indicated that the traits most followers believe are important are intelligence and dominance. More research on the follower's beliefs of necessary traits will be helpful in furthering the understanding of this theory.

Traditional criticisms of Trait theory include: it has failed to create a definitive list of leadership traits; it fails to take the situation into account; it is not a useful approach for the training and development of leaders as the traits it examines are not easily changed or acquired. Critical theorists have noted that the research focuses almost exclusively on male leaders and male respondents. Other critics have noted the failure of this theory to acknowledge that leadership traits are a receiver characteristic. The follower must accept these traits as necessary and/or sufficient for effective leadership, or the leader will face difficulty in persuading others to follow. Lastly, **charisma**, **creativity** and flexibility are not included in Trait theory, yet they are the focus of later leadership theories.

See also: **charisma**, **effectiveness**, **gender and leadership**, **great man theory**, **leadership development**

Further reading: Boyatzis 1982; Stogdill 1948, 1974

TRANSACTIONAL LEADERSHIP

Marco Tavanti

Transactional leadership is most often explained as a cost-benefit exchange between leaders and their **followers** (Kuhnert and Lewis 1987). The transaction or exchange involves something of value between what the leader possesses or controls and what the follower wants in return for his/her services (Yukl and Van Fleet 1992). Transactional leadership involves leaders clarifying goals and objectives, communicating to organize tasks and activities with the cooperation of their employees to ensure that wider organizational goals are met (Bass 1974: 341). The success of this type of leader–follower relationship depends on the acceptance of hierarchical differences and the ability to work through this mode of exchange. Transactional leadership is based on the assumption that subordinates and systems work better under a clear chain of command. The implicit belief in the leader–follower relationship is that people are motivated by rewards and penalties (Kuhnert 1994) and that interpersonal relations can be characterized as more or less rational exchanges between agents exercising the power of choice. Despite numerous leadership studies highlighting the limitations of this approach, transactional leadership remains popular among leaders and managers. Along the spectrum leadership versus management, this approach is clearly closer to the management end (MacKenzie *et al.* 2001).

In his seminal work on leadership, James MacGregor Burns (1978) defines transactional leadership as the first form of interaction between leaders and followers. On the opposite side of transforming leadership, transactional leadership occurs when one person takes the initiative in making contact with others for the purpose of an exchange of valued things. The relations of most leaders and followers are transactional: leaders approach followers with an eye to exchanging one thing for another: jobs for votes, or subsidies for campaign contributions (Burns 1978: 19). In his historical review of political leadership practices exemplified by numerous case studies, Burns defines this exchange as economic or political or psychological in nature. The relationship leader–follower revolves around the bargaining process and the maintenance of it. This is also the limit of this leadership approach, which does not attempt to push the relation beyond bargaining, contracts and exchanges.

Barnard M. Bass (1985) further elaborated on Burns's conceptualization of transactional-transformational leadership. Bass argued that transactional and **transformational leadership** are not two opposite ends of the spectrum but are two separate concepts. According to Bass, the best leaders are both transformational and transactional. Although his leadership model has undergone various revisions, the most recent version considers four dimensions of transformational leadership, three dimensions of transactional leadership and a non-leadership dimension, or laissez-faire. Apart from its emphasis on transformational leadership exemplified by **charisma**, or idealized **influence**, inspirational **motivation**, intellectual stimulation and individualized consideration, three important distinctions identify transactional approaches to leadership. The first dimension, contingent reward, is the degree to which the leader sets up constructive transactions or exchanges with followers. The leader using this dimension clarifies expectations and establishes the rewards for meeting these expectations.

The second and third dimensions of transactional leadership are two types of management-by-exception. Management-by-exception occurs when the leader intervenes to make a correction when something goes wrong (Bass 1985). The two types of management-by-exception are active and passive. Howell and Avolio (1993) observe that the difference between them lies in the timing of the leader's intervention. Active leaders monitor follower behaviour, anticipate problems and take corrective actions before the behaviour creates serious difficulties (Northouse 2004: 179). Passive leaders wait until the behaviour has created problems before taking action. A substantial difference is that in the active form the leader looks for deviations, whereas in the passive form, the leader waits for problems to emerge (Hater and Bass 1988).

The distinction between transactional and transformational is commonly emphasized in leadership studies. In spite of the fact that transformational theories have been a popular topic in leadership literature, transactional leadership constitutes a foundation for it and the two approaches are not necessarily in opposition to one another (Northouse 2004; Tracey and Hinkin 1998). Nonetheless, most advocates of the distinction persist in describing leaders as one or the other. While transactional leaders motivate followers to comply with the leader's requests and organizational role through an exchange process, transformational leaders motivate followers by encouraging them to transcend their self-interests for the sake of the organization and shared goals. According to Barnard M. Bass, transactional leaders predetermine what their followers should do to realize their personal and organizational aims, while transformational leaders motivate and stimulate their followers to surpass their own self-interests and direct themselves to a higher level of motivation linked to the interests of the team, organization or larger community (Bass and Avolio 1994). Critics might object that insofar as transformational leaders prioritize these so-called higher order goals, they are pre-determining the followers' moral choices.

The distinction between transactional leadership and laissez-faire is less clearly defined (Bass 1985; Judge and Piccolo 2004). Laissez-faire leadership is the avoidance or absence of leadership. Laissez-faire leaders are indifferent and have a 'hands-off' approach toward the workers and their performance. These leaders, unlike most transactional leadership approaches, ignore the needs of others, do not respond to problems or do not monitor performance. Leaders who score high on laissez-faire leadership avoid making decisions, hesitate in taking action and are absent when needed. Although laissez-faire leadership bears some resemblance to passive forms of management by exception, researchers have argued that laissez-faire leadership should be treated separately from the other transactional dimensions because it represents the absence of any leadership (transformational or transactional) (Avolio 1999; Bass 1998).

Transactional leaders exhibit specific leadership skills usually associated with the ability to obtain results, to control through structures and processes, to solve problems, to plan and organize, and work within the structures and boundaries of the organization. As the transactional style revolves around the formulation and maintenance of a contract, negotiation skills are essential for this type of leadership. The exchange will successfully happen only on the basis of clear and effective communication skills. While leaders need to clearly define job descriptions and task assignments, subordinates must be able to show results and fulfil the leader's expectations. Effective transactional leaders are capable of (1) clarifying what is expected of the employees' performance, (2) explaining how to meet such expectations, (3) spelling out the criteria of the evaluation of their performance, (4) providing feedback on whether the employee is meeting the objective and (5) allocating rewards that are contingent to their meeting the objectives (Bass 1974: 339).

The transactional and leader–follower exchange theories represent a significant step beyond the 'leader-oriented' approaches most often focused exclusively on the leader's actions and attitudes. In a general sense, transactional leadership exemplifies the most common dynamic of social exchange between leadership and followership (Bass 1974: 319). The question remains as to what is the dynamic in this exchange process that produces satisfactory results for the leaders, followers and organizations involved? Many transactional leadership studies have shown that the nature of the exchange process between leaders and subordinates can highly influence the group performance and morale. Bass considers the leader–follower interactive effects from the perspective of an effective transactional leader who acts as a source of feedback, as communicator, as a model and a source of influence (Bass 1974: 339). He also explores how subordinates use effective tactics to influence and gain feedback and how transactional leadership mutually influences both leaders and followers. Building on Bass's work, George Grean and his associates (1977) studied how a more positive exchange between leader and follower characterized as a true partnership with a large degree of freedom for the subordinate generates higher subordinate satisfaction, reduced turnover and produced greater identification with the organization (Grean *et al.* 1977).

The style of a transactional leader is creating clear structures, expectations and rewards. Whereas transformational leadership has more of a 'selling' style, transactional leadership, once the contract is in place, takes a 'telling' style. The Multifactor Leadership Questionnaire (MLQ) developed by Bass is the most commonly used instrument to assess an individual's transformational, transactional and laissez-faire leadership styles (Avolio *et al.* 1999; Bass and Avolio 1990). Although individual leaders exhibit tendencies toward transactional or transformational leadership styles, most leaders show characteristics of both styles. While transformational leadership motivates subordinates through a shared vision and **responsibility**, transactional leadership motivates followers by appealing to their self-interests. Its principles are to motivate by the exchange process.

The limits of transactional leadership hinge on the behaviourist assumption that a 'rational person' is largely motivated by money and simple rewards, and hence his behaviour is predictable. In practice this assumption often ignores complex emotional factors and social values present in work environments and interpersonal relationships. For example, transactional leadership may operate successfully in a work environment where leaders' and workers' personalities are compatible, but it could result in conflict between task-oriented and person-oriented personalities. Transactional leadership works well in a supply-and-demand situation of much employment, coupled with the effects of deeper needs, but it may be insufficient when the demand for a skill outstrips the supply. Transactional leadership behaviour is used to one degree or another by most leaders. However, it can be quite limiting if it is the only leadership style used. As the old saying goes, 'if the only tool in your workbox is a hammer . . . you will perceive every problem as a nail'. Today, most leaders would agree that material rewards and fear of punishment may not be the best approach to motivate their workers. Because transactional leadership encourages specific exchanges and a close connection between goals and rewards, workers are not motivated to give anything beyond what is clearly specified in their contract.

See also: **behavioural theories of leadership, effectiveness, leader–follower relations, transformational leadership**

Further reading: Avolio and Bass 2001; Burns 1978, 2003; Northouse 2004

TRANSFORMATIONAL LEADERSHIP

Terry L. Price

James MacGregor Burns's (1978) book *Leadership* is generally considered to be the seminal text in the field of leadership studies. The book's central accomplishment is the articulation of a normative conception of leadership, what Burns calls transforming leadership.

Transforming leadership is normative in the sense that it does not simply describe how leaders do in fact behave but, rather, prescribes how they ought to behave. Burns claims that leaders must do more than cater to whatever wants and desires people happen to have. Transforming leadership thus aims to move beyond people's wants and desires, thereby engaging their real needs and values. As he puts it, '[T]he ultimate test of moral leadership is its capacity to transcend the claims of the multiplicity of everyday wants and needs and expectations' (1978: 46). By raising both leaders and **followers** 'to higher levels of motivation and morality' (1978: 20), transforming leadership, Burns thinks, passes this test.

Transforming leadership is introduced as an alternative to much more common, transactional varieties of leadership. (See the entry on **transactional leadership** for a fuller discussion.) Burns characterizes transactional leadership in terms of the notion of exchange:

> Such leadership occurs when one person takes the initiative in making contact with others for the purpose of an exchange of valued things. The exchange could be economic or political or psychological in nature: a swap of goods or of one good for money; a trading of votes between candidate and citizen or between legislators; hospitality to another person in exchange for willingness to listen to one's troubles.
>
> (Burns 1978: 19)

The morality associated with transactional leadership is thus the **ethics** of choice and individualism that characterizes the market and contemporary politics. Actors are held accountable for the means they use to achieve their ends, but not necessarily for the ends of profit or **power** at which they aim.

Burns's analysis of this form of leadership points to two distinct moral weaknesses (Hicks and Price 1999). First, particular instances of transactional leadership are motivated simply by people's wants and desires. This form of leadership uncritically responds our preferences, that is, even when they are grounded in base motivations or an underdeveloped moral sense. Yet the mere fact that a person has a want or a desire does not generate the kind of moral **authority** necessary for a normative conception of leadership. Second, transactional leadership fails to foster and maintain genuine relationships between people. The interactions of the marketplace or the voting booth are fleeting, disjointed and generally impersonal. The exchanges that characterize this form of leadership thus fail to '[bind] leader and follower together in [the] mutual and continuing pursuit of a higher purpose' (1978: 20) to which leadership should aspire. To use Burns's terms, transactional leadership is preoccupied with modal values (the value of the means) to the neglect of end-values (the value of the ends).

According to Burns, then, good leadership implies a moral **responsibility** to respond to people's needs and values in a way that is conducive to the highest forms of human relations. How does transforming leadership move beyond potentially suspect motivational and moral states to discharge its moral responsibility? With respect to **motivation**, Burns appeals directly to Abraham Maslow's (1954) hierarchy of needs. Transforming leadership transcends satisfaction of basic physiological and security needs to meet 'higher' needs for belonging and esteem. With respect to morality, Burns draws on the work of Lawrence Kohlberg (1981, 1984) and suggests that transforming leaders promote real moral maturity. Self-interest and blind obedience to authority, which characterize Kohlberg's preconventional and conventional stages of moral development, give way to respect for universal moral principles, the defining feature of his postconventional stages of moral development. In short, morally responsible leadership transforms individuals to make their good consistent with the good of the group.

The collectivist nature of transforming leadership has been the target of serious criticism (Hicks and Price 1999). One such criticism holds that this form of leadership fails to show sufficient respect for the existing motivational and moral states of individual followers. In particular, critics claim that transformational leadership ignores the moral importance of follower dissent. Some followers, that is, will remain unmoved by the merits of particular end-values or the 'higher' motivational and moral states that Burns endorses. As Michael Keeley poses the question: 'If not all social participants have the same goals, if transformational leaders are not able to persuade everyone to voluntarily accept a common vision, what is the likely status of people who prefer their own goals and visions?' (1995: 77). Keeley foresees a tyranny of the majority, suggesting that 'unless leaders are able to transform *everyone* and create absolute unanimity of interests (a very special case), transformational leadership produces simply a majority will that represents the interests of the strongest faction' (1995: 77). Defenders of transforming leadership argue that we can draw upon its rich resources to respond to this sort of critique. J. Thomas Wren, for example, holds that the strength of transforming leadership is precisely in its allegiance to 'the supremacy of follower interests', a commitment that encourages leaders to find 'a common interest among relevant stakeholders' (1998: 163–4).

In organizational contexts, Bernard Bass (Bass 1985; Bass and Riggio 2006) is the chief advocate of transformational leadership. Bass's empirical work uses the Multifactor Leadership Questionnaire to identify four components of transformational leadership: idealized **influence (charisma)**, inspirational motivation, intellectual stimulation and individualized consideration (Yukl 2002). To critics such as Michael Carey, who charges that when 'the gifts of charisma, inspiration, consideration and intellectual strength are abused for the self-interest of the leader, the effect on followers ceases to be liberating and moral, and becomes instead oppressive and ideological' (1992: 232), Bass defends the ethics of this form of leadership by pointing to the altruism associated with it. Bass and Steidlmeier (1999) respond that leadership is truly transformational only if it is focused on the interests of followers, not on a leader's self-interest. Here, Bass and Steidlmeier distinguish between authentic transformational leadership and pseudo-transformational leadership. Authentic transformational leaders are committed to altruistic values and, moreover, conform their behaviour to these values, whereas pseudo-transformational leaders are engaged in the pursuit of self-interest. Following Aristotle (1985), we might say that some pseudo-transformational leaders are incontinent and that others are simply base. Incontinent pseudo-transformational leaders may have commitments to altruistic values, but they fail to conform their behaviour to these values. Base pseudo-transformational leaders simply lack a commitment to altruistic values. Their values are the values of egoism and self-interest (Price 2003).

Unfortunately, the distinction between authentic and pseudo-transformational leadership does not dispense with its ethical problems. First, the distinction fails to show that transformational leadership cannot be unethical. In fact, by differentiating between ethical and unethical varieties of transformational leadership, it shows just the opposite. Calling leadership inauthentic, then, does not negate the claim that it is transformational. In this context, to say that leadership is inauthentic simply means that it is unethical. Moral authenticity is not necessary for the conceptual authenticity of transformational leadership, unless we assume that morality is itself part of the concept of transformational leadership. Defenders of transformational leadership cannot make this assumption because so doing begs the question. In other words, since critics of transformational leadership contend that this form of leadership can be unethical, its defenders cannot simply assert – as a matter of definition – that transformational leadership must be ethical after all.

Second, not even the notion of authentic transformational leadership is immune to moral objection (Price 2003). Leadership can be unethical, despite the fact that it is altruistic. In the pursuit of group interests, altruistic leaders sometimes make moral exceptions of themselves and exclude members of other groups. Another way to put this point is to say that they sometimes sacrifice modal values in pursuit of end-values. In these cases, the authentic transformational leader makes an exception of himself – albeit for the interests of group members, not for his self-interest. Yet the altruism that characterizes this leader's behaviour is hardly sufficient to meet the demands of morality. Noble ends, that is, do not release leaders from all moral restrictions on means. In other cases, the authentic transformational leader fails to extend the protections of morality to the members of other groups – albeit for the interests of the members in the leader's group. But, again, morality demands more than altruism. The good of a leader's group can compete with the legitimate good of other groups just as it can compete with moral restrictions on means (Price 2006).

Vocal opposition to transformational leadership is evidence not of its intellectual defeat but, rather, of the paramount place of this form of leadership within leadership studies. No normative conception of leadership comes close to transformational leadership in terms of conceptual sophistication and empirical analysis. Moreover, its influence extends across leadership contexts: politics, business and nonprofits. The importance that scholars of transformational leadership such as Burns and Bass consistently attach to morality and values is also a large part of the explanation of the centrality of leadership ethics within the field of leadership studies.

See also: **ethics**, **leader–follower relations**, **motivation**, **strategic visioning**, **transactional leadership**

Further reading: Bass 1985; Bass and Riggio 2006; Bass and Steidlmeier 1999; Burns 1978, 2003

TRUST

Jon Aarum Andersen

The importance of trust related to human actions is generally acknowledged. Organizations are confronted by rapid changes that imply uncertainty for people at work. Uncertainty about the future makes trust important. However, there is no agreement on how to define it. Some definitions are widely used. Rotter defines trust as 'a generalized expectancy held by any individual or group that the word, promise, verbal, or written statement of another individual or group can be relied on' (1971: 444). Rotter sees trust as a relatively stable personality characteristic, while social psychologists view trust as an expectation that is specific to a transaction and the person with whom one is transacting. Sabel defines trust as 'the mutual confidence that no party in the relationship will exploit the vulnerability of the others' (1993: 1133). Gambetta defines trust as 'a specific level of subjective probability that an agent or group will do a specific action before he (she) can monitor such an act . . . and in a situation where this action influences his own action' (1988: 217).

Bhattacharya *et al.* (1998) conclude that trust is a multidimensional concept. It is impossible to think that individuals have innate levels of trust which are independent of the environment, the actions of one another, the nature of outcomes and the consequences of those outcomes to specific individuals. Trust is not a clearly defined attribute of an individual's behaviour, as it is not only dependent on actions but also on outcomes and consequences. Nonetheless, mechanisms for controlling behaviour and inducing trust tend to be defined around the trust which one individual has for another, regardless of the trustworthiness of 'the system'.

Dunn (1988) and McAllister (1995) argue that there are two distinct concepts of trust. One is based on calculative decisions (judgements of the other parties' competence and reliability); the other is based on emotions (affective bonds between individuals). Work on trust can be divided into four main groups: (1) trust as an individual attribute, (2) trust as behaviour, (3) trust as a situational feature and (4) trust as an institutional arrangement (Sitkin and Roth 1993). Lewicki and Bunker (1995) studied how trust was *perceived*: as an individual characteristic, as a characteristic of interpersonal transactions or as an institutional phenomenon. Bigley and Pearce (1998) classify the theoretical contribution to trust in relation to the problem being addressed: (1) interaction between unknown actors, (2) interaction between known actors within ongoing relationships, and (3) organization of economic transactions. Some aspects seem to capture the essence of the trust concept. These are: risk, knowledge, vulnerability and uncertainty and **ethics**.

Risk: Several researchers agree that the concept of risk is vital to the understanding of trust. Giddens (1990) writes that trust requires consciousness about risky circumstances. Trust relations are those in which the risk that one party takes is dependent on the actions of another person (Coleman 1990). Sheppard and Sherman (1998) claim that risk is the core in actions and how humans ought to think about trust. Much research on trustworthiness has focused on the characteristics of others that are likely to mitigate the risks present in relationships.

Knowledge: Trust concerns expectations that may come to nothing. According to Luhmann (1988), trust exists when the individual is conscious of the various alternatives when he or she decides upon a specific course of action. Giddens (1990) says that the basic condition for trust is lack of complete information. Trust is related to events that have not happened yet. It has to do with circumstances that we do not have any direct knowledge about. Rotter (1980) sees trust as a disposition that would be most predictive in situations where individuals are relatively unknown to each other. Gambetta (1988), however, perceives trust as a calculated decision to cooperate with other specific people, based on information about the personal qualities and social constraints of those people.

Vulnerability and uncertainty: Trust and distrust have almost always been associated with the idea of actor vulnerability (Bigley and Pearce 1998; Sennett 1998). Gambetta (1988) claims that for trust to be relevant, there must be a possibility for exit, deceit and defection. Trust is present in situations characterized by uncertainty. Trust cannot exist without some possibility of error to occur.

Ethics: Trust and ethics need to be built together (Wood *et al.* 2002). Trust demands high ethical standards, and is an ethical construct. O'Neill (2002) defines ethics related to trust as the lack of deception, which is a major moral failure. Deceivers do not treat others as moral equals; they exempt themselves from obligations that they rely on others to live up to. Trust is a condition for interaction between morally autonomous individuals (Seligman 1997). Since trust has to be placed without guarantees, it is inevitably sometimes misplaced: others let us down and we let others down (O'Neill 2002). Trust is partly a product of one's own capability to judge the reliability of a potential partner (Sheppard and Sherman 1998).

Trust emerges under circumstances of risk and uncertainty, lack of knowledge and information, vulnerability and ethical consideration: it is a vital reserve under such circumstances. Research appears to support the distinction between the rational and emotional bases for trust (e.g. McAllister 1995).

The literature on trust and control in organizations has largely focused on managers. Some scholars present trust and control as a constant sum. Handy (1977) considers trust in subordinates and control over their work on the part of the manager in this way. Managers thus face a 'trust–control' dilemma. When the managers' trust in their subordinates reduces, they must increase their supervision and control (Casson 1991). The idea of role associated with a position provides the link to the leader–subordinate relationship (Seligman 1997). Bonds of trust develop informally as people learn on whom they can depend (Sennett 1998). Positive events tend to be attributed to the individuals one trusts, while negative events are linked to distrusted persons.

If subordinates trust their managers, the attribution of motives will be positive (Kramer 1996). If the subordinates feel that they are treated with respect, dignity and in a fair way, they tend to see their managers as worthy of their trust. The trust vested in managers by their subordinates depends upon the ability to judge the trustworthiness of the managers. A condition for the creation of trust is that the relevant behaviour is predictable, transparent and readily interpreted (Bass 1990a; Yukl 2002). Andersen (2005) found that: (1) managers enjoy different degrees of trust, (2) trust is induced through actions and (3) trust relations require knowledge about each other and about the organization. Trust in managers differs between the closest subordinates and other employees.

Definitions are needed when trust is to be measured empirically. Rotter's (1967) instrument aims at measuring the concept of trust and not what causes it. The Organisational Trust Inventory (OTI) aims at measuring the degree of trust between departments or between organizations (Cummings and Bromiley 1996) as does the questionnaire developed by Luo (2002). Andersen (2005) applied a questionnaire to measure the degree of trust in managers and the causes for subordinates' trust.

Trust is important and useful in a range of organizational activities (Mayer et al. 1995; Morris and Moberg 1994). It is co-related to good (non-negative) outcomes, and appears to be a crucial component of leadership. Without trust, it may be difficult to communicate a vision to subordinates or to maintain cohesion when visions, objectives, threats and opportunities are unclear. Rotter (1967) claims that the **effectiveness** of our organizations to a large extent depends on people in organizations being prepared to trust others. The higher the level of trust, the easier employees accept decisions made by managers (Creed and Miles 1996; Tyler and Degoey 1996). Trust can explain the outcome of many organizational activities, such as leadership, ethical behaviour, teamwork, goal setting, performance appraisal, development of labour relations and negotiations. Conditions leading to changes in organizations increase the importance of trust because organizational performance and the wellbeing of the employees are affected in a positive way (Mishra 1996; Schein 1985; Gilkey 1991).

See also: **change and continuity**, **ethics**, **group dynamics**, **leader–follower relations**, **strategic visioning**

Further reading: Andersen 2005; Bhattacharya *et al.* 1998; Gambetta 1988; Giddens 1990; Kramer and Tyler 1996

WISDOM

Tim Harle

Where shall wisdom be found? Not, it would appear, in the typical management school syllabus (Dunphy and Pitsis 2003: 170) or many books on knowledge management (Lloyd 2005). However, there are signs of renewed interest. Sternberg (1990) promoted a broad-ranging study of wisdom and it can now attract the epithet 'pragmatic' (Baltes and Staudinger 2000). Wisdom has been identified as a possible source of competitive advantage (Bierly *et al.* 2000) and canvassed as a leadership competence (Harle 2005). In the popular literature, the 15 years between the publication of Stephen Covey's *Seven Habits* and his *Eighth Habit* (Covey 1989, 2004) saw a 10-fold growth of index entries for 'wisdom' – from two to 20.

Wisdom's elusive nature is reflected in attempts at definition. Describing it as 'the traditional goal of philosophy', a standard reference work considers it to be 'some amalgam of knowledge, spiritual profundity, Stoical ability to put up with the evils of the world, and practical ability' (Blackburn 2005: 389). This last aspect is seen in the classical tradition, where Aristotle distinguished *phronesis*, practical wisdom, from *sophia*, or more theoretical aspects. In the leadership literature, *phronesis* has long featured in the writings of Adair (e.g. Adair 2002: 73).

The Greeks had no monopoly on wisdom. A non-exhaustive list of influential traditions might note the contributions from China (e.g. Lao-Tzu, founder of Taoism), from India (the Vedas, various schools of Buddhism, Hinduism), from the Ancient Near East (whose wisdom literature provides our opening question (Job 28.12)), from a number of indigenous communities (e.g. Warner and Grint 2006) and from the perspective of gender (Boyle and Roan 2005).

At the risk of gross oversimplification, the main strands may be referred to as Eastern and Western. Some see differences between these thought forms (Takahashi and Bordia 2000), while others have called for a more nuanced understanding (Case and Gosling 2007; McKenna and Rooney 2004). Perhaps we see here a legacy of dualism: contemporary authors look beyond an either/or mindset to hold different contributions in tension. In twentieth-century management literature, Taylorism left little room for wisdom: praxis and rationalism stood in contrast to humanistic, even spiritual, approaches.

In a postmodern context, growing awareness of cultures other than the dominant Western model encouraged exploration. Thus Case and Gosling (2007) explore how, in a postmodern age, the contributions of a premodern era can speak wisely. Regretting the exclusion of non-rational concepts, they find less of a distinction between practical and theoretical aspects of wisdom. With McKenna and Rooney (2004), they call for wisdom to find a place in business education. The possible topics for such a curriculum provide a useful framework for considering wisdom's place in contemporary leadership discourse.

First, the relation of wisdom to knowledge. Lloyd (2005) rightly points out that the link is more elusive than the next step in a data–information–knowledge **hierarchy**. Referring to cultural legacies from the Greeks to Zen Buddhism, Nonaka and Takeuchi (1995) highlighted the difference between explicit and tacit knowledge. They located the success of Japanese companies in their ability to process the latter, while Western organizations concentrated on the former. Emphasizing the importance of a dynamic approach, they drew attention to the need to socialize knowledge. This leads to the next consideration.

Wisdom is often at its most powerful in a community. Jewish wisdom literature stems from communities; native traditions often note the importance of elders and the power of story in transmitting the tradition. Research indicates that individuals are weak carriers of wisdom (Baltes and Staudinger 2000: 130f.). The links with learning organizations are suggestive: team learning was at the apex of Senge's model (Senge 1990: 233–69). The importance of the collective for learning has been noted by Grint (2005), where 'inverse learning' forms a powerful challenge to traditional ideas about training for leadership: 'the follower is teacher to the leader' (2005: 105). The dyadic relation between leaders and those around them provides the next theme.

Wisdom involves a degree of self-understanding. Best known through the Delphic maxim, know thyself, both classical Greek and contemporary spiritual approaches emphasize the importance of **self-awareness**. Sternberg's research indicates that wise people 'know what they do not know' (1990: 157): a challenge to leaders who demonstrate a degree of honest vulnerability where omniscience is so often an unwritten prerequisite. If writings on **emotional intelligence** (e.g. Goleman *et al.* 2002) seek to understand relationships with others, advocates of spiritual intelligence seek a new understanding of self which 'leads from reflection, through understanding, to wisdom' (Zohar and Marshall 2000: 244). Meanwhile, Brown (2005: 72–104) has written of 'relational wholeness' in the context of interpersonal integrity.

This leads to a concluding application which ties many of the strands around wisdom together: **ethics**, where values and practice meet. Sternberg's Balance Theory of Wisdom emphasizes the importance of virtue, or behaviour which is valued socially, although Baltes and Staudinger (2000) note the absence of empirical evidence relating wisdom and behaviour. Robertson emphasizes the importance of consistency: indeed, his 'maturity-in-complexity' (2005: 74–89) provides a suggestive contemporary rephrasing of what is summed up by wisdom.

See also: **emotional intelligence, empowerment, leadership development, philosophical approaches to leadership, self-awareness**

Further reading: Baltes and Staudinger 2000; Case and Gosling 2007; Dunphy and Pitsis 2003; Goldberg 2005; Sternberg and Jordan 2005

Note

1 In twenty-first century speeches and reports the 'cold war' threat seems to have been replaced by the 'globalisation' threat (cf. the Cox report). The core arguments seem eerily analogous.

BIBLIOGRAPHY

Abell, D.F. (2006) 'The Future of Strategy is Leadership', *Journal of Business Research*, 59, 310–14.

Adair, J. (1989) *Great Leaders*, Talbot Adair Press, Guildford.

—— (2001) *The Leadership of Jesus and its Legacy Today*, Canterbury Press, Norwich.

—— (2002) *Effective Strategic Leadership*, Macmillan, London.

—— (2005) *How to Grow Leaders*, Kogan Page, London.

Adams, J.S. (1963) 'Toward an Understanding of Inequity', *Journal of Abnormal Social Psychology*, 67, 422–36.

Adorno, T., Frenkel-Brunswik, E., Levinson, J. and Sanford, R.N. (1964) *The Authoritarian Personality*, John Wiley & Sons, New York.

Albert, S. and Whetten, D. (1985) 'Organizational Identity', *Research in Organizational Behavior*, 7, 263–95.

Allen, S. J. (2006) 'An Exploration of Theories of Action in Leadership Development: A Case Study', *Dissertation Abstracts International*.

Alvesson, M. and Berg, P.O. (1992) *Corporate Culture and Organisational Symbolism*, Walter de Gruyter, Berlin.

Alvesson, M. and Willmott, H. (2002) 'Producing the Appropriate Individual: Identity Regulation as Organizational Control', *Journal of Management Studies*, 39, 619–44.

Anand, V., Ashforth, B. and Joshi, M. (2004) 'Business as Usual: the Acceptance and Perpetuation of Corruption in Organizations', *Academy of Management Executive*, 19, 9–23.

Anastasi, A. and Urbina, S. (1997) *Psychological Testing*, 7th international edn, Prentice Hall, Upper Saddle River, NJ.

Andersen, J.A. (2000) 'Leadership and Leadership Research', in D.F. Dahiya (ed.), *Current Issues in Business Disciplines, Vol. 5: Management II*, Spellbound Publications, New Delhi, pp. 2267–87.

—— (2005) 'Trust in Managers: A Study of Why Swedish Subordinates Trust Their Managers', *Business Ethics – A European Review*, 14, 392–404.

—— (2006) 'Leadership, Personality and Effectiveness', *Journal of Socio-Economics*, 35, 1078–91.

Antonakis, J., Avolio, B.J. and Sivasubramaniam, N. (2003) 'Context and Leadership: An Examination of the Nine-factor Full-range Leadership Theory Using Multifactor Leadership Questionnaire (MLQ Form 5X)', *Leadership Quarterly*, 14, 261–95.

Argyris, C. (1999) *On Organizational Learning*, Blackwell, London.

Argyris, C. and Schön, D.A. (1978) *Organizational Learning: A Theory of Action Perspective*, Addison-Wesley, Boston, MA.

Aristotle (1946) *The Politics of Aristotle*, trans. E. Barker, Clarendon Press, Oxford.

—— (1952) *The Works of Aristotle*, vol. 1, Encyclopedia Britannica, Chicago. Reprinted for *Great Books of the Western World*, ed. W.D. Ross, *The Works of Aristotle*, by arrangement with Oxford University Press.

—— (1981) *Politics*, trans. T.A. Sinclair, rev. and re-presented by T.J. Saunders, Penguin Books, New York.

—— (1985) *Nicomachean Ethics*, trans. T. Irwin, Hackett Publishing Company, Indianapolis, IN.

Arnstein, S.R. (1969) 'A Ladder of Citizen Participation', *Journal of American Institute of Planners*, 35, 26–34.

Arvonen, J. (2002) *Change, Production and Employees: An Integrated Model of Leadership*, Department of Psychology, Stockholm University, Stockholm.

Ashforth, B. and Mael, F. (1989) 'Social Identity Theory and the Organization', *Academy of Management Review*, 14, 20–39.

Austin, R. and Devin, L. (2003) *Artful Making: What Managers Need to Know about How Artists Work*, Pearson, Upper Saddle River, NJ.

Autry, J. (2001) *The Servant Leader*, Prima, Roseville, CA.

Avolio, B.J. (1999) *Full Leadership Development*, Sage, Thousand Oaks, CA.

—— (2004) 'Examining the Full Range Model of Leadership: Looking Back to Transform Forward', in D. Day, S. Zaccaro and S. Halpin (eds), *Leader Development for Transforming Organizations: Growing Leaders for Tomorrow*, Lawrence Erlbaum Associates, Mahwah, NJ, pp. 71–98.

—— (2005) *Leadership Development in Balance*, Lawrence Erlbaum Associates, Mahwah, NJ.

Avolio, B.J. and Bass, B.M. (eds) (2001) *Developing Potential Across a Full Range of Leadership TM: Cases on Transactional and Transformational Leadership*, Lawrence Erlbaum Associates, Mahwah, NJ.

Avolio, B.J. and Gardner, W. (2005) 'Authentic Leadership Development: Getting to the Root of Positive Forms of Leadership', *The Leadership Quarterly*, 16, 315–38.

Avolio, B.J., Yammarino, F.J. and Bass, B.M. (1991) 'Identifying Common Methods Variance with Data Collected from a Single Source: An Unresolved Sticky Issue', *Journal of Management*, 17, 571–87.

Avolio, B.J., Bass, B.M. and Jung, D.I. (1999) 'Re-examining the Components of Transformational and Transactional Leadership using the Multifactor Leadership Questionnaire', *Journal of Occupational and Organizational Psychology*, 72, 441–62.

Avolio, B.J., Sosik, J.J., Jung, D.I. and Berson, Y. (2003) 'Leadership Models, Methods, and Applications', in W.C. Borman, D.R. Ilgen, R.J. Klimoski and I.B. Weiner (eds), *Handbook of Psychology: Industrial and Organizational Psychology*, vol. 12, Wiley, New York, pp. 277–307.

Babbie, E.R. (1990) *Survey Research Methods*, 2nd edn, Wadsworth, Belmont, CA.

Babiak, P. (1995) 'When Psychopaths go to Work: A Case Study of an Industrial Psychopath', *Applied Psychology: An International Review*, 44, 171–88.

—— (1996) 'Psychopathic Manipulation in Organizations: Pawns, Patrons and Patsies', in D.J. Cooke, A.E. Forth, J.P. Newman and R.D. Hare (eds), *Issues in Criminological and Legal Psychology: No. 24, International Perspective on Psychopathy*, British Psychological Society, Leicester, pp. 12–17.

Babiak, P. and Hare, R. (2006) *Snakes in Suits*, Regan Books, New York.

Badaracco, J.L. Jr (2001) 'We Don't Need Another Hero', *Harvard Business Review*, 79, 120–26.

—— (2002a) *Leading Quietly: An Unorthodox Guide to Doing the Right Thing*, Harvard Business School Press, Boston, MA.

—— (2002b) 'The Quiet Leader – and How to Be One', *Harvard Business School: Working Knowledge Newsletter*, 11 February.

—— (2004) 'Beyond Heroic Moral Leadership', *Conversations on Leadership of the Center for Public Leadership*, Harvard College Publications, Boston, MA.

Baltes, P. and Staudinger, U. (2000) 'A Metaheuristic (Pragmatic) to Orchestrate Mind and Virtue Towards Excellence', *American Psychologist*, 55, 122–36.

Barbuto, J. and Wheeler, D. (2006) 'Scale Development and Construct Clarification of Servant Leadership', *Group and Organization Management*, 31, 300–26.

Barker, R. (2001) 'The Nature of Leadership', *Human Relations*, 54, 469–94.

—— (2002) *On the Nature of Leadership*, University Press of America, Lanham, MD.

Barnett, R.E. (1998) *The Structure of Liberty: Justice and the Rule of Law*, Oxford University Press, Oxford.

Bar-On, R. (1997) *Bar-On Emotional Quotient Inventory (EQ-i): Technical Manual*, Multi-Health Systems, Toronto.

Bar-On, R. and Parker, J.D.A. (eds) (2000) *The Handbook of Emotional Intelligence: Theory, Development, Assessment and Application at Home, School, and in the Workplace*, Jossey-Bass, San Francisco, CA.

Barrett, F. (2000) 'Cultivating an Aesthetic of Unfolding', in S. Linstead and H. Hopfl (eds), *The Aesthetics of Organization*, Sage, London, pp. 228–45.

Barry, D. (1997) 'Telling Changes: From Narrative Family Therapy to Organizational Change and Development', *Journal of Organizational Change Management*, 10, 30–46.

Bass, B.M. (1960) *Leadership, Psychology and Organizational Behaviour*, Harper, New York.

—— (1974) *Bass and Stogdill's Handbook of Leadership: Theory, Research and Managerial Applications*, The Free Press, New York.

—— (1985) *Leadership and Performance Beyond Expectations*, Free Press, New York.

—— (1988) 'Evolving Perspectives on Charismatic Leadership', in J.A. Conger and R.N. Kanungo (eds), *Charismatic Leadership. The Elusive Factor in Organizational Effectiveness*, Jossey-Bass, San Francisco, pp. 40–77.

—— (1990a) 'From Transactional to Transformational Leadership: Learning to Share the Vision', *Organizational Dynamics*, 18, 19–31.

—— (1990b) *Bass & Stogdill's Handbook of Leadership: Theory, Research and Managerial Applications*, 3rd edn, The Free Press, New York.

—— (1998) *Transformational Leadership: Industrial, Military, and Educational Impact*, Lawrence Erlbaum Associates, Mahwah, NJ.

—— (2000) 'The Future of Leadership in Learning Organizations', *Journal of Leadership Studies*, 7, 18–40.

Bass, B.M. and Avolio, B.J. (1990) *Multifactor Leadership Questionnaire*, Consulting Psychologist Press, Palo Alto, CA.

—— (1993) 'Transformational Leadership and Organizational Culture', *Public Administration Quarterly*, 17, 112–22.

—— (1994) *Improving Organizational Effectiveness Through Transformational Leadership*, Sage Publications, Thousand Oaks, CA.

Bass, B.M. and Steidlmeier, P. (1999) 'Ethics, Character, and Authentic Transformational Leadership Behavior', *Leadership Quarterly*, 10, 181–217.

Bass, B.M. and Riggio, R.E. (2006) *Transformational Leadership*, 2nd edn, Lawrence Erlbaum, Mahwah, NJ.

Baum, J., Locke, E. and Kirkpatrick, S. (1998) 'A Longitudinal Study of the Relation of Vision and Vision Communication to Venture Growth in Entrepreneurial Firms', *Journal of Applied Psychology*, 83, 43–54.

Baumeister, R.F., Chesner, S.P., Senders, P.S. and Tice, D.M. (1988) 'Who's in Charge Here? Group Leaders do Lend Help in Emergencies', *Personality and Social Psychology Bulletin*, 14, 17–22.

Beazley, H. (forthcoming) *Servant-leadership in Corporate America*, John Wiley & Sons, New York.

Beazley, H., Beggs, J. and Spears, L. (2003) *The Servant Leader Within: A Transformative Path*, Paulist Press, Mahwah, NJ.

Beer, M. and Eisenstat, R. (2000) 'The Silent Killers of Strategy Implementation and Learning', *Sloan Management Review*, 41, 29–41.

Bell, D. (1979) *Power, Influence, and Authority*, Oxford University Press, New York.

Bendell, J. (2002) 'Psychos in Suits', *Open Democracy*. Available at www.opende mocracy.net/themes/article-6-260.jsp

Benjamin, J. (1990) *Psychoanalysis, Feminism and the Problem of Domination*, Virago, London.

—— (2004) 'Beyond Doer and Done To: An Intersubjective View of Thirdness', *Psychoanalytic Quarterly*, LXXIII, 5–46.

Bennett, N., Wise, C., Woods, P. and Harvey, J. (2003) *Distributed Leadership*, National College for School Leadership, Nottingham. Also published as Woods *et al.* (2004) 'Variabilities and Dualities in Distributed Leadership', *Educational Management, Administration and Leadership*, 32, 439–57.

Bennis, W.G. and Nanus, B. (1985) *Leaders: the Strategies for Taking Charge*, Harper & Row, New York.

Bentley, E. (1944) *A Century of Hero-worship: A Study of the Idea of Heroism in Carlyle and Nietzsche, with Notes on Wagner, Spengler, Stefan George, and D.H. Lawrence*, 2nd edn, Beacon Press, Boston, MA.

Berger, J. and Zelditch, M., Jr (1998) *Status, Power, and Legitimacy: Strategies and Theories*, Transaction, New Brunswick, NJ.

Bergson, H. (1912) *An Introduction to Metaphysics*, T.E. Hulme (trans.) and T.A. Goudge (intro.), Hackett, Indianapolis, IN.

—— (1983) *Creative Evolution*, A. Mitchell (trans.), University Press of America, Lanham, MD.

Berlin, I. (1994) 'The Romantic Revolution: A Crisis in the History of Modern Thought', in *The Sense of Reality*, Farrar, Straus and Giroux, New York, pp. 168–93.

Bernstein, A. (2001) *Emotional Vampires: Dealing with People who Drain you Dry*, McGraw-Hill, New York.

Bhattacharya, R., Devinney, T.M. and Pillutla, M.M. (1998) 'A Formal Model of Trust Based on Outcomes', *Academy of Management Review*, 23, 459–72.

Bierly, P., Kessler, E. and Christensen, E. (2000) 'Organizational Learning, Knowledge and Wisdom', *Journal of Organizational Change Management*, 13, 595–618.

Bigley, G.A. and Pearce, J.L. (1998) 'Straining for Shared Meaning in Organisation Science: Problems of Trust and Distrust', *Academy of Management Review*, 23, 405–21.

Bills, T. and Genasi, C. (2003) *Creative Business: Achieving Your Goals Through Creative Thinking and Action*, Palgrave, London.

Bilton, C. (2007) *Management and Creativity: From Creative Industries to Creative Management*, Blackwell, Oxford.

Bion, W.R. (1961) *Experiences in Groups*, Tavistock, London.

Blackburn, S. (2005) *Oxford Dictionary of Philosophy*, 2nd edn, Oxford University Press, Oxford.

Blake, R.R. and Mouton, J.S. (1964) *The Managerial Grid*, Gulf, Houston, TX.

—— (1969) *Building a Dynamic Corporation Through Grid Organizational Development*, Addison-Wesley, Reading, MA.

—— (1978) *The New Managerial Grid*, Gulf, Houston, TX.

—— (1985) *The Managerial Grid III*, Gulf, Houston, TX.

Blake, R.R. and McCanse, A.A. (1991) *Leadership Dilemmas – Grid Solutions*, Gulf, Houston, TX.

Blanchard, K.H. and Hersey, P. (1996) 'Great Ideas Revisited', *Training and Development*, 50, 2–47.

Blanchard, K.H., Carlos, J.P. and Randolph, A. (2001) *The 3 Keys to Empowerment: Release the Power within People for Astonishing Results*, Berrett-Koehler, San Francisco, CA.

Blank, W., Weitzel, J.R. and Green, S.G. (1990) 'A Test of the Situational Leadership Theory', *Personnel Psychology*, 43, 579–97.

Block, P. (1996) *Stewardship: Choosing Service Over Self-Interest*, Berrett-Koehler, San Francisco, CA.

Boal, K. and Hooijberg, R. (2001) 'Strategic Leadership Research: Moving On', *Leadership Quarterly*, 11, 515–49.

Bolden, R. (ed.) (2006) *Leadership Development in Context*. Leadership South West Research Report, Centre for Leadership Studies, University of Exeter. Available at www.centres.ex.ac.uk/cls/lsw/lswreports.php, accessed 3/8/2007.

Bolman, L. and Deal, T. (1991) *Reframing Organizations: Artistry, Choice, and Leadership*, Jossey-Bass, San Francisco, CA.

Bookman, A. and Morgen, S. (eds) (1988) *Women and the Politics of Empowerment*, Temple University Press, Philadelphia, PA.

Bowers, D.G. and Seashore, S.E. (1966) 'Predicting Organizational Effectiveness with a Four-Factor Theory of Leadership', *Administrative Science Quarterly*, 11, 238–63.

Boyatzis, R.E. (1982) *The Competent Manager*, John Wiley, New York.

Boyle, M. and Roan, A. (2005) 'Too Wise or Too Womanly?: the Paradox of Gendered Wisdom', paper presented at 4th International Critical Management Studies Conference, Cambridge, July 2005.

Bradford, D. and Cohen, A. (1998) *Power Up*, John Wiley & Sons, New York.

Brown, M. (2005) *Corporate Integrity: Rethinking Organizational Ethics and Leadership*, Cambridge University Press, Cambridge.

Bryman, A. (1992) *Charisma and Leadership in Organizations*, Sage, London.

—— (1993) 'Charismatic Leadership in Business Organizations', *Leadership Quarterly*, 4, 289–304.

Buber, M. (1970) *I and Thou*, T. and T. Clark, Edinburgh (German orig. *Ich und Du*, 1922).

Bullen, P. (1987) 'Charismatic Political Domination'. Available at http://paul.bullen.com/BullenCharisma.html (accessed 31 January 2007).

Bungay, S. (2005) 'The Road to Mission Command: The Genesis of a Mission Command Philosophy', *The British Army Review*, 137, 22–8.

Burns, J.M. (1978) *Leadership*, Harper & Row, New York.

—— (1984) *Leadership*, Harper & Row, New York.

—— (2003) *Transforming Leadership: A New Pursuit of Happiness*, Atlantic Monthly Press, New York.

Burns, J.S. (2000) 'A River Runs Through It: A Metaphor for Teaching Leadership Theory', *The Journal of Leadership Studies*, 7, 41–55.

—— (2002) 'Chaos Theory and Leadership Studies: Exploring Uncharted Seas', *Journal of Leadership and Organizational Studies*, 9, 42–56.

Cacioppe, R. (1998) 'An Integrated Model and Approach for the Design of Effective Leadership Development Programs', *Leadership and Organization Development Journal*, 19, 44–53.

Capra, F. (1996) *The Web of Life*, Doubleday, New York.

Carey, M.R. (1992) 'Transformational Leadership and the Fundamental Option for Self-Transcendence', *Leadership Quarterly*, 3, 217–36.

Carlyle, T. (1969) *Thomas Carlyle on Heroes and Hero-Worship and the Heroic in History*, AMS Press, New York.

Carnegie, D. (1936) *How to Win Friends and Influence People*, Simon & Schuster, New York.

Carr, W. (ed.) (2002) *The New Dictionary of Pastoral Studies*, SPCK, London.

Carrette, J. and King, R. (2004) *Selling Spirituality: the Silent Takeover of Religion*, Routledge, London.

Carter, C. (1979) *Authority and Democracy*, Routledge and Kegan Paul, London.

Cary, S.G. (1955) *Speak Truth to Power: A Quaker Search for an Alternative to Violence* [Report] The American Friends Service Committee. Available at www.quaker.org/sttp.html (accessed 26 April 2006).

Case, P. (1999) 'Remember Reengineering: The Rhetorical Appeal of a Managerial Salvation Device', *Journal of Management Studies*, 36, 419–41.

Case, P. and Gosling, J. (2007) 'Wisdom of the Moment: Premodern Perspectives on Organizational Action', *Social Epistemology*, 21, 2.

Casson, M.C. (1991) *Economics of Business Culture: Game Theory, Transaction Costs and Economic Performance*, Clarendon Press, Oxford.

Cavaiola, A. and Lavender, N. (2000) *Toxic Coworkers*, New Harbinger, Oakland, CA.

CCL (1998) *The Center for Creative Leadership Handbook of Leadership Development*, C.D. McCauley and E. Van Velsor (eds), John Wiley & Sons, New York.

—— (2002) *Leadership Skills: Derailment*, Center for Creative Leadership.

CEML (2002) *Managers and Leaders: Raising Our Game*, Council for Excellence in Management and Leadership, London.

Chaleff, I. (1995) *The Courageous Follower – Standing Up To and For Our Leaders*, Berrett-Koehler, San Francisco, CA.

Chapman, J. (2003) 'Hatred and Corruption of Task', *Organisational and Social Dynamics*, 3, 40–60.

Charan, R. and Colvin, G. (1999) 'Why CEOs Fail', *Fortune*, 21 June.

Chauncey, A.A. (1967) 'What Does a Representative Represent?', *Social Work*, 21, 5–9.

Chemers, M.M. (2000) 'Leadership Research and Theory: A Functional Integration', *Group Dynamics*, 4, 27–43.

Cherniss, C. and Goleman, D. (eds) (2001) *The Emotionally Intelligent Workplace: How to Select for, Measure, and Improve Emotional Intelligence in Individuals, Groups, and Organizations*, Jossey-Bass, San Francisco, CA.

Chia, R. (1999) 'A "Rhizomic" Model of Organizational Change and Transformation: Perspectives from a Metaphysics of Change', *British Journal of Management*, 10, 209–27.

Chrislip, D. and Larson, C. (1994) *Collaborative Leadership*, Jossey-Bass, San Francisco, CA.

Christenson, D. and Walker, D.H.T. (2004) 'Understanding the Role of "Vision" in Project Success', *Project Management Journal*, 35, 39–52.

Churchill, G.A., Jr (1979) 'A Paradigm for Developing Better Measures of Marketing Constructs', *Journal of Marketing Research*, 16, 64–73.

Ciulla, J.B. (1995) 'Leadership Ethics: Mapping the Territory', *Business Ethics Quarterly*, 5, 5–24.

—— (1996) 'Leadership and the Problem of Bogus Empowerment', in *Ethics and Leadership Working Papers*, Academy of Leadership University of Maryland, College Park, MD. Available at www.academy.umd.edu/Publications/klspdocs/jciul_p1.htm (accessed 31 May 2006).

—— (2004) 'Ethics and Leadership Effectiveness', in J. Antonakis, A.T. Cianciolo and R.J. Sternberg (eds), *The Nature of Leadership*, Sage, Thousand Oaks, CA, pp. 302–27.

—— (2005) 'The State of Leadership Ethics and the Work that Lies Before Us', *Business Ethics: A European Review*, 323–35.

—— (2006) 'Ethics: The Heart of Leadership', in T. Maak and N.M. Pless (eds), *Responsible Leadership*, Routledge, Abingdon, pp. 17–32.

Clegg, S.R. (1989) *Frameworks of Power*, Sage, London.

Cleveland, H. (1985) *The Knowledge Executive*, Dutton, New York.

Coleman, J.S. (1990) *Foundations of Social Theory*, Belknap Press of Harvard University, Cambridge, MA.

Collins, J.C. and Porras, J.I. (1991) 'Organizational Vision and Visionary Organizations', *California Management Review*, 34, 30–52.

—— (1997) *Built to Last: Successful Habits of Visionary Companies*, Harper Business, New York.

Conchie, B. (2004) 'The Seven Demands of Leadership', *Gallup Management Journal*, May.

Confucius (1963) 'Selections from the Analects', in Wing-tsit Chan (ed. and trans.), *A Source Book in Chinese Philosophy*, Princeton University Press, Princeton, NJ.

Conger, J.A. (1988) 'Behavioral Dimensions of Charismatic Leadership', in J.A. Conger and R.N. Kanungo (eds), *Charismatic Leadership*, Jossey-Bass, San Francisco, CA, pp. 78–89.

—— (1989) *The Charismatic Leader: Behind the Mystique of Exceptional Leadership*, Jossey-Bass, San Francisco, CA.

—— (1990) 'The Dark Side of Leadership', *Organizational Dynamics*, 19, 44–55.

—— (1992) *Learning to Lead: The Art of Transforming Managers into Leaders*, Jossey-Bass, San Francisco, CA.

—— (1993) 'Max Weber's Conceptualization of Charismatic Authority: Its Influence on Organizational Research', *Leadership Quarterly*, 4, 277–88.

—— (1998) 'The Necessary Art of Persuasion', *Harvard Business Review*, May–June, 87–95.

Conger, J.A. and Kanungo, R.N. (1988) *Charismatic Leadership: The Elusive Factor in Organisational Effectiveness*, Jossey-Bass, San Francisco, CA.

—— (1998) *Charismatic Leadership in Organizations*, Sage, Thousand Oaks, CA.

Conger, J. and Benjamin, B. (1999) *Building Leaders: How Successful Companies Develop the Next Generation*, Jossey-Bass, San Francisco, CA.

Cooper, R.K. (1996/1997) *EQ Map*, AIT and Essi Systems, San Francisco, CA.

Couto, Richard A. (1993) 'What's Political About Self-Help?', *Social Policy*, 23, 39–43.

Covey, S. (1989) *The Seven Habits of Highly Effective People*, Simon & Schuster, London.

—— (2004) *The Eighth Habit: From Effectiveness to Greatness*, Simon & Schuster, London.

Cox, G. (2005) *The Cox Review of Creativity in Business*, HM Treasury, London. Available at www.hm-treasury.gov.uk/cox.

Creed, W.E.D. and Miles, R.E. (1996) 'Trust in Organisations: A Conceptual Framework', in R.M. Kramer and T.R. Tyler (eds), *Trust in Organisations: Frontiers of Theory and Research*, Sage, London, pp. 16–39.

Creswell, J.W. (2003) *Research Design: Qualitative, Quantitative, and Mixed Methods Approaches*, 2nd edn, Sage, Thousand Oaks, CA.

Cummings, L.L. and Bromiley, P. (1996) 'The Organisational Trust Inventory (OTI): Development and Validation', in R.M. Kramer and T.R. Tyler (eds), *Trust in Organisations: Frontiers of Theory and Research*, Sage, London, pp. 302–33.

Daft, R. (2005) *The Leadership Experience*, 3rd edn, Thompson-Southwestern Publishing, Belmont, CA.

Davies, M., Stankov, L. and Roberts, R.D. (1998) 'Emotional Intelligence: In Search of an Elusive Construct', *Journal of Personality and Social Psychology*, 75, 989–1015.

Dawis, R.V. (1987) 'Scale Construction', *Journal of Counseling Psychology*, 34, 481–9.

Day, D. (2001) 'Leadership Development: A Review in Context', *Leadership Quarterly*, 11, 581–613.

de Brabandere, L. (2005) *The Forgotten Half of Change: Achieving Greater Creativity through Changes in Perception*, Dearborn, Chicago, IL.

De Cock, C. (1996) 'Thinking Creatively about Creativity: What Can We Learn From Recent Developments in the Philosophy of Science?', *Creativity and Innovation Management*, 5, 204–11.

De Cock, C. and Rehn, A. (2006) 'On Novelty and Being Novel (editorial)', *Creativity and Innovation Management*, 15, 123–6.

de Jouvenel, B. (1945/1993) *On Power*, Liberty Fund, Indianapolis, IN.

de Tocqueville, A. (1835/1956) *Democracy in America*, New American Library, New York.

Deal, T. and Kennedy, A. (1982) *Corporate Cultures: the Rites and Rituals of Corporate Life*, Addison-Wesley, London.

Dearborn, K. (2002) 'Studies in Emotional Intelligence Redefine our Approach to Leadership Development', *Public Personnel Management*, 31, 523–30.

Delahoussaye, M. (2001) 'Leadership in the 21st Century', *Training*, 8, 60–72.

Deleuze, G. (1994) *Difference and Repetition*, P. Patton (trans.), Athlone Press, London.

Den Hartog, D.N., House, R.J., Hanges, P.J., Ruiz Quintanilla, S.A. and Dorfman, P.W. (1999) 'Culture Specific and Cross-culturally Generalizable Implicit Leadership Theories: Are Attributes of Charismatic/Transformational Leadership Universally Endorsed?', *Leadership Quarterly*, 10, 219–56.

Denison, D.R., Hooijberg, R. and Quinn, R.E. (1995) 'Paradox and Performance: Toward a Theory of Behavioral Complexity in Managerial Leadership', *Organization Science*, 6, 524–40.

Dennis, R. and Winston, B. (2003) 'A Factor Analysis of Page and Wong's Servant Leadership Instrument', *Leadership and Organizational Development Journal*, 24, 455–59.

Dennis, R. and Bocarnea, M. (2005) 'Development of the Servant Leadership Assessment Instrument', *Leadership and Organizational Development Journal*, 26, 600–15.

Densten, I. and Gray, J. (2001) 'The Links between Followership and the Experiential Learning Model', *The Journal of Leadership Studies*, 8, 70–6.

DeVellis, R.F. (1991) *Scale Development: Theory and Applications*, Sage, Newbury Park, CA.

Dibben, M. and Cobb, J. (eds) (2003) 'Process Studies and Organisation Theory', special issue of *Process Studies*, 32.

Dibben, M.R. and Kelly, T. (eds) (2007) *Applied Process Thought: Frontiers of Theory and Research*, Ontos, Frankfurt.

Dixon, N. (1976) *On the Psychology of Military Incompetence*, Jonathan Cape, London.

Dolezalek, H. (2005) '2005 Industry Report', *Training*, 42, 14–28.

Dollard, K., Marett-Crosby, A. and Wright, T. (2002) *Doing Business with Benedict*, Continuum, London.

Dorfman, P.W. (2004) 'International and Cross-Cultural Leadership', in B.J. Punnett and O. Shenkar (eds), *Handbook of International Management Research*, 2nd edn, University of Michigan Press, Ann Arbor, MI, pp. 265–355.

Dorfman, P.W. and Howell, J.P. (1988) 'Dimensions of National Culture and Effective Leadership Patterns: Hofstede Revisited', in G. McGoun (ed.), *Advances in International Comparative Management*, vol. 3, JAI Press, Greenwich, CT, pp. 127–49.

Doris, J.M. (2005) *Lack of Character: Personality and Moral Behavior*, Cambridge University Press, Cambridge.

Dotlich, D. and Cairo, P. (2003) *Why CEOs Fail*, Jossey-Bass, San Francisco, CA.

Dotlich, D., Noel, J. and Walker, N. (2004) *Leadership Passages: the Personal and Professional Transitions that Make or Break a Leader*, Jossey-Bass, San Francisco, CA.

Dow, T.E. (1978) 'An Analysis of Weber's Work on Charisma', *British Journal of Sociology*, 29, 83–93.

Dowding, H., Air Chief Marshal Lord (1940) Letter of 16 May.

Drath, W. (2001) *The Deep Blue Sea: Rethinking the Source of Leadership*, Jossey-Bass, San Fransisco, CA.

Drath, W. and Palus, C. (1994) *Making Common Sense: Leadership as Meaning-making in a Community of Practice*, Centre for Creative Leadership, Greensboro, NC.

Drucker, P. (1999) *Management Challenges for the 21st Century*, Butterworth-Heinemann, Oxford.

—— (2004) 'What Makes an Effective Executive', *Harvard Business Review*, June, 58–63.

DSM-IV (1994) *Diagnostic and Statistical Manual of Mental Disorders*, American Psychiatric Association, Washington, DC.

Dunn, J. (1988) 'Trust and Political Agency', in D. Gambetta (ed.), *Trust: Making and Breaking Co-Operative Relations*, Basil Blackwell, Oxford, pp. 213–37.

Dunphy, D. and Pitsis, T. (2003) 'Wisdom', in C. Barker and R. Coy (eds), *The Seven Heavenly Virtues of Leadership*, McGraw-Hill, Sydney.

Dutton, J., Dukerich, J. and Harquail, C. (1994) 'Organizational Images and Member Identification', *Administrative Science Quarterly*, 43, 293–327.

Eagly, A.H. and Karau, S.J. (2002) 'Role Congruity Theory of Prejudice Toward Female Leaders', *Psychological Review*, 109, 573–98.

Ekvall, G. and Arvonen, J. (1991) 'Change-centered Leadership: An Extension of the Two-Dimensional Model', *Scandinavian Journal of Management*, 7, 17–26.

Ely, R. (2003) 'Leadership: Overview', in Ely, R., Foldy, E., Scully, M. and the Centre for Gender in Organizations, Simmons School of Management (eds), *Reader in Gender, Work and Organization*, Blackwell, Oxford, pp. 153–8.

Ely, R., Foldy, E., Scully, M. and the Centre for Gender in Organizations (2003) *Reader in Gender, Work and Organization*, Simmons School of Management (eds), Blackwell, Oxford.

Emory, W.C. (1980) *Business Research Methods*, Richard Irwin, Burr Ridge, IL.

Engestrom, Y. (1999) 'Activity Theory and Individual and Social Transformation', in Y. Engestrom, R. Miettinen and R.-L. Punamaki (eds), *Perspectives on Activity Theory*, Cambridge University Press, Cambridge.

Erkut, S. and Winds of Change Foundation (2001) 'Inside Women's Power: Learning from Leaders', CRW Special Report no. 28, Center for Women, Wellesley College, Wellesley, MA.

Etzioni, A. (1961) *A Comparative Analysis of Complex Organizations: On Power, Involvement, and their Correlates*, Free Press, New York.

Fairhurst, G. and Sarr, R. (1996) *The Art of Framing: Managing the Language of Leadership*, Jossey-Bass, San Francisco, CA.

Farling, M., Stone, A. and Winston, B. (1999) 'Servant Leadership: Setting the Stage for Empirical Research', *Journal of Leadership Studies*, 6, 49–72.

Fiedler, F.E. (1967) *A Theory of Leadership Effectiveness*, McGraw-Hill, New York.

—— (1973) 'The Contingency Theory and the Dynamics of Leadership Process', *Advances in Experimental Social Psychology*, 11, 60–112.

—— (1974) 'The Contingency Model: New Directions for Leadership Utilization', *Journal of Contemporary Business*, 3, 65–79.

—— (1978) 'The Contingency Model and the Dynamics of the Leadership Process', *Advances in Experimental Social Psychology*, 12, 59–112.

—— (1993) 'The Leadership Situation and the Black Box in Contingency Theories', in M. Chemers and R. Ayman (eds), *Leadership, Theory, and Research: Perspectives and Directions*, Academic Press, New York, pp. 1–28.

Fiedler, F.E. and Chemers, M.M. (1974) *Leadership and Effective Management*, Scott, Foresman and Co., Glenview, IL.

Fielding, K.S. and Hogg, M.A. (1997) 'Social Identity, Self-categorization, and Leadership: A Field Study of Small Interactive Groups', *Group Dynamics*, 1, 39–51.

Fineman, S. (2000) *Emotion in Organizations*, Sage, London.

Finkelstein, S. (2003) *Why Smart Executives Fail*, Penguin Books, New York.

Finkelstein, S. and Hambrick, D.C. (1996) *Strategic Leadership: Top Executives and Their Effects on Organisations*, West Publishing Company, Eagan, MN.

Fleishman, E.A. and Harris, E.F. (1962) 'Patterns of Leadership Behavior Related to Employee Grievances and Turnover', *Personnel Psychology*, 15, 43–56.

Fletcher, J.K. (2003) 'The Greatly Exaggerated Demise of Heroic Leadership: Gender, Power and the Myth of the Female Advantage', in R. Ely, E. Foldy, M. Scully and the Centre for Gender in Organizations, Simmons School of Management (eds), *Reader in Gender, Work and Organization*, Blackwell, Oxford, pp. 204–10.

Follett, M.P. (1919) 'Community is a Process', *The Philosophical Review*, 28, 576–88.

Forsyth, D.R. (2006) *Group Dynamics*, Thompson/Wadsworth, Belmont, CA.

Foster, W. (1986) *Paradigms and Promises*, Prometheus Books, Buffalo, NY.

Foucault, M. (1977) *Discipline and Punish: The Birth of the Prison*, Penguin, Harmondsworth.

—— (1980) *Power/Knowledge*, Harvester, Brighton.

Fowler, F.J. (1993) *Survey Research Methods*, 2nd edn, Sage, Newbury Park, CA.

Frankl, V.E. (1959) *Man's Search for Meaning: An Introduction to Logotherapy*, Beacon Press, Boston, MA.

—— (1969) *The Will to Meaning: Foundations and Applications of Logotherapy*, The World Publishing Company, New York.

Frederick, W.R. and Rodrigues, A.F. (1994) 'A Spanish Acquisition in Eastern Germany: Culture Shock', *Journal of Management Development*, 13, 42–8.

Fredrickson, Barbara L. (1998) 'What Good are Positive Emotions?', *Review of General Psychology*, 2, 300–19.

—— (2001) 'The Role of Positive Emotions in Positive Psychology: The Broaden & Build Theory of Positive Emotions', *American Psychologist*, 56, 218–26.

Fredrickson, Barbara L. and Losada, M.F. (2005) 'Positive Affect and the Complex Dynamics of Human Flourishing', *American Psychologist*, 60, 678–786.

Freiberg, K. and Freiberg, J. (1996) *Nuts*, Bard Press, Austin, TX.

French, J., Jr and Raven, B.H. (1959) 'The Bases of Social Power', in D. Cartwright (ed.), *Studies of Social Power*, Institute for Social Research, Ann Arbor, MI, pp. 150–67.

—— (1960) 'The Bases of Social Power', in D. Cartwright and A. Zander (eds), *Group Dynamics: Research and Theory*, Harper & Row, New York.

Freud, S. (1923) *Das Ich und das Es*, Internationaler Psycho-analytischer Verlag, Leipzig.

Friedlander, F. (1970) 'The Primacy of Trust as a Facilitator of Further Group Accomplishment', *Journal of Applied Behavioral Science*, 6, 387–400.

Friedman, R.B. (1990) 'On the Concept of Authority in Political Philosophy', in J. Raz (ed.), *Authority*, New York University Press, New York.

Fromm, E. (1994) *Escape from Freedom*, Henry Holt and Company, New York.

Frost, P. (2003) *Toxic Emotions at Work*, Harvard Business School Press, Boston, MA.

Frost, P. and Robinson, S. (1999) 'The Toxic Handler', *Harvard Business Review*, July–Aug, 97–106.

Furnham, A. and Taylor, J. (2004) *The Dark Side of Behaviour at Work*, Palgrave Macmillan, Basingstoke.

Gambetta, D. (1988) 'Can We Trust Trust?', in D. Gambetta (ed.), *Trust: Making and Breaking Co-operative Relations*, Basil Blackwell, Oxford, pp. 213–37.

Gardner, H. (1983) *Frames of Mind: The Theory of Multiple Intelligences*, Basic Books, New York.

Gardner, H. with Laskin, E. (1995) *Leading Minds: An Anatomy of Leadership*, Basic Books, New York.

Gardner, J. (1990) *On Leadership*, Free Press, New York.

Geen, R.G. (1995) *Human Motivation: A Social Psychological Approach*, Cole, Belmont, CA.

Gemmill, G. and Oakley, J. (1992) 'Leadership: An Alienating Social Myth', *Human Relations*, 45, 113–29.

Gergen, D. (2005) 'Does Leadership Matter?', *US News & World Report*, 13 Oct, 139, 91.

Gerstner, L.V., Jr (2003) *Who Says Elephants Can't Dance?*, HarperCollins, London.

Gibb, C.A. (1954) 'Leadership', in G. Lindzey (ed.), *Handbook of Social Psychology*, vol. 2, Addison-Wesley, Reading, MA, pp. 877–917.

—— (1969) 'Leadership', in L. Gardner and E. Aronson (eds), *The Handbook of Social Psychology*, vol. 4, Addison-Wesley, Cambridge, MA, pp. 205–81.

Gibb, J.R. (1978) *Trust: A New View of Personal and Organizational Development*, Guild of Tutors Press, Los Angeles, CA.

Giber, D., Carter, L. and Goldsmith, M. (eds) (2000) *Linkage Inc.'s Best Practices in Leadership Development Handbook*, Jossey-Bass Pfeiffer, San Francisco, CA.

Giddens, A. (1990) *The Consequences of Modernity*, Polity Press, Cambridge.

—— (1991) *Modernity and Self-Identity*, Polity Press, Cambridge.

Gilbert, M. (2004) *Winston Churchill's War Leadership*, Vintage, London.

Gilkey, R. (1991) 'The Psychodynamics of Upheaval: Intervening in Merger and Acquisition Transitions', in M.F.R. Kets de Vries (ed.), *Organisations on the Couch*, Jossey-Bass, San Francisco, CA, pp. 331–61.

Gilligan, C. (1982) *In a Different Voice: Psychological Theory and the Women's Movement*, Harvard Press, Cambridge, MA.

Giuliani, R. (2002) *Leadership* (with K. Kurson), Hyperion, New York.

Goffman, E. (1959) *The Presentation of Self in Everyday Life*, Doubleday, New York.

Gogatz, A. and Mondejar, R. (2005) *Business Creativity: Breaking the Invisible Barriers*, Palgrave Macmillan, Basingstoke.

Goldberg, E. (2005) *The Wisdom Paradox*, Free Press, London.

Goleman, D. (1995) *Emotional Intelligence: Why It Can Matter More Than IQ*, Bantam Books, New York.

—— (1998a) 'What Makes a Leader?', *Harvard Business Review*, 76, 92–102.

—— (1998b) *Working with Emotional Intelligence*, Bantam Books, New York.

Goleman, D., Boyatzis, R. and McKee, A. (2002) *The New Leaders: Transforming the Art of Leadership into the Science of Results*, Little Brown, London. [Published in the USA as *Primal Leadership: Realizing the Power of Emotional Intelligence*, HBSP, Boston, MA.]

Gosling, J. (2006) 'Quietness as a Virtue of Leadership', *Professional Manager*, Jan, 37.

Gosling, J. and Mintzberg, H. (2003) 'The Five Minds of a Manager', *Harvard Business Review*, November.

Graeff, C. (1983) 'The Situational Leadership Theory: A Critical View', *Academy of Management Review*, 8, 285–91.

Graen, G. and Uhl-Bien, M. (1995) 'Relationship-Based Approach to Leader-ship: Development of Leader-Member Exchange (LMX) Theory of Leadership Over 25 Years: Applying a Multi-Level Multi-Domain Perspec-tive', *The Leadership Quarterly*, 6, 219–47.

Graen, G.B. and Hui, C. (1999) 'Transcultural Global Leadership in the Twenty-first Century: Challenges and Implications for Development', in W.H. Mobley (ed.), *Advances in Global Leadership*, vol. 1, JAI Press, Stamford, CT, pp. 9–26.

Graham, J.W. (1988) 'Transformational Leadership: Fostering Follower Autonomy, Not Automatic Leadership', in J.G. Hunt, B.R. Baligia and C.A. Schiesheim (eds), *Emerging Leadership Vistas*, DC Heath, Lexington, MA, pp. 73–9.

—— (1991) 'Servant-leadership in Organizations: Inspirational and Moral', *Leadership Quarterly*, 2, 43–54.

Gramsci, A. (1957/1992) *The Modern Prince and Other Writings*, L. Marks (trans.), International Publisher, New York.

Grant, J.S. and Davis, L.L. (1997) 'Selection and Use of Content Experts for Instrument Development', *Research in Nursing and Health*, 20, 269–74.

Grean, G., Cashman, J., Ginsburgh, S. and Schiemann, W. (1977) 'Effects of Linking-pin Quality of Work Life of Lower Participants', *Administrative Science Quarterly*, 22, 491–504.

Green, S. and Cooper, P. (1998) 'Sage, Visionary, Prophet and Priest: Leadership Styles of Knowledge Management and Wisdom', in G. Hamel *et al.* (eds), *Strategic Flexibility: Managing in a Turbulent Environment*, John Wiley & Sons, Chichester.

Greenberg, J. (1996) *The Quest for Justice on the Job: Essays and Experiments*, Sage, London.

Greenleaf, R. (1970) *The Servant as Leader*, Paulist Press, New York.

—— (1974) *Trustees as Servants*, Paulist Press, New York.

—— (1977a) *The Institution as Servant*, Paulist Press, New York.

—— (1977b) *Servant-Leadership: A Journey into the Nature of Legitimate Power and Greatness*, Paulist Press, New York.

—— (1979) *Teacher as Servant*, Paulist Press, New York.

—— (1996) 'The Crisis of Leadership', in M. Frick and L. Spears (eds), *On Becoming a Servant Leader*, Jossey-Bass, San Francisco, CA, pp. 287–98.

—— (1998) *The Power of Servant Leadership*, L. Spears (ed.), Barrett-Koehler, San Francisco, CA.

Greer, D. (1999) Personal Interview, 8 January, Derry, Northern Ireland.

Greising, D. (1999) *I'd Like the World to Buy a Coke: the Life and Leadership of Roberto Goizueta*, Wiley, New York.

Grint, K. (2000) *The Arts of Leadership*, Oxford University Press, Oxford.

—— (2004) 'Problems, Problems, Problems: The Irony and Social Construction of "Leadership"', paper presented at *Studying Leadership: 3rd International Work-shop*, Centre for Leadership Studies, Exeter.

—— (2005) *Leadership: Limits and Possibilities*, Palgrave Macmillan, Basingstoke.

Gronn, P. (2000) 'Distributed Properties: A New Architecture for Leadership', *Educational Management and Administration*, 28, 317–38.

—— (2002a) 'Distributed Leadership as a Unit of Analysis', *The Leadership Quarterly*, 13, 423–51.

—— (2002b) 'Distributed Leadership', in K. Leithwood, P. Hallinger, K. Seashore-Louis, G. Furman-Brown, P. Gronn, W. Mulford and K. Riley (eds), *Second International Handbook of Educational Leadership and Administration*, Kluwer, Dordrecht.

Guillet de Monthoux, P. (2004) *The Art Firm: Aesthetic Management and Metaphysical Marketing from Wagner to Wilson*, Stanford Business Books, Stanford, CT.

Hackman, J.R. and Wageman, R. (2005) 'When and How Team Leaders Matter', in B.M. Staw and R.M. Kramer (eds), *Research in Organizational Behavior*, 26, 37–74.

Hadot, P. (1995) *Philosophy as a Way of Life*, Blackwell, Oxford.

Hamilton, F. and Bean, C. (2005) 'The Importance of Context, Beliefs and Values in Leadership Development', Special Issue on Leadership and Ethics, A. Marturano and J. Gosling (eds), *Business Ethics: A European Review*, 14, 336–47.

Handy, C. (1977) *Understanding Organizations*, Penguin, Harmondsworth.

Hardy, C. (1995) *Power and Politics in Organizations*, Aldershot, Dartmouth.

—— (1996) 'Understanding Power: Bringing About Strategic Change', *British Journal of Management*, 7, S3–S16.

Hare, R. and Babiak, P. (2006) *Snakes in Suits*, Regan Books, New York.

Harkins, P. (1999) *Powerful Conversations: How High Impact Leaders Communicate*, McGraw-Hill, New York.

Harle, T. (2005) 'Serenity, Courage and Wisdom: Changing Competencies for Leadership', *Business Ethics: European Review*, 14, 348–58.

Harman, G. (1999) 'Moral Philosophy Meets Social Psychology: Virtue Ethics and the Fundamental Attribution Error', *Proceedings of the Aristotelian Society*, 99, 315–31.

Harris, A. (2003) 'Teacher Leadership as Distributed Leadership: Heresy, Fantasy or Possibility?', *School Leadership and Management*, 23, 313–24.

Harris, P.R. and Moran, R.T. (1987) *Managing Cultural Differences*, Gulf, Houston, TX.

Harrison, R. (1972) 'How to Describe Your Organization', *Harvard Business Review*, 5, 119–28.

Harter, N. (2003) 'Between Great Men and Leadership: William James on the Importance of Individuals', *Journal of Leadership Education*, 2, 3–12.

—— (2006) *Clearings in the Forest*, Purdue University Press, West Lafayette, IN.

Harter, N. and Evanecky, D. (2002) 'Fairness in Leader-Member Exchange Theory: Do We All Belong on the Inside?', *Leadership Review*. Available at www.leadershipreview.org

Harter, N., Ziolkowski, F. and Wyatt, S. (2006) 'Leadership and Inequality', *Leadership*, 2, 275–93.

Harvey, J. (1988a) *The Abilene Paradox*, Lexington Books, Lexington, MA.

—— (1988b) *The Abilene Paradox and Other Meditations on Management: Compassionate Insights into the Craziness of Organizational Life*, University Associates, San Diego, CA.

Haslam, S.A. (2004) *Social Psychology: A Social Identity Approach*, 2nd edn, Sage, London.

Hatch, M.J., Kostera, M. and Kozminski, A.K. (2004) *The Three Faces of Leadership: Manager, Artist, Priest*, Blackwell, Oxford.

Hater, J.J. and Bass, B.M. (1988) 'Superiors' Evaluations and Subordinates' Perceptions of Transformational and Transactional Leadership', *Journal of Applied Psychology*, 73, 695–702.

Heifetz, R.A. (1994) *Leadership Without Easy Answers*, Belknap Press of Harvard University, Cambridge, MA.

—— (2007) 'The Scholarly/Practitioner Challenge of *Leadership*', in Richard Couto (ed.), *Reflections on Leadership*, University Press of America, Lanham, MD, pp. 31–45.

Heifetz, R.A. and Linsky, M. (2002) *Leadership on the Line*, Harvard Business Review, Cambridge, MA.

Heller, R. (1998) *How to Delegate*, DK Publications, New York.

Hemphill, J.K. and Coons, A.E. (1957) 'Development of the Leader Behavior Description Questionnaire', in R.M. Stogdill and A.E. Coons (eds), *Leader Behavior: Its Description and Measurement*, Bureau of Business Research, Ohio State University, Columbus, OH, pp. 6–38.

Henry, P. (ed.) (2002) *Benedict's Dharma: Buddhists Reflect on the Rule of St Benedict*, Continuum, London.

Heraclitus (1979) 'Fragments', in C. Kahn, *The Art and Thought of Heraclitus: An Edition of the Fragments with Translation and Commentary*, Cambridge University Press, Cambridge.

Hersey, P. and Blanchard, K.H. (1969) 'Life Cycle Theory of Leadership', *Training and Development Journal*, 23, 26–33.

—— (1974) 'So You Want To Know Your Leadership Style?', *Training and Development Journal*, 28, 22–37.

—— (1982) *Management of Organizational Behavior*, 4th edn, Prentice Hall, Upper Saddle River, NJ.

—— (1993) *Management of Organizational Behavior: Utilizing Human Resources*, 6th edn, Prentice Hall, Englewood Cliffs, NJ.

Hersey, P., Blanchard, K.H. and Johnson, D.E. (2000) *Management of Organizational Behaviour*, Prentice-Hall, New York.

Herzberg, F. (1966) *Work and the Nature of Man*, World Publishing, Cleveland, OH.

Hesse, H. (1991) *The Journey to the East*, Farrar, Straus and Giroux, New York.

Hicks, D. (2003) *Religion and the Workplace: Pluralism, Spirituality, Leadership*, Cambridge University Press, Cambridge.

Hicks, D.A. and Price, T.L. (1999) 'What Do People Really Need: An Ethical Challenge for Leaders and Scholars', in *The Selected Proceedings of the Leaders/Scholars Association*, James MacGregor Burns Academy of Leadership, College Park, pp. 53–61.

Hickson, D.J. and Pugh, D.S. (2001) *Management Worldwide: Distinctive Styles Amid Globalization*, Penguin, London.

Higgs, M. and Dulewicz, S.V. (1999) *Making Sense of Emotional Intelligence*, NFER-Nelson, Windsor.

Higgs, M. and Rowland, D. (2002) 'Does it Need Emotional Intelligence to Lead Change?', *Journal of General Management*, 27, 62–76.

Hinkin, T.R. (1995) 'A Review of Scale Development Practices in the Study of Organizations', *Journal of Management*, 21, 967–88.

Hobbes, T. (1651/1991) *Leviathan*, R. Tuck (ed.), Cambridge University Press, Cambridge.

Hofstede, G. (1980) *Culture's Consequences: International Differences in Work-Related Values*, Sage, Newbury Park, CA.

—— (2004) *Cultures and Organizations: Software of the Mind*, McGraw-Hill, New York.

Hogan, R. and Hogan, J. (2001) 'Assessing Leadership: A View from the Dark Side', *International Journal of Selection and Assessment*, 9, 40–51.

Hogan, R. and Kaiser, R.B. (2005) 'What We Know About Leadership', *Review of General Psychology*, 9, 169–80.

Hogg, M.A. (2001) 'A Social Identity Theory of Leadership', *Personality and Social Psychology Review*, 5, 184–200.

Hollander, E.P. (1993) 'Legitimacy, Power, and Influence: A Perspective on Relational Features of Leadership', in M. Chemers and R. Ayman (eds), *Leadership Theory and Research: Perspectives and Directions*, Academic Press, San Diego, CA, pp. 29–47.

—— (2004) 'Idiosyncrasy Credit', in George R. Goethals, Georgia J. Sorenson and James MacGregor Burns (eds), *Encyclopedia of Leadership*, vol. 4, Sage, Thousand Oaks, CA, pp. 695–700.

—— (2007) 'Relating *Leadership* to Active Followership', in Richard Couto (ed.), *Reflections on Leadership*, University Press of America, Lanham, MD, pp. 57–66.

Honneth, A. (1995) *The Struggle for Recognition and the Moral Grammar of Social Conflicts*, Polity Press, Cambridge.

Hook, S. (1943) *The Hero in History: A Study in Limitation and Possibility*, Beacon Press, Boston, MA.

Hopfl, H.M. (1999) 'Power, Authority and Legitimacy', *Human Resource Development International*, 2, 217–34.

Höpfl, H.J. and Linstead, S. (eds) (2000) *The Aesthetics of Organization*, Sage, London.

Hornstein, H.A. (1986) *Managerial Courage: Revitalizing Your Company Without Sacrificing Your Job*, John Wiley & Sons, New York.

Hosking, D.M. (1988) 'Organizing, Leadership and Skilful Process', *Journal of Management Studies*, 25, 147–66.

House, R.J. (1971) 'A Path-Goal Theory of Leadership Effectiveness', *Administrative Science Quarterly*, September, 32–9.

—— (1977) 'A 1976 Theory of Charismatic Leadership', in J.G. Hunt and L.L. Larson (eds), *Leadership: The Cutting Edge*, Southern Illinois University Press, Carbondale, IL, pp. 189–207.

House, R.J. and Mitchell, T.R. (1974) 'A Path-Goal Theory of Leader Effectiveness', *Journal of Contemporary Business*, 3, 81–97.

—— (1997) 'Path-Goal Theory of Leadership', in R.P. Vecchio (ed.), *Leadership: Understanding the Dynamics of Power and Influence in Organizations*, Notre Dame University Press, Notre Dame, IN, pp. 259–73.

House, R.J. and Aditya, R. (1997) 'The Social Scientific Study of Leadership: Quo Vadis?', *Journal of Management*, 23, 409–74.

House, R.J., Hanges, P.M., Javidan, M., Dorfman, P. and Gupta, V. (2004) *Culture, Leadership and Organizations: The GLOBE Study of 62 Societies*, Sage, Thousand Oaks, CA.

Howard, S. and Welbourn, D. (2004) *The Spirit at Work Phenomenon*, Azure, London.

Howell, J.M. (1988) 'Two Faces of Charisma: Socialized and Personalized Leadership in Organizations', in J.A. Conger and R.N. Kanungo (eds), *Charismatic Leadership: The Elusive Factor in Organizational Effectiveness*, Jossey-Bass, San Francisco, CA, pp. 213–36.

Howell, J.M. and Avolio, B.J. (1993) 'Transformational Leadership, Transactional

Leadership, Locus of Control, and Support for Innovation: Key Predictors of Business Unit Performance', *Journal of Applied Psychology*, 78, 891–902.

Hoyt, C., Goethals, G. and Riggio, R. (2006) 'Leader–Follower Relations: Group Dynamics and the Role of Leadership', in G. Goethals and G. Sorenson (eds), *A Quest for a General Theory of Leadership: A Multidisciplinary Experiment*, Edward Elgar, Cheltenham, pp. 96–122.

Hughes, R.L., Ginnett, R.C. and Curphy, G.J. (2002) *Leadership: Enhancing the Lessons of Experience*, 4th edn, McGraw-Hill, New York.

Hummel, R. (1994) *The Bureaucratic Experience: A Critique of Life in the Modern Organization*, 4th edn, St Martin's Press, New York.

Humphreys, J. (2005) 'Contextual Implications for Transformational and Servant Leadership: A Historical Investigation', *Management Decision*, 43, 1410–31.

Hunsaker, P.L. (2001) *Training in Management Skills*, Prentice Hall, Upper Saddle River, NJ.

Hunt, J.G. (2004) 'What is Leadership?', in J. Antonakis, A. Cianciaola and R.J. Sternberg (eds), *The Nature of Leadership*, Sage, Thousand Oaks, CA.

Hunt, S.D. (1991) *Modern Marketing Theory*, South-Western Publishing, Cincinnati, OH.

Huppe, F.F. (1994) *Successful Delegation: How to Grow Your People, Build Your Team, Free Up Your Time, and Increase Profits and Productivity*, Career Press, Hawthorne, NJ.

Jackson, N. and Carter, P. (2000) *Rethinking Organisational Behaviour*, Prentice-Hall, London.

Jacques, E. (1951) *The Changing Culture of the Factory*, Tavistock, London.

Janis, I.L. (1982) *Groupthink: Psychological Studies of Policy Decisions and Fiascos*, 2nd edn, Houghton Mifflin, Boston, MA.

Jaques, E. (2002) *Social Power and the CEO: Leadership and Trust in a Sustainable Free Enterprise System*, Quorum Books, Westport, CT.

Jaworski, J. (1998) *Synchronicity: The Inner Path of Leadership*, Berrett-Koehler, San Francisco, CA.

Jennings, E.E. (1960) *An Anatomy of Leadership: Princes, Heroes, and Supermen*, McGraw-Hill, New York.

Jones, D.H. (1999) *Moral Responsibility in the Holocaust: A Study in the Ethics of Character*, Rowman and Littlefield, Lanham, MD.

Jones, D. (2005) *NEXT to Me: Luck, Leadership and Living with Parkinson's*, Nicholas Brealey, London.

Jones, J. and Eicher, J. (1999a) *Post-heroic Leadership Assessment Others: Packet of Five*, Human Resource Development Partners, New York.

—— (1999b) *Post-heroic Leadership Assessment Self: Packet of Five*, Human Resource Development Partners, New York.

—— (1999c) *Post-heroic Leadership Leaders Guide*, Human Resource Development Partners, New York.

Jones, S. and Gosling, J. (2005) *Nelson's Way: Leadership Lessons from the Great Commander*, Nicholas Brealey, London.

Joseph, E. and Winston, B. (2005) 'A Correlation of Servant Leadership, Leader Trust and Organizational Trust', *Leadership and Organizational Development Journal*, 26, 6–22.

Judge, T.A. and Piccolo, R.F. (2004) 'Transformational and Transactional Leadership: A Meta-Analytic Test of Their Relative Validity', *Journal of Applied Psychology*, 89, 755–68.

Jupp, J. and Grint, K. (2005) *Air Force Leadership: Beyond Command*, The Royal Air Force Leadership Centre, Lincolnshire.

Kanungo, R.N. and Mendonca, M. (1996) *Ethical Dimensions of Leadership*, Sage, London.

Karau, S.J. and Williams, K.D. (1993) 'Social Loafing: A Meta-analytic Review and Theoretical Integration', *Journal of Personality and Social Psychology*, 65, 681–706.

Katz, D. and Kahn, R.L. (1952) 'Some Recent Findings in Human-relations Research in Industry', in E. Swanson, T. Newcomb and E. Hartley (eds), *Readings in Social Psychology*, Holt, New York, pp. 650–65.

Kauffman, S. (1995) *At Home in the Universe*, Oxford University Press, Oxford.

Keegan, J. (1987) *The Mask of Command*, Penguin Books, London.

Keeley, M. (1995) 'The Trouble with Transformational Leadership: Toward a Federalist Ethic for Organizations', *Business Ethics Quarterly*, 5, 67–96.

Kellerman, B. (1984) *Leadership: Multidisciplinary Perspectives*, Prentice Hall, Englewood Cliffs, NJ.

—— (2004a) *Bad Leadership: What It Is, How It Happens, Why It Matters*, Belknap Press, Cambridge, MA.

—— (2004b) 'Leadership Warts and All', *Harvard Business Review*, 82, 40–5.

Kelley, M. (1995) 'The New Leadership', in L. Spears (ed.), *Reflections on Leadership: How Robert K. Greenleaf's Theory of Servant-leadership Influenced Today's Top Management Thinkers*, John Wiley & Son, New York, pp. 169–78.

Kelley, R. (1988) 'In Praise of Followers', *Harvard Business Review*, Nov.

—— (1992) *The Power of Followership*, Doubleday, New York.

Kelley, T. (2001) *The Art of Innovation: Lessons in Creativity from IDEO, America's Leading Design Firm*, Currency, New York.

Kelman, H.C. (1958) 'Compliance, Identification, and Internalization: Three Processes of Opinion Change', *Journal of Conflict Resolution*, 2, 51–60.

Kerlinger, F.N. (1973) *Foundations of Behavioral Research*, 2nd edn, Holt, Rhinehart, and Winston, New York.

Kets de Vries, M. (1979) 'Managers Can Drive Their Subordinates Mad', *Harvard Business Review*, July–August, 125–34.

—— (1985) 'The Dark Side of Entrepreneurship', *Harvard Business Review*, 63, 160–7.

—— (1989a) 'Leaders Who Self-destruct: the Causes and Cures', *Organizational Dynamics*, 17, 5–17.

—— (1989b) *Prisoners of Leadership*, John Wiley Inc., New York.

—— (1991) 'Whatever Happened to the Philosopher-King? The Leader's Addiction to Power', *Journal of Management Studies*, 28, 339–51.

—— (1995) *Life and Death in the Executive Fast Lane*, Jossey-Bass, San Francisco, CA.

—— (2001) *The Leadership Mystique*, Prentice Hall, London.

—— (2004a) 'Organizations on the Couch', *European Management Journal*, 22, 183–200.

—— (2004b) *Lessons on Leadership by Terror: Finding Shaka Zulu in the Attic*, New Horizons in Leadership Series, Edward Elgar, Cheltenham.

Kets de Vries, M. and Balazs, K. (2005) 'A Clinical Perspective on Organizational Consultation', *Organizational Dynamics*, 34, 1–17.

Khurana, R. (2002) *Searching for a Corporate Savior: The Irrational Quest for Charismatic CEOs*, Princeton University Press, Princeton, NJ.

Kidder, L.H. (1981) *Selltiz, Wrightsman, and Cook's Research Methods in Social Relations*, 4th edn, Holt, Rinehart and Winston, New York.

Kieffer, C.H. (1984) 'Citizen Empowerment: A Developmental Perspective', *Prevention in Human Services (Studies in Empowerment: Steps Toward Understanding and Action)*, 3, 9–36.

Kilburg, R. (2000) *Executive Coaching*, American Psychological Association, Washington, DC.

Kirkpatrick, D. (1994) *Evaluating Training Programs: The Four Levels*, Berrett-Koehler, San Francisco, CA.

Kirton, G. and Greene, A.-M. (2000) *The Dynamics of Managing Diversity: a Critical Approach*, Butterworth-Heinemann, Oxford.

Klein, K.J. and House, R.J. (1995) 'On Fire: Charismatic Leadership and Levels of Analysis', *Leadership Quarterly*, 6, 183–98.

Klein, K.J. and Ziegert, J.C. (2004) 'Leader Development and Change Over Time: A Conceptual Integration and Exploration of Research Challenges', in D. Day, S. Zaccaro and S. Halpin (eds), *Leader Development for Transforming Organizations: Growing Leaders for Tomorrow*, Lawrence Erlbaum Associates, Mahwah, NJ, pp. 359–82.

Kluckhohn, F.R. and Strodtbeck, F.L. (1961) *Variations in Value Orientations*, Harper Collins, New York.

Koestler, A. (1964) *The Act of Creation*, Hutchinson, London.

Kofodimos, J. (1989) *Why Executives Lose their Balance*, Center for Creative Leadership, Greensboro, NC.

—— (1990) 'Why Executives Lose their Balance', *Organizational Dynamics*, 19, 58–73.

Kohlberg, L. (1981) *Essays on Moral Development: The Philosophy of Moral Development*, vol. 1, Harper and Row, San Francisco, CA.

—— (1984) *Essays on Moral Development: The Psychology of Moral Development*, vol. 2, Harper and Row, San Francisco, CA.

Korman, A.K. (1974) '"Consideration", "Initiating Structures" and Organizational Criteria – A Review', *Personnel Psychology*, 27, 555–68.

Kotter, J.P. (1995) 'Leading Change: Why Transformation Efforts Fail', *Harvard Business Review*, 73, 59–67.

—— (1999) *John P. Kotter On What Leaders Really Do*, Harvard Business School Press, Boston, MA.

Kouzes, J. and Posner, B. (1987) *The Leadership Challenge*, Jossey-Bass, San Francisco, CA.

—— (1995) *The Leadership Challenge*, Jossey-Bass, San Francisco, CA.

—— (2003) *The Leadership Challenge*, Jossey-Bass, San Francisco, CA.

Kramer, R.M. (1996) 'Divergent Realities and Convergent Disappointments in the Hierarchical Relation: Trust and the Intuitive Auditor at Work', in R.M. Kramer and T.R. Tyler (eds), *Trust in Organisations: Frontiers of Theory and Research*, Sage, London, pp. 216–46.

—— (2002) 'When Paranoia Makes Sense', *Harvard Business Review*, 80, 66.

Kramer, R.M. and Tyler, T.R. (eds) (1996) *Trust in Organisations: Frontiers of Theory and Research*, Sage, London.

Kuhnert, K.W. (1994) 'Transforming Leadership: Developing People Through Delegation', in B.M. Bass and B.J. Avolio (eds), *Improving Organizational Effectiveness Through Transformational Leadership*, Sage, Thousand Oaks, CA, pp. 10–25.

Kuhnert, K.W. and Lewis, P. (1987) 'Transactional and Transformational Leadership: A Constructive/Developmental Analysis', *Academy of Management Review*, 12, 648–57.

Kumar, S. (2002) *You Are Therefore I Am: A Declaration of Dependence*, Green Books, Dartington.

Kunda, G. (1992) *Engineering Culture*, Temple University Press, Philadelphia, PA.

Ladkin, D. (forthcoming) 'Leading Beautifully: How Mastery Coherence and Purpose Contribute to Inspirational Leadership Performance'.

Langley, A. (1999) 'Strategies for Theorizing from Process Data', *Academy of Management Review*, 24, 691–710.

Larson, J.R., Jr, Christensen, C., Abbott, A.S. and Franz, T.M. (1996) 'Diagnosing Groups: Charting the Flow of Information in Medical Decision-making Teams', *Journal of Personality and Social Psychology*, 71, 315–30.

Larwood, L., Falbe, C.M., Kriger, M.P. and Miesing, P. (1995) 'Structure of Organisational Vision', *Academy of Management Journal*, 38, 740–69.

Lasch, C. (1977) *Haven in a Heartless World: The Family Besieged*, Basic Books, New York.

—— (1979) *The Culture of Narcissism: American Life in an Age of Diminishing Expectations*, Norton, New York.

Latane, B. (1981) 'The Psychology of Social Impact', *American Psychologist*, 36, 343–56.

Laub, J. (1999) 'Assessing the Servant Organization: Development of the Servant Organizational Leadership Assessment (SOLA) Instrument', Unpublished Dissertation, Florida Atlantic University.

Lawler, E.J. (1975) 'An Experimental Study of Factors Affecting the Mobilization of Revolutionary Coalitions', *Sociometry*, 38, 163–79.

Lawler, E.L. III (1966) 'Ability as a Moderator of the Relationship between Job Attitudes and Job Performance', *Personnel Psychology*, 19, 153–64.

Lawrence, P.R. and Lorsch, J.W. (1967) *Organization and Environment: Managing Differentiation and Integration*, Harvard University Graduate School of Business Administration, Boston, MA.

Leary, M. (1989) 'Self-presentational Processes in Leadership Emergence and Effectiveness', in R. Giacalone and P. Rosenfeld (eds), *Impression Management in the Organization*, Lawrence Erlbaum Associates, Hillsdale, NJ.

Leary, M., Barnes, B., Robertson, R. and Miller, R. (1986) 'Self-presentations of Small Group Leaders: Effects of Role Requirements and Leadership Orientation', *Journal of Personality and Social Psychology*, 51, 742–8.

Lee-Kelley, L. (2002) 'Situational Leadership', *Journal of Management Development*, 21, 461–76.

Leslie, J. and Van Velsor, E. (1996) *A Look at Derailment Today: North America and Europe*, Center for Creative Leadership, Greensboro, NC.

Leuner, B. (1966) 'Emotional Intelligence and Emancipation' [Translated English title], *Praxis der Kinderpsychologie und Kindersyychiatrie*, 15, 196–203.

Levin, I.M. (2000) 'Vision Revisited: Telling the Story of the Future', *Journal of Applied Behavioural Science*, 36, 91–107.

Levine, D. (1995) 'The Italian Tradition', in *Visions of the Sociological Tradition*, The University of Chicago Press, Chicago, IL, pp. 231–49.

Levinson, D., Darrow, C., Klein, E., Levinson, M. and McKee, B. (1978) *The Seasons of a Man's Life*, Ballantine Books, New York.

Levinson, H. (1978) 'The Abrasive Personality', *Harvard Business Review*, May–June, 86–94.

Lewicki, R.J. and Bunker, B. (1995) 'Trust in Relationships: A Model of Trust Development and Decline', in B. Bunker and J. Rubin (eds), *Conflict, Cooperation and Justice*, Jossey-Bass, San Francisco, CA, pp. 133–73.

Lewin, K. (1951) *Field Theory in Social Science*, Harper, New York.

Lewin, K., Lippitt, R. and White, R. (1939) 'Patterns of Aggressive Behavior in Experimentally Created "Social Climates"', *Journal of Social Psychology*, 10, 271–99.

Lewin, R. and Regine, B. (2001) *Weaving Complexity & Business: Engaging the Soul at Work*, Texere, New York.

Likert, R. (1961) *New Patterns of Management*, McGraw-Hill, New York.

—— (1967) *The Human Organization: Its Management and Value*, McGraw-Hill, New York.

Lin, M. (2000) *Boundaries*, Simon & Schuster, New York.

Linstead, S. and Grafton-Small, R. (1992) 'On Reading Organisation Culture', *Organization Studies*, 13, 331–55.

Lipman-Blumen, J. (2005a) *The Allure of Toxic Leaders: Why We Follow Destructive Bosses and Corrupt Politicians – and How We Can Survive Them*, Oxford University Press, New York.

—— (2005b) 'The Allure of Toxic Leaders: Why Followers Rarely Escape their Clutches', *Ivey Business Journal*, 69.

Lipton, M. (2003) *Guiding Growth: How Vision Keeps Companies on Course*, Harvard Business School Publishing, Boston, MA.

Lissack, M.R. (2002) *The Interaction of Complexity and Management*, Quorum Books, Westport, CT.

Livers, A.B. and Caver, K.A. (2005) 'Leadership Development Across Race', in C.D. McCauley and E. Van Velsor (eds), *The Center for Creative Leadership Handbook of Leadership Development*, Jossey-Bass, San Francisco, CA, pp. 304–30.

Lloyd, B. (2005) *Wisdom, Knowledge Management and Leadership: Linking the Past, Present and Future*. Available at www.collectivewisdominitiative.org/papers/lloyd_wisdom.htm (accessed 28 April 2006).

Locke, E.A. and Latham, G.P. (1990) *A Theory of Goal Setting and Task Performance*, Prentice Hall, Englewood Cliffs, NJ.

—— (2002) 'Building a Practically Useful Theory of Goal Setting and Task Motivation: A 35-year Odyssey', *American Psychologist*, 57, 705–17.

Locke, J. (1690/1988) *Two Treatises on Government*, P. Laslett (ed.), Cambridge University Press, Cambridge.

Lombardo, M. and McCall, M. (1984) *Coping with an Intolerable Boss*, Center for Creative Leadership, Greensboro, NC.

Lombardo, M. and McCauley, C. (1988) *The Dynamics of Management Derailment*, Center for Creative Leadership, Greensboro, NC.

Lombardo, M., Ruderman, M. and McCauley, C. (1988) 'Explanations of Success and Derailment in Upper-level Management Positions', *Journal of Business and Psychology*, 2, 199–216.

London, M. (2002) *Leadership Development: Paths to Self-insight and Professional Growth*, Lawrence Erlbaum Associates, Mahwah, NJ.

Lord, R.G. and Maher, K.J. (1991) *Leadership and Information Processing: Linking Perceptions and Performance*, Harper Collins, Boston, MA.

Lord, R.G., Foti, R.J. and Phillips, J.S. (1982) 'A Theory of Leadership Categorization', in J.G. Hunt, U. Sekaran and C. Schreisheim (eds), *Leadership: Beyond Establishment Views*, Southern Illinois University Press, Carbondale, IL.

Lord, R.G., Klimoski, R.J. and Kanfer, R. (2002) *Emotions in the Workplace: Understanding the Structure and Role of Emotions in Organizational Behaviour*, Jossey-Bass, San Francisco, CA.

Lovell, T. (2003) 'Resisting with Authority: Historical Specificity, Agency and the Performative Self', *Theory, Culture and Society*, 20, 1–17.

Lowman, R. (1993) *Counselling and Psychotherapy of Work Dysfunctions*, American Psychological Association, Washington, DC.

Lubit, R. (2002) 'The Long-term Organizational Impact of Destructively Narcissistic Managers', *Academy of Management Executive*, 16, 127–38.

Ludeman, K. and Erlandson, E. (2004) 'Coaching the Alpha Male', *Harvard Business Review*, May, 58–68.

Ludwig, D. and Longenecker, C. (1993) 'The Bathsheba Syndrome: The Ethical Failure of Successful Leaders', *The Journal of Business Ethics*, 12, 265–73.

Luft, J. and Ingham, H. (1955) *The Johari Window: A Graphic Model for Interpersonal Relations*, Western Training Lab, University of California, Los Angeles, CA.

Luhmann, N. (1988) 'Familiarity, Confidence and Trust: Problems and Alternatives', in D. Gambetta (ed.), *Trust: Making and Breaking Co-operative Relations*, Basil Blackwell, Oxford, pp. 213–37.

Lukes, S. (1974) *Power: A Radical View*, Macmillan, London.

—— (1987) 'Perspectives on Authority', in R. Pennock and J. Chapman (eds), *Authority Revisited: NOMOS XXIX*, NYUP, New York, reprinted in J. Raz (ed.) (1990), *Authority*, Basil Blackwell, London.

Luo, Y. (2002) 'Building Trust in Cross-cultural Collaborations: Toward a Contingency Perspective', *Journal of Management*, 28, 669–94.

Lussier, R.N. and Achua, C.F. (2001) *Leadership: Theory, Application, Skill Development*, South-Western College Publishing, Cincinnati, OH.

McAllister, D.J. (1995) 'Affect- and Cognition-based Trust as Foundations for Interpersonal Cooperation in Organisations', *Academy of Management Journal*, 38, 24–59.

MacBeath, J. (2005) 'Leadership as Distributed: A Matter of Practice', *School Leadership and Management*, 25, 349–66.

McCall, M. (1998) *High Flyers*, Harvard Business School Press, Boston, MA.

McCall, M. and Lombardo, M. (1983a) *Off the Track: Why and How Successful Executives Get Derailed*, Center for Creative Leadership, Greensboro, NC.

McCall, M. and Lombardo, M. (1983b) 'What Makes a Top Executive?', *Psychology Today*, 17, 26–31.

McCall, M.W., Jr (1976) 'Leadership Research: Choosing Gods and Devils on the Run', *Journal of Occupational Psychology*, 49, 139–53.

McCalley, R. (2002) *Patterns of Management Power*, Quorum Books, Westport, CT.

McCauley, C.D. (2001) 'Leader Training and Leader Development', in S.J. Zaccaro and R.J. Klimoski (eds), *The Nature of Organizational Leadership: Understanding the Performance Imperatives Confronting Today's Leaders*, Jossey-Bass, San Francisco, CA, pp. 347–83.

McCauley, C., Moxley, R. and VanVelsor, E. (1998) *The Center for Creative Leadership Handbook of Leadership Development*, Jossey-Bass, San Francisco, CA.

McClelland, D.C. (1975) *Power: The Inner Experience*, Irvington, New York.

McClelland, D.C. (1985) *Human Motivation*, Scott Foresman, Glenview, IL.

Maccoby, M. (2000) 'Narcissistic Leaders: the Incredible Pros, the Inevitable Cons', *Harvard Business Review*, Jan, 69–77.

—— (2004) 'Why People Follow the Leader: the Power of Transference', *Harvard Business Review*, Sept, 76–85.

McCormack, M.H. (1984) *What They Don't Teach You at Harvard Business School*, Bantam Books, New York.

Macdonald, J.H. (trans.) (1996) *Tao Te Ching*. Available at www.wam.umd.edu/~stwright/rel/tao/TaoTeChing.html#57 (Accessed 22 June 2006).

McFarlin, D. and Sweeney, P. (2000) *Where Egos Dare*, Kogan Page, London.

McGill, M. and Slocum, J., Jr (1997) 'A Little Leadership, Please', *Organizational Dynamics*, 26, 39–49.

McGregor, D. (1960) *The Human Side of Enterprise*, McGraw-Hill, New York.

Machiavelli, N. (1532/1991) *The Prince*, R. Price (trans.), Cambridge University Press, New York.

—— (1531/1992) 'Discourses on the First Ten Books of Titius Livius', in M.L. Morgan (ed.), *Classics of Moral and Political Theory*, 3rd edn, Hacket Publishing Co., Indianapolis, IN, pp. 467–87.

McKenna, B. and Rooney, D. (2004) 'Managing Wisely: An Historical Survey of Philosophy and Psychology Shows Us How', Unpublished manuscript, University of Queensland.

MacKenzie, S.B., Podsakoff, P.M. and Rich, G.A. (2001) 'Transformational and Transactional Leadership and Salesperson Performance', *Journal of the Academy of Marketing Science*, 29, 115–34.

MacKinnon, D.W. (1978) *In Search of Human Effectiveness*, The Creative Education Foundation, Buffalo, NY.

Martin, J. (2001) *Organizational Culture: Mapping the Terrain*, Sage, London.

Martocchio, J.J. and Baldwin, T.T. (1997) 'The Evolution of Strategic Organizational Training: New Objectives and Research Agenda', *Research in Personnel and Human Resources Management*, 15, 1–46.

Marx, K. (1970) *Economic and Philosophic Manuscripts of 1844*, D. Struik (ed. intro.), Lawrence & Wishart, London.

Maslow, A.H. (1943) 'A Theory of Human Motivation', *Psychological Review*, 50, 370–96.

—— (1954) *Motivation and Personality*, Harper and Brothers, New York.

—— (1966) 'Comments on Dr. Frankl's Paper', *Journal of Humanistic Psychology*, 6, 107–12.

—— (1969) *Toward a Psychology of Being*, 2nd edn, D. Van Nostrand, New York.

Matthews, G., Zeinder, M. and Roberts, R.D. (2002) *Emotional Intelligence: Science and Myth*, MIT Press, Cambridge, MA.

Mayer, J.D. and Salovey, P. (1997) 'What is Emotional Intelligence?', in P. Salovey and D. Sluyter (eds), *Emotional Development and Emotional Intelligence: Implications for Educators*, Basic Books, New York, pp. 3–31.

Mayer, J.D., Salovey, P. and Caruso, D.R. (2000) 'Emotional Intelligence', in R.J. Sternberg (ed.), *Handbook of Intelligence*, 2nd edn, Cambridge University Press, New York, pp. 396–420.

Mayer, R.C., Davis, J.H. and Schoorman, F.D. (1995) 'An Integrative Model of Organisational Trust', *Academy of Management Review*, 20, 709–34.

Mazlish, B. (1990) *The Leader, the Led, and the Psyche*, Wesleyan University Press, Hanover, NH.

Mead, G.H. (1934/1962) *Mind, Self, & Society*, C. Morris (ed.), University of Chicago Press, Chicago, IL.

Meindl, J.M. (1995) 'The Romance of Leadership as a Follower-centric Theory: Social Constructionist Approach', *Leadership Quarterly*, 6, 329–41.

Mengel, T. (2004) 'From Responsibility to Values-Oriented Leadership – 6 Theses on Meaning and Values in Personal Life and Work Environments', International Network on Personal Meaning. *Positive Living E-Zine*, 11 August, Available at www.meaning.ca/articles04/mengel-responsibility.htm

Messick, D.M. (2005) 'On the Psychological Exchange Between Leaders and Followers', in D.M. Messick and R.M. Kramer (eds), *The Psychology of Leadership: New Perspectives and Research*, Lawrence Erlbaum Associates, Mahwah, NJ, pp. 81–96.

Michels, R. (1915/1949) *Political Parties*, E. Paul and C. Paul (eds), Free Press, Glencoe, IL.

Milgram, S. (1974) *Obedience to Authority: An Experimental View*, Harper & Row, New York.

Mill, J.S. (1987) *Utilitarianism and Other Essays*, Alan Ryan (ed.), Penguin, New York, pp. 276–97.

Miller, A. (1949/1998) *Death of a Salesman*, Penguin, London.

Miller, E. (1993) *From Dependency to Autonomy: Studies in Organisation and Change*, Free Association Books, London.

Mintzberg, H. (1978) 'Patterns in Strategy Formation', *Management Science*, 24, 934–48.

Mintzberg, H. (1998) 'Covert Leadership: Notes on Managing Professionals: Knowledge Workers Respond to Inspiration, Not Supervision', *Harvard Business Review*, 76, 140–7.

Mishra, A. (1996) 'Organisational Responses to Crisis: the Centrality of Trust', in R.M. Kramer and T.R. Tyler (eds), *Trust in Organisations: Frontiers of Theory and Research*, Sage, London, pp. 261–88.

Mitchell, G.J. (1999) *Making Peace*, Knopf, New York.

Mitroff, I. and Denton, E. (1999) *A Spiritual Audit of Corporate America: A Hard Look at Spirituality, Religion, and Values in the Workplace*, Jossey-Bass, San Francisco, CA.

Mock, F.L. (1995) *A Strong Clear Vision: Maya Lin* (DVD).

Moody-Adams, M.M. (1994) 'Culture, Responsibility, and Affected Ignorance', *Ethics*, 104, 291–309.

Morgan, G. (1986) *Images of Organizations*, Sage, New York.

Morrell, M. and Capparell, S. (2001) *Shackleton's Way: Leadership Lessons from the Great Antarctic Explorer*, Nicholas Brealey, London.

Morris, J.H. and Moberg, D.J. (1994) 'Work Organisations and Contexts for Trust and Betrayal', in T. Sarbin, R. Carney and C. Eoyang (eds), *Citizen Espionage: Studies in Trust and Betrayal*, Praeger, Westport, CT, pp. 163–87.

Mosca, G. (1939) *The Ruling Class*, H. Kahn (trans.), McGraw-Hill, New York.

Mumford, M.D. and Gustafson, S.B. (1988) 'Creativity Syndrome: Integration, Application, and Innovation', *Psychological Bulletin*, 103, 27–43.

Murphy, S.E. and Riggio, R.E. (2003) 'Introduction to the Future of Leadership Development', in S. Murphy and R. Riggio (eds), *The Future of Leadership Development*, Lawrence Erlbaum Associates, Mahwah, NJ, pp. 11–28.

Murphy, S.M., Wayne, S.J., Liden, R.C. and Erdoban, B. (2003) 'Understanding

Social Loafing: The Role of Justice Perceptions and Exchange Relationships', *Human Relations*, 56, 61–84.

Nahavandi, A. (2005) *The Art and Science of Leadership*, Prentice Hall, Upper Saddle River, NJ.

Nanus, B. (1992) *Visionary Leadership*, Jossey-Bass, San Francisco, CA.

Nash, L. and McLennan, S. (2001) *Church on Sunday, Work on Monday: The Challenge of Fusing Christian Values with Business Life*, Jossey-Bass, San Francisco, CA.

Nelson, R.B. (1994) *Empowering Employees Through Delegation*, Irwin Professional, Burr Ridge, IL.

Nietzsche, F. (1969) *Thus Spoke Zarathustra*, Penguin, London.

Nisbett, R.E. and Ross, L. (1980) *Human Inference: Strategies and Shortcomings of Social Judgment*, Prentice Hall, Englewood Cliffs, NJ.

Nolan, P. (1999) Personal Interview, 7 January, Belfast, Northern Ireland.

Nonaka, I. and Takeuchi, H. (1995) *The Knowledge-Creating Company: How Japanese Companies Create the Dynamics of Innovation*, Oxford University Press, New York.

Northouse, P. (2001) *Leadership, Theory and Practice*, 2nd edn, Sage, Thousand Oaks, CA.

—— (2004) *Leadership: Theory and Practice*, 3rd edn, Sage, Thousand Oaks, CA.

Nozick, R. (1990) *Philosophical Explanations*, Simon & Schuster, New York.

Nunnally, J.C. (1978) *Psychometric Theory*, McGraw-Hill, New York.

Nye, R. (1977) *The Anti-democratic Sources of Elite Theory: Pareto, Mosca, Michels*, Sage, Beverly Hills, CA.

O'Brien, F. and Meadows, M. (2000) 'Corporate Visioning: A Survey of UK Practice', *Journal of Operational Research Society*, 51, 36–44.

O'Loughlin, J. (2004) *The Real Warren Buffett: Managing Capital, Leading People*, Nicholas Brealey, London.

O'Neil, H. and Fisher, Y. (2004) 'A Technology to Support Leader Development: Computer Games', in D. Day, S. Zaccaro and S. Halpin (eds), *Leader Development for Transforming Organizations: Growing Leaders for Tomorrow*, Lawrence Erlbaum Associates, Mahwah, NJ, pp. 41–69.

O'Neill, O. (2002) *A Question of Trust. The BBC Reith Lectures 2002*, Cambridge University Press, Cambridge.

Offermann, L. (2004a) 'Empowerment', in G.R. Goethals, G.J. Sorenson and J.M. Burns (eds), *Encyclopedia of Leadership*, vol. 4, Sage, Thousand Oaks, CA, pp. 434–37.

—— (2004b) 'When Followers Become Toxic', *Harvard Business Review*, 82, 54–60.

Offner, A.K., Kramer, T.J. and Winter, J.P. (1996) 'The Effects of Facilitation, Recording, and Pauses on Group Brainstorming', *Small Group Research*, 27, 283–98.

Oldham, J. and Morris, L. (1995) *The New Personality Self-Portrait*, Bantam Books, New York.

Oliver, Q. (1998) *Working for 'YES': The Story of the May 1998 Referendum in Northern Ireland*, The 'YES' Campaign, Belfast, Northern Ireland.

Orme, G. and Bar-On, R. (2002) 'The Contribution of Emotional Intelligence to Individual and Organisational Effectiveness', *Competency & Emotional Intelligence*, 9, 23–8.

Osborn, A.F. (1953) *Applied Imagination*, Scribner's Sons, New York.

Osland, J. and Bird, A. (2000) 'Beyond Sophisticated Stereotyping: Cultural Sensemaking in Context', *Academy of Management Executive*, 14, 65–79.

Owen, H. (1987) *Spirit-Transformation and Development in Organizations*, Abbot, Potomac, MD.

Oxford English Dictionary. Available at www.oed.com

Padilla, A., Hogan, R. and Kaiser, R. (2005) *The Toxic Triangle: Destructive Leaders, Vulnerable Followers, and Conducive Environments*, Department of Business Management, North Carolina State University, Raleigh, NC.

Page, D. and Wong, P. (2000) 'A Conceptual Framework for Measuring Servant Leadership', in S. Adjuibolosoo (ed.), *The Human Factor in Shaping the Course of History and Development*, Oxford University Press, Oxford, pp. 69–109.

Paine, L.S. (2003) *Value Shift: Why Companies Must Merge Social and Financial Imperatives to Achieve Superior Performance*, McGraw-Hill, New York.

Palestini, R.H. (2006) *Path to Leadership: the Heroic Follower*, Rowman & Littlefield, New York.

Pareto, V. (1991) *The Rise and Fall of Elites*, H. Zetterberg (trans.), Transaction, New Brunswick, NJ.

Parker, M. (2000) *Organizational Culture and Identity*, Sage, London.

Parks, S.D. (2005) *Leadership Can Be Taught*, Harvard Business School Press, Boston, MA.

Parnes, S.J. (1985) *A Facilitating Style of Leadership*, Bearly, Buffalo, NY.

Paulhus, D. and Williams, K. (2002) 'The Dark Triad of Personality: Narcissism, Machiavellianism, and Psychopathy', *Journal of Research in Psychology*, 36, 556–63.

Pawar, B.S. and Eastman, K. (1997) 'The Nature and Implications of Contextual Influences on Transformational Leadership: A Conceptual Examination', *Academy of Management Review*, 22, 80–109.

PDI (1992) 'Competence, Potential, and Jeopardy', Personnel Decisions Inc., Minneapolis, MN.

Perren, L. and Burgoyne, J. (2001) *Management and Leadership Abilities: An Analysis of Texts, Testimony and Practice*, Council for Excellence in Management and Leadership, London.

Peters, T. (1987) *Thriving on Chaos: Handbook for a Management Revolution*, Alfred A. Knopf Inc., New York.

Peters, T. and Waterman, R. (1982) *In Search of Excellence: Lessons from America's Best Run Companies*, Harper & Row, New York.

Petri, H.L. and Govern, J.M. (2004) *Motivation: Theory, Research, and Applications*, 5th edn, Wadsworth Publishing, Belmont, CA.

Pfeffer, J. (1994) *Managing with Power: Politics and Influence in Organizations*, Harvard Business School Press, Boston, MA.

Pierce, J.L. and Newstrom, J.W. (1994) *Leaders & the Leadership Process*, Irwin, Chicago, IL.

Plato (1992) *Republic*, G.M.A. Grube (trans.), Hackett Publishing, Indianapolis, IN.

Podsakoff, P.M. and Organ, D. (1986) 'Self-reports in Organizational Research: Problems and Prospects', *Journal of Management*, 12, 531–44.

Ponder, R.D. (2005) *Leadership Made Easy*, Entrepreneur Press, Madison, WI.

Popper, M. and Lipshitz, R. (1993) 'Putting Leadership Theory to Work: A Conceptual Framework for Theory-based Leadership Development', *Leadership & Organization Development Journal*, 14(7), 23–7.

Portny, S.E. (2002) 'The Delegation Dilemma: When Do You Let Go?', *The Information Management Journal*, 36.

Price, R.H. (1990) 'Wither Participation and Empowerment?', *American Journal of Community Psychology*, 18, 163–7.

Price, T.L. (2000) 'Explaining Ethical Failures of Leadership', *The Leadership and Organization Development Journal*, 21, 177–84.

—— (2003) 'The Ethics of Authentic Transformational Leadership', *Leadership Quarterly*, 14, 67–81.

—— (2004) 'Philosophy', in G.R. Goethals, G. Sorenson and J.M. Burns (eds), *Encyclopedia of Leadership*, Sage, Thousand Oaks, CA, pp. 1195–9.

—— (2006) *Understanding Ethical Failures in Leadership*, Cambridge University Press, New York.

Proctor, T. (2005) *Creative Problem Solving for Managers: Developing Skills for Decision Making and Innovation*, Routledge, London.

Puccio, G., Firestien, R.L., Coyle, C. and Masucci, C. (2006) 'A Review of the Effectiveness of CPS Training: A Focus on Workplace Issues', *Creativity and Innovation Management*, 15, 19–33.

Quallich, S.A. (2005) 'A Bond of Trust: Delegation', *Urologic Nursing*, 25, 120–3.

Quick, J. and Tetrick, L (2003) *Handbook of Occupational Health Psychology*, American Psychological Association, Washington, DC.

Quinn, R.E., Faerman, S.R., Thompson, M.P. and McGrath, M.R. (2003) *Becoming a Master Manager: A Competency Framework*, 3rd edn, John Wiley & Sons, Hoboken, NJ.

Ramirez, R. (1991) *The Beauty of Social Organization*, Accedo, Munich.

Rappaport, J. (1985) 'The Power of Empowerment Language', *Social Policy*, 16, 15–21.

Raz, J. (1979) *The Authority of Law: Essays on Laws and Morality*, Clarendon Press, Oxford.

—— (1985) 'The Justification of Authority', *Philosophy and Public Affairs*, 14, 2–29.

—— (ed.) (1990) *Authority*, Basil Blackwell, London.

Reddin, W.J. (1967) 'The 3-D Management Style Theory', *Management Development Journal*, April, 8–17.

—— (1970) *Managerial Effectiveness*, McGraw-Hill, New York.

Reed, P. (1993) 'Organisation Culture: A Potentially Powerful Management Research Tool but a Disappointing Management Control Mechanism', Unpublished paper presented at the British Academy of Management Annual Conference, Milton Keynes, 20–22 Sept.

Reiss, S. and Haverkamp, S.H. (2005) 'Motivation in Developmental Context: A New Method for Studying Self-actualization', *Journal of Humanistic Psychology*, 45, 41–53.

Rescher, N. (1996) *Process Metaphysics: An Introduction to Process Philosophy*, SUNY, Albany, NY.

Rice, K.E. (1967) *Learning for Leadership: Interpersonal and Intergroup Relations*, Tavistock, London.

Rickards, T. (1999) *Creativity and the Management of Change*, Blackwell, Oxford.

Rickards, T. and De Cock, C. (1994) 'Training for Creativity: Findings in a European Context', *Interfaces*, 24, 59–65.

—— (1999) 'Sociological Paradigms and Organizational Creativity', in R.E. Purser and A. Montuori (eds), *Social Creativity*, vol. 2, Hampton Press, Cresskill, NJ, pp. 235–56.

Rickards, T. and Moger, S. (2006) 'Creative Leaders: A Decade of Contributions from Creativity and Innovation Management Journal', *Creativity and Innovation Management*, 15, 4–18.

Rickards, T., Runco, M. and Moger, S. (forthcoming) *Routledge Companion of Creativity*, Routledge, London.

Riggio, R.E. (2004) 'Charisma', in G.R. Goethals, G.J. Sorenson and J.M. Burns (eds), *Encyclopedia of Leadership*, vol. 1, Sage, Thousand Oaks, CA, pp. 158–62.

Robbins, S.R. and Duncan, R.B. (1988) 'The Role of the CEO and Top Management in the Creation and Implementation of Strategic Vision', in D. C. Hambrick (ed.), *The Executive Effect: Concepts and Methods for Studying Top Managers*, JAI Press, Greenwich, CT.

Roberts, K.H. and O'Reilly, C.A., III (1976) 'Failures in Upward Communication in Organizations: Three Possible Culprits', *Academy of Management Journal*, 17, 205–15.

Roberts, R. (2002) *Religion, Theology and the Human Sciences*, Cambridge University Press, Cambridge.

Robertson, P. (2005) *Always Change a Winning Team: Why Reinvention and Change are Prerequisites for Business Success*, Marshall Cavendish Business, London.

Rogers, C.R. (1961) *On Becoming a Person*, 2nd edn, Houghton Mifflin, Boston, MA.

Roper, J. (2001) *American Presidents: Heroic Leadership from Kennedy to Clinton*, Edinburgh University Press, Edinburgh.

Ropo, A., Eriksson, P. and Hunt, J.G. (1997) 'Editorial – Reflections on Conducting Processual Research on Management and Organizations', *Scandinavian Journal of Management*, Special Issue on Processual Research, 13, 331–5.

Rosenbach, W.E. and Taylor, R.L. (eds) (1998) *Contemporary Issues in Leadership*, 4th edn, Westview Press, Boulder, CO.

Rost, J. (1991) *Leadership for the Twenty-first Century*, Praeger, Westport, CT.

Rotter, J.B. (1967) 'A New Scale for Measurement of Interpersonal Trust', *Journal of Personality*, 35, 651–65.

—— (1971) 'Generalized Expectations for Interpersonal Trust', *American Psychologist*, 26, 443–52.

—— (1980) 'Interpersonal Trust, Trustworthiness and Gullibility', *American Psychologist*, 35, 1–17.

Rousseau, J.-J. (1755/1973) *The Social Contract and Discourses*, G.D.H. Cole (trans.), J.H. Brumfitt and J.C. Hall (rev.), J.M. Dent Ltd, London.

Russell, R. (2001) 'The Role of Values in Servant Leadership', *Leadership and Organizational Development Journal*, 22, 76–83.

Russell, R. and Stone, A. (2002) 'A Review of Servant Leadership Attributes: Developing a Practical Model', *Leadership and Organizational Development Journal*, 23, 145–57.

Rustow, D. (1970) 'The Study of Leadership', in D. Rustow (ed.), *Philosophers and Kings: Studies in Leadership*, George Braziller, New York, chapter 1.

Ryan, K.D. and Oestreich, D.K. (1998) *Driving Fear Out of the Workplace: Creating the High-trust, High-performance Organization*, 2nd edn, Jossey-Bass, San Francisco, CA.

Sabel, C.F. (1993) 'Studied Trust: Building New Forms of Cooperation in a Volatile Economy', *Human Relations*, 46, 1133–70.

Salaman, G. (2004) 'Competencies of Managers, Competences of Leaders', in

J. Storey (ed.), *Leadership in Organizations: Current Issues and Key Trends*, Routledge, London.

Salas, E. and Cannon-Bowers, J.A. (2001) 'The Science of Training: A Decade of Progress', *Annual Review of Psychology*, 52, 471–99.

Salovey, P. and Mayer, J.D. (1990) 'Emotional Intelligence', *Imagination, Cognition and Personality*, 9, 185–211.

Sankowsky, D. (1995) 'The Charismatic Leader as Narcissist: Understanding the Abuse of Power', *Organizational Dynamics*, 23, 57–71.

Schein, E.H. (1985) *Organization Culture and Leadership*, Jossey-Bass, San Francisco, CA.

Schell, B. (1999) *Management in the Mirror: Stress and Emotional Dysfunction in Lives at the Top*, Quorom Books, Westport, CT.

Schlenker, B.R. (1980) *Impression Management: The Self-concept, Social Identity, and Interpersonal Relations*, Brooks/Cole, Monterey, CA.

—— (1985) 'Introduction: Foundations of the Self in Social Life', in B.R. Schlenker (ed.), *The Self and Social Life*, McGraw-Hill, New York.

Schmitt, N.W. and Klimoski, R.J. (1991) *Research Methods in Human Resource Management*, South-Western Publishing, Cincinnati, OH.

Schoenfeldt, L.F. (1984) 'Psychometric Properties of Organizational Research Instruments', in T.S. Bateman and G.R. Ferris (eds), *Method and Analysis in Organizational Research*, Reston Publishing, Reston, VA.

Schriesheim, C.A., Powers, K.J., Scandura, T.A., Gardiner, C.C. and Lankau, M.J. (1993) 'Improving Construct Measurement in Management Research: Comments and a Quantitative Approach for Assessing the Theoretical Content Adequacy of Paper-and-pencil Survey-type Instruments', *Journal of Management*, 19, 385–417.

Schroeder, J.E. (2005) 'The Artist and the Brand', *European Journal of Marketing*, 39, 1291–305.

Schwab, D.P. (1980) 'Construct Validity in Organizational Behavior', in L.L. Cummings and B.M. Staw (eds), *Research in Organizational Behavior*, vol. 2, JAI Press, Greenwich, CT, pp. 3–43.

Schwartzmann, H.B. (1993) *Ethnography in Organizations*, Sage, London.

Scott, W.R. (1987) *Organizations: Rational, Natural, and Open Systems*, 2nd edn, Prentice Hall, Englewood Cliffs, NJ.

Sekaran, U. (1992) *Research Methods for Business: A Skill-building Approach*, John Wiley, New York.

Seldon, A. (2005) *Blair*, Gardners Books, London.

Seligman, A.B. (1997) *The Problem of Trust*, Princeton University Press, Princeton, NJ.

Sendjaya, S. and Sarros, J. (2002) 'Servant Leadership: Its Origin, Development, and Applications in Organizations', *Journal of Leadership and Organizational Studies*, 9, 57–65.

Senge, P. (1990) *The Fifth Discipline: The Art and Practice of the Learning Organization*, Century Business, London.

Senge, P., Kleiner, A., Roberts, C., Ross, R., Rother, G. and Smith, B. (1999) *The Dance of Change*, Doubleday, New York.

Senge, P., Scharmer, C.O., Jaworski, J. and Flowers, B.S. (2004) *Presence: An Exploration of Profound Change in People, Organizations and Society*, Society for Organizational Learning, Currency Doubleday, London.

Sennett, R. (1980) *Authority*, Alfred A. Knopf, New York.

—— (1998) *The Corrosion of Character*, W.W. Norton, New York.

Shamir, B. (1991) 'The Charismatic Relationship: Alternative Explanations and Predictions', *Leadership Quarterly*, 2, 81–104.

Shaw, J.B. (1990) 'A Cognitive Categorization Model for the Study of Intercultural Management', *Academy of Management Review*, 15, 626–45.

Shaw, P. (2002) *Changing Conversations in Organizations: A Complexity Approach to Change*, Routledge, London.

Sheppard, B.H. and Sherman, D.M. (1998) 'The Grammars of Trust: A Model and General Implications', *Academy of Management Review*, 23, 422–37.

Shils, E. (1965) 'Charisma, Order, and Status', *American Sociological Review*, 30, 199–213.

Showkier, J. (2002) 'The Business Case for Servant-Leadership', in L. Spears and M. Lawrence (eds), *Focus on Leadership: Servant-Leadership for the 21st Century*, John Wiley & Sons, New York, pp. 123–41.

Shriberg, A., Lloyd, C., Shriberg, D. and Williamson, M.L. (1997) *Practicing Leadership*, John Wiley & Sons, New York.

Shriberg, A., Shriberg, D.L. and Kumari, R. (2005) *Practicing Leadership: Principles and Applications*, 3rd edn, John Wiley & Sons, Hoboken, NJ.

Silverman, S. (1968) 'Review of Miller and Rice: Systems of Organization', *British Journal of Industrial Relations*, 6, 393–97.

Silverthorne, C. and Ting-Hsin, W. (2001) 'Situational Leadership Style as a Predictor of Success and Productivity among Taiwanese Business Organizations', *The Journal of Psychology*, 135, 399–412.

Sims, B. (1997) *Servanthood: Leadership for the Third Millennium*, Cowley Publications, Boston, MA.

Sinclair, A. (2004) *Doing Leadership Differently: Gender, Power and Sexuality in a Changing Business Culture*, Melbourne University Press, Melbourne.

Sitkin, S.B. and Roth, N.L. (1993) 'Explaining the Limited Effectiveness of Legalistic "Remedies" for Trust/Distrust', *Organisation Science*, 4, 367–403.

Slaski, M. and Cartwright, S. (2002) 'Health Performance and Emotional Intelligence: An Exploratory Study of Retail Managers', *Stress and Health*, 18, 63–8.

Slater, R. (2000) *Jack Welch and the GE Way: Management Insights and Leadership Secrets of the Legendary CEO*, McGraw-Hill, New York.

Sloan, E. (1994) 'Assessing and Developing Versatility: Executive Survival Skill for the Brave New World', *Counselling Psychology Journal*, 46, 24–31.

Smircich, L. and Morgan, G. (1982) 'Leadership: The Management of Meaning', *The Journal of Applied Behavioral Science*, 18, 257–74.

Smith, B., Montagno, R. and Kuszmenko, T. (2004) 'Transformational and Servant Leadership: Content and Contextual Comparisons', *Journal of Leadership and Organizational Studies*, 10, 80–91.

Smith, N. and Quirk, M. (2004) 'From Grace to Disgrace: the Rise & Fall of Arthur Andersen', *Journal of Business Ethics Education*, 1, 93–132.

Smith, P. and Peterson, M. (1988) *Leadership, Organization and Culture*, Sage, London.

Smith, P.B., Misumi, J., Tayeb, M., Peterson, M. and Bond, M. (1989) 'On the Generality of Leadership Style Measures Across Cultures', *Journal of Occupational Psychology*, 62, 97–109.

Solomon, R.C. (2004) 'Ethical Leadership, Emotions, and Trust: Beyond "Charisma"', in J.B. Ciulla (ed.), *Ethics the Heart of Leadership*, 2nd edn, Quorum Books, Westbury, CT, pp. 83–102.

Sonquist, J.A. and Dunkelberg, W.C. (1977) *Survey and Opinion Research: Procedures for Processing and Analysis*, Prentice-Hall, London.

Spears, L. (1995) 'Introduction: Servant-leadership and the Greenleaf Legacy', in L. Spears (ed.), *Reflections on Leadership*, John Wiley & Sons, New York, pp. 1–16.

Spears, L. and Lawrence, M. (eds) (2004) *Practicing Servant-leadership: Succeeding Through Trust, Bravery and Forgiveness*, Jossey-Bass, San Francisco, CA.

Spector, P.E. (1987) 'Method Variance as an Artifact in Self-reported Affect and Perceptions at Work: Myth or Significant Problem?', *Journal of Applied Psychology*, 72, 438–43.

Sperry, L. (2002) *Effective Leadership*, Brunner-Routledge, New York.

Spillane, J.P. (2006) *Distributed Leadership*, Jossey-Bass, San Francisco, CA.

Spillane, J.P., Halverson, R. and Diamond, J.B. (2004) 'Towards a Theory of Leadership Practice: a Distributed Perspective', *Journal of Curriculum Studies*, 36, 3–34.

Spreitzer, G. (2003) 'Leadership Development in the Virtual Workplace', in S. Murphy and R. Riggio (eds), *The Future of Leadership Development*, Lawrence Erlbaum Associates, Mahwah, NJ, pp. 71–86.

Stacey, R.D. (1996) *Complexity and Creativity in Organizations*, Berrett-Koehler, San Francisco, CA.

Stein, M. (2005) 'The Othello Conundrum: the Inner Contagion of Leadership', *Organization Studies*, 26, 1405–19.

Sternberg, R. (ed.) (1990) *Wisdom: Its Nature, Origins and Development*, Cambridge University Press, Cambridge.

Sternberg, R. and Jordan, J. (eds) (2005) *A Handbook of Wisdom: Psychological Perspectives*, Cambridge University Press, Cambridge.

Stogdill, R.M. (1948) 'Personal Factors Associated with Leadership: A Survey of the Literature', *Journal of Psychology*, 25, 35–71.

—— (1963) *Manual for the Leader Behaviour Description Questionnaire XII*, Bureau of Business Research, Ohio State University, Columbus, OH.

—— (1974) *Handbook of Leadership*, Free Press, New York.

Stone, A., Russell, R. and Patterson, K. (2004) 'Transformational Versus Servant Leadership: A Difference in Leader Focus', *The Leadership and Organizational Development Journal*, 25, 349–61.

Stone-Romero, E.F., Weaver, A.E. and Glenar, J.L. (1995) 'Trends in Research Design and Data Analytic Strategies in Organizational Research', *Journal of Management*, 21, 141–57.

Strati, A. (1999) *Organization and Aesthetics*, Sage, London.

Sulkowicz, K. (2004) 'Worse than Enemies: the CEO's Destructive Confident', *Harvard Business Review*, Feb.

Sunstein, C.R. (2003) *Why Societies Need Dissent*, Harvard University Press, Cambridge, MA.

Sutton, R.I. and Hargadon, A. (1996) 'Brainstorming Groups in Context: Effectiveness in a Product Design Firm', *Administrative Science Quarterly*, 41, 685–718.

Sveningsson, S. and Alvesson, M. (2003) 'Managing Managerial Identities', *Human Relations*, 56, 10, 1163–93.

Takahashi, M. and Bordia, P. (2000) 'The Concept of Wisdom: A Cross-Cultural Comparison', *International Journal of Psychology*, 35, 1–9.

Tannenbaum, R. and Schmidt, W.H. (1973) 'How to Choose a Leadership Pattern', *Harvard Business Review*, May–June, 162–80.

Tarnas, R. (1991) *The Passion of the Western Mind*, Ballantine Books, New York.

Taylor, H.L. (1991) *Delegate: The Key to Successful Management*, Warner Books, New York.

Taylor, S.S. and Hansen, H. (2005) 'Finding Form: Looking at the Field of Organizational Aesthetics', *Journal of Management Studies*, 42, 1211–31.

Tedeschi, J. and Melburg, V. (1984) 'Impression Management and Influence in the Organization', in S. Bachrach and E.J. Lawler (eds), *Research in the Sociology of Organizations*, vol. 3, JAI Press, Greenwich, CT, pp. 31–58.

Temes, P. (2005) 'Dirty Hands, Necessary Sin, and the Ethics of Leaders', in J.B. Ciulla, T.L. Price and S.E. Murphy (eds), *The Quest for Moral Leaders: Essays in Leadership Ethics*, Edward Elgar, Cheltenham, chapter 6.

Thomas, D.C. and Inkson, K. (2004) *Cultural Intelligence: People Skills for Global Business*, Berett-Koehler, San Francisco, CA.

Thomas, J. and Hansen, M. (eds) (2002) *Handbook of Mental Health in the Workplace*, Sage, Thousand Oaks, CA.

Thorndike, R.L. and Stein, S. (1937) 'An Evaluation of the Attempts to Measure Social Intelligence', *Psychological Bulletin*, 34, 275–84.

Thorndike, R.L. and Hagen, E. (1969) *Measurement and Evaluation in Psychology and Education*, 3rd edn, John Wiley, New York.

Tichy, N. and Devanna, M.A. (1986) *The Transformational Leader*, John Wiley & Sons, New York.

Tichey, N. and Cohen, E. (1997) *The Leadership Engine: How Winning Companies Build Leaders at Every Level*, Harper Collins, New York.

Tourish, D. (2005a) 'Charismatic Leadership and Corporate Cultism at Enron: the Elimination of Dissent, the Promotion of Conformity and Organizational Collapse', *Leadership*, 1, 455–80.

—— (2005b) 'Transformational Leadership and the Perils of Coercive Persuasion', paper presented at the 4th International Conference on Studying Leadership, Lancaster, December.

Tracey, J.B. and Hinkin, T.R. (1998) 'Transformational Leadership or Effective Managerial Practices?', *Group & Organization Management*, 23, 220–36.

Trompenaars, F. (1997) *Riding the Waves of Culture: Understanding Cultural Diversity in Business*, Nicholas Brealey, London.

Trompenaars, F. and Hampden-Turner, C. (1997) *Riding the Waves of Culture: Understanding Cultural Diversity in Business*, 2nd edn, Nicholas Brealey, London.

Tsoukas, H. and Chia, R. (2002) 'On Organizational Becoming: Rethinking Organizational Change', *Organization Science*, 13, 567–82.

Tuccari, F. (1991) *Carisma e Leadership nel Pensiero di Max Weber*, Franco Angeli, Milan.

Tucker, R. (1968) 'The Theory of Charismatic Leadership', *Daedalus*, 97, 731–56.

Turner, J. (1984) 'Social Identification and Psychological Group Formation', in H. Tajfel (ed.), *The Social Dimension, Vol. 2*, Cambridge University Press, Cambridge.

Turner, J.C. (2005) 'Explaining the Nature of Power: A Three-process Theory', *European Journal of Psychology*, 35, 1–22.

Tyler, T. and Degoey, P. (1996) 'Trust in Organisational Authorities: the Influence of Motive Attributions on Willingness to Accept Decisions', in R.M.

Kramer and T.R. Tyler (eds), *Trust in Organizations: Frontiers of Theory and Research*, Sage, London, pp. 331–57.

Tyler, T.R. and Lind, E.A. (1992) 'A Relational Model of Authority in Groups', *Advances in Experimental Social Psychology*, 25, 115–91.

Van Creveld, M. (1985) *Command in War*, Harvard University Press, Cambridge, MA.

Van de Ven, A. and Poole, S. (1995) 'Explaining Development and Change in Organizations', *The Academy of Management Review*, 20, 510–40.

—— (2005) 'Alternative Approaches for Studying Organizational Change', *Organization Studies*, 26, 1377–404.

Van Velsor, E. and Leslie, B. (1995) 'Why Executives Derail: Perspectives Across Time and Cultures', *Academy of Management Executive*, 9, 62–72.

Vecchio, R.P. (2002) 'Leadership and Gender Advantage', *Leadership Quarterly*, 13, 643–71.

Vecchio, R.P. and Boatwright, K. (2002) 'Preferences for Idealized Styles of Supervision', *Leadership Quarterly*, 13, 327–43.

Vicere, A. and Fulmer, R. (1996) *Leadership by Design*, Harvard Business School Press, Boston, MA.

Vinnicombe, S. and Singh, V. (2005) *Female FTSE Index and Report (2005): New Look Women Directors Add Value to FTSE 100 Boards*, School of Management Cranfield University, Cranfield.

Voegelin, E. (1956) *Order and History*, vol. 1, Louisiana State University Press, Baton Rouge, LA.

—— (1957) *Order and History*, vols 2 and 3, Louisiana State University Press, Baton Rouge, LA.

—— (1999) *The Collected Works of Eric Voegelin*, vol. 26, D. Walsh (ed.), University of Missouri Press, Columbia, MO.

—— (2001) *The Collected Works of Eric Voegelin*, vol. 13, J. Cockerill and B. Cooper (eds), University of Missouri Press, Columbia, MO.

Vroom, V.H. (1964) *Work and Motivation*, John Wiley & Sons, New York.

Vroom, V.H. and Yetton, P.W. (1973) *Leadership and Decision-making*, University of Pittsburgh Press, Pittsburgh, PA.

Vroom, V.H. and Jago, A.G. (1988) *The New Leadership: Managing Participation in Organizations*, Prentice Hall, Englewood Cliffs, NJ.

Waldroop, J. and Butler, T. (2000) 'Managing Away Bad Habits', *Harvard Business Review*, 78, 89–98.

Walton, M. (2005a) *Executive Behaviour in Context*, School of Management, University of Bradford.

—— (2005b) 'It Ain't What You Do Its The Way That You Do It . . . Or Is It?', *6th International Conference on HRD Research and Practice across Europe*, Leeds, UK.

—— (in press) 'In Consideration of a Toxic Workplace', in A. Kinder, R. Hughes and C. Cooper (eds), *Employee Wellbeing Support: A Workplace Resource*, John Wiley & Sons, Chichester.

Warner, L. and Grint, K. (2006) 'American Indian Ways of Leading and Knowing', *Leadership*, 2, 225–44.

Watson, T.J. (2002) *Organising and Managing Work: Organisational, Managerial and Strategic Behaviour in Theory and Practice*, Prentice Hall, London.

Wayne, S. and Green, S. (1993) 'The Effects of Leader–Member Exchange on

Employee Citizenship and Impression Management Behavior', *Human Relations*, 46, 1431–40.

Weaver, R. (1948) *Ideas have Consequences*, University of Chicago Press, Chicago, IL.

Weber, M. (1947) *The Theory of Social and Economic Organization*, A.R. Henderson and T. Parsons (eds), Hodge & Co., London.

—— (1968) *Economy and Society: An Outline of Interpretative Sociology*, University of California Press, Berkeley, CA.

Wechsler, D. (1943) 'Nonintellective Factors in General Intelligence', *Journal of Abnormal Psychology*, 38, 100–4.

—— (1958) *The Measurement and Appraisal of Adult Intelligence*, 4th edn, The Williams and Wilkins Co., Baltimore, MD.

Weick, K. (1995) *Sensemaking in Organizations*, Sage, Thousand Oaks, CA.

—— (2001) 'Leadership as the Legitimation of Doubt', in W. Bennis, G. Schweiter and T. Cumming (eds), *The Future of Leadership*, Jossey-Bass, San Francisco, CA, pp. 91–102.

Westley, F. and Mintzberg, H. (1989) 'Visionary Leadership and Strategic Management', *Strategic Management Journal*, 10, 17–32.

Wheatley, M. (1992) *Leadershp and the New Science*, 2nd edn, Berrett-Koehler, San Francisco, CA.

—— (1999) *Leadership and the New Science: Discovering Order in a Chaotic World*, Berrett-Koehler, San Francisco, CA.

—— (2005) *Finding Our Way: Leadership for an Uncertain Time*, Berrett-Koehler, San Francisco, CA.

—— (2007) 'A New Paradigm for a New Leadership', in Richard Couto (ed.), *Reflections on Leadership*, University Press of America, Lanham, MD, pp. 105–15.

Whitehead, A.N. (1920a) *The Concept of Nature*, Cambridge University Press, Cambridge.

—— (1920b) *Symbolism, Its Meaning and Effect*, The 1927 Barbour-Page Lectures, given at the University of Virginia, Fordham University Press, Bronx, NY.

—— (1925) *Science and Modern World*, Cambridge University Press, Cambridge.

—— (1933) *Adventures of Ideas*, Free Press, New York.

—— (1938) *Modes of Thought*, Columbia University Press, New York.

—— (1978) *Process and Reality*, D.R. Griffin and D.W. Sherburne (eds), Free Press, New York.

Williams, B.A.O. (1981) *Moral Luck*, Cambridge University Press, Cambridge.

Williams, F. (1999) 'Good-enough Principles for Welfare', *Journal Social Policy*, 28, 667–87.

Williams, L.J. and Brown, B.K. (1994) 'Method Variance in Organizational Behavior and Human Resources Research: Effects on Correlations, Path Coefficients, and Hypothesis Testing', *Organizational Behavior and Human Decision Processes*, 57, 185–209.

Willmott, H. (1993) 'Strength is Ignorance, Slavery is Freedom: Managing Culture in Modern Organizations', *Journal of Management Studies*, 30, 515–52.

Wilson, D.C. (1992) *A Strategy of Change*, Routledge, London.

Wilson, D.C. and Rosenfeld, R.H. (1998) *Managing Organizations*, 2nd edn, McGraw-Hill, London.

Wilson, I. (1992) 'Realizing the Power of Strategic Vision', *Long Range Planning*, 25, 18–28.

Winckelmann, J. (ed.) (1956) *Wirtschaft und Gesellschaft* (Critical edn), J.C.B. Mohr, Tubingen.

Wolf, S. (1990) *Freedom Within Reason*, Oxford University Press, Oxford.

Wood, G., McDermott, P. and Swan, W. (2002) 'The Ethical Benefits of Trust-based Partnering: the Example of the Construction Industry', *Business Ethics: A European Review*, 11, 4–13.

Wood, M. (2005) 'The Fallacy of Misplaced Leadership', *Journal of Management Studies*, 42, 1101–21.

Wood, M. and Ferlie, E. (2003) 'Journeying from Hippocrates with Bergson and Deleuze', *Organization Studies*, 24, 47–68.

Woodruff, P. (2001) *Reverence: Renewing a Forgotten Virtue*, Oxford University Press, New York.

Woods, P.A. (2004) 'Democratic Leadership: Drawing Distinctions with Distributed Leadership', *International Journal of Leadership in Education*, 7, 3–26.

Wren, D.A. (2005) *The History of Management Thought*, 5th edn, John Wiley & Sons, Hoboken, NJ.

Wren, J.T. (1998) 'James Madison and the Ethics of Transformational Leadership', in J.B. Ciulla (ed.), *Ethics, the Heart of Leadership*, Praeger, Westport, CT, pp. 145–68.

Wright, K., Rowitz, L. and Merkle, A. (2001) 'A Conceptual Model for Leadership Development', *Journal of Public Health Management & Practice*, 7, 60–6.

Wright, L. and Smye, M. (1996) *Corporate Abuse*, Macmillan, New York.

Yagil, D. (2002) 'Substitution of Leaders' Power Bases by Contextual Variables', *International Journal of Organizational Theory and Behaviour*, 5, 383–99.

Yarmolinsky, A. (2006) 'The Challenge of Change in Leadership', in Richard A. Couto (ed.), *Reflections on Leadership*, University Press of America, Lanham, MD, pp. 39–46.

Yukl, G. (1998) *Leadership in Organizations*, 4th edn, Prentice Hall, Upper Saddle River, NJ.

—— (1999) 'An Evaluation of Conceptual Weaknesses in Transformational and Charismatic Leadership Theories', *The Leadership Quarterly*, 10, 285–305.

—— (2002) *Leadership in Organisations*, 5th edn, Prentice Hall, Upper Saddle River, NJ.

Yukl, G. and Van Fleet, D.D. (1992) 'Theory and Research on Leadership in Organizations', in M.D. Dunnette and L.M. Hough (eds), *Handbook of Industrial and Organizational Psychology*, Consulting Psychologists Press, Palo Alto, CA, pp. 147–97.

Zaleznik, A. and Kets de Vries, M. (1985) *Power and the Corporate Mind*, Bonus Books, Chicago, IL.

Zigarmi, P., Zigarmi, D. and Blanchard, K.H. (1985) *Leadership and the One Minute Manager: Increasing Effectiveness through Situational Leadership*, HarperCollins, London.

Zikmund, W.G. (1991) *Business Research Methods*, 3rd edn, Dryden Press, Chicago, IL.

Zimbardo, P. (1969) *The Cognitive Control of Motivation*, Scott Foresman, Glenview, IL.

Zimmerman, M. (1990a) 'Toward a Theory of Learned Hopefulness: A Structural Model Analysis of Participation and Empowerment', *Journal of Research in Personality*, 24, 71–86.

—— (1990b) 'Taking Aim on Empowerment Research: On the Distinction

Between Individual and Psychological Conceptions', *American Journal of Community Psychology*, 18, 169–77.

Zimmerman, M. and Rappaport, J. (1988) 'Citizen Participation, Perceived Control, and Psychological Empowerment', *American Journal of Community Psychology*, 16, 725–50.

Zohar, D. and Marshall, I. (2000) *SQ – Spiritual Intelligence: the Ultimate Intelligence*, Bloomsbury, London.

—— (2004) *Spiritual Capital: Wealth We Can Live By*, Berrett-Koehler, San Francisco, CA.

Zola, Irving K. (1987) 'The Politicization of the Self-Help Movement', *Social Policy*, 18, 32–3.

INDEX

NOTE: Page numbers in **bold** denote entries and their authors.

Business:
The Key Concepts
Mark Vernon

A practical guide to the essentials of business. This book provides everything you need to know about the key concepts and terms, from accountability to zero-sum game.

Everything from management, economics and finance to marketing, organizational behaviour and operations, is covered in just the right amount of detail to make things clear and intelligible.

- Detailed yet approachable.
- Considers new developments in business, notably e-business and contemporary business ethics.
- Covers established subjects, taking an international and strategic perspective that balances theory and practice.
- Suggests further reading for many concepts and also includes an extensive bibliography.

Whether you're already in business and you could do with a handy reference guide or you're a student needing an introduction to the fundamentals, *Business: The Key Concepts* is the perfect companion.

ISBN 10: 0–415–25324–1

ISBN 13: 978–0–415–25324–6

Available at all good bookshops
For ordering and further information please visit
www.routledge.com

Management:
The Basics
Morgen Witzel

'A valuable addition to the management lexicon — I would urge students of management to read this book.'
James Pickford, *Editor of FT Mastering, Financial Times*

'Witzel has an engaging style which makes this an excellent text for students on introductory business and management courses.'
Kerry Carson, *University of Louisiana, USA*

Management: The Basics provides an easy, jargon-free introduction to the fundamental principles and practices of modern management. Using examples ranging from people management at Cadbury and the Enron crisis to the marketing of fried chicken in China, it explains key aspects of:

- planning effective business strategy to meet goals
- how successful marketing works
- how organizations are structured and function
- how to understand corporate finance
- what affects how people work and effective human resources management
- the importance of knowledge and culture.

This informative and accessible guide is ideal for anyone who wants to understand what management is and how it works.

Morgen Witzel is Honorary Senior Fellow at the School of Business and Economics, University of Exeter, and editor-in-chief of *Corporate Finance Review*.

ISBN: 978–0–415–32018–4

Available at all good bookshops
For ordering and further information please visit
www.routledge.com

Finance:
The Basics
Erik Banks

This book is for anyone who would like to get to grips with the world of finance. *Finance: The Basics* provides the reader with the opportunity to become comfortable with applying and relating financial concepts to daily activities, the financial press and the financial market as well as gaining a solid working knowledge of the key drivers in the financial marketplace. Topics covered include:

- the world of finance
- investment funds
- corporate finance
- the global financial market.

Written in a jargon free style, *Finance: The Basics* covers the essential elements of this broad topic. Simple, yet comprehensive explanations of the primary elements involved in this field of study are offered.

ISBN: 978–0–415–38463–6

Available at all good bookshops
For ordering and further information please visit
www.routledge.com